# The Rhetoric of National Dissent in Thomas Bernhard, Peter Handke, and Elfriede Jelinek

*Studies in German Literature, Linguistics, and Culture*

Edited by James Hardin
(*South Carolina*)

MATTHIAS KONZETT

# THE RHETORIC OF NATIONAL DISSENT

## IN THOMAS BERNHARD, PETER HANDKE, AND ELFRIEDE JELINEK

CAMDEN HOUSE

First published 2000
by Camden House

Camden House is an imprint of Boydell & Brewer Inc.
PO Box 41026, Rochester, NY 14604–4126 USA
and of Boydell & Brewer Limited
PO Box 9, Woodbridge, Suffolk IP12 3DF, UK

ISBN: 1–57113–204–x

**Library of Congress Cataloging-in-Publication Data**

Konzett, Matthias, 1960–
The rhetoric of national dissent in Thomas Bernhard, Peter Handke, and Elfriede Jelinek / Matthias Konzett.
p. cm. – (Studies in German literature, linguistics, and culture)
Includes bibliographical references and index.
ISBN 1–57113–204–x (alk. paper)
1. Austrian literature — 20th century — History and criticism. 2. Austria — In literature. 3. Politics and literature — Austria. 4. Literature and society — Austria. 5. Social problems in literature. 6. Bernhard, Thomas — Political and social views. 7. Handke, Peter — Political and social views. 8. Jelinek, Elfriede, 1946– — Political and social views. I. Title. II. Studies in German literature, linguistics, and culture (Unnumbered)

PT3818.K67 2000
830.9'32436—dc21

99–088927

A catalogue record for this title is available from the British Library.

This publication is printed on acid-free paper.
Printed in the United States of America.

*For my friend and teacher*
*Angel Medina*

*Contents*

# *Acknowledgments*

I WOULD LIKE TO THANK the following people who have contributed to this study through advice, suggestions and helpful conversations: Dagmar Lorenz, Reinhold Heller, Peter Jansen, Katie Trumpener, Peter Demetz, and Wendelin Schmidt-Dengler.

I would also like to thank Günter Brus for his kind permission to reprint the photograph that is used on the dust jacket of this book. The photograph, taken by Ludwig Hoffenreich, documents Brus's performance *Wiener Stadtspaziergang* (Viennese Stroll) from 1965.

As one of the leading Austrian avant-garde artists, Brus staged in public his protest and disagreement with the tacit structures of consensus that inform Austria's postwar society. The image depicts the artist painted in a white suit with a jagged black seam drawn through the middle of his body, suggesting rupture, discontinuity, and dissent. He is walking in front of Austria's government building amidst a crowd of typical Viennese bourgeois. Redefining Vienna's popular pastime, Brus turns the casual stroll of the bourgeois into one of conscious assertion of difference from mass consensus. His work, which anticipates and parallels the work of Bernhard, Handke, and Jelinek, has had a significant influence on the development of a rhetoric of national dissent.

M. K.
January 2000

# *Preface*

THE TITLE OF THIS STUDY, *The Rhetoric of National Dissent*, suggests the sense of unease that Thomas Bernhard, Peter Handke and Elfriede Jelinek bring to Austria's regained national identity after an intense historical period of nationalism and mono-ethnic cultural definition. In this work, I look at three writers who have dominated the literary scene of Austria and Germany during the past three decades, replacing former household names like Heinrich Böll, Günter Grass and Christa Wolf. All three writers have written numerous successful novels and plays, ranking presently among the most performed and discussed authors on the German stage. Unlike Böll, Grass or Wolf, however, Bernhard, Handke and Jelinek are rarely seen as entirely politically motivated authors. Their sophisticated aesthetics has invited largely formal and one-dimensional discussions at the expense of accounting for their complex critical stances on public issues such as nationhood, critical memory and cultural identity that are central to their works.

Criticizing postwar normalization, these writers attack and expose a lingering rhetoric of national consensus that helped shape the fascist paradigms of Austro-German culture and politics. While appreciative of postwar democratic reforms, Bernhard, Handke and Jelinek alert us to the latent patterns of consensus rhetoric that inform present Austrian and European welfare states in their effort to neutralize conflicting social and cultural claims. They articulate a unique model of dissent, combining avant-garde and mainstream techniques of writing that cut across different modes of literary discourse and reception. Their literature exposes and attacks conventions of pre-arranged consensus and harmonization that block the ongoing negotiations necessary for the development of multi-cultural awareness.

Each writer, as my study shows, poses the question of national dissent differently. Bernhard exposes a coercive climate of historical amnesia and national self-canonization from within Austria's cultural institutions. In contrast to Handke's work, Bernhard's later works exhibit increasing political clarity and engagement. Handke focuses on what I call post-ideological voices that are suppressed in the account of the history of the marginal individual. Recently, he has unsuccessfully extended this analysis to larger collective questions and made serious political errors by lapsing back into untenable ideological statements that blatantly ignore the historical and political reality of the former Yugoslavia. Finally, Jelinek confronts the commodity value and marketability of all cultural identity. In doing so, Jelinek maps out a complex and critical path for younger Jewish ethnic writers such as Robert

Schindel and Doron Rabinovici, who carry the legacy of national dissent in a new direction. All writers discussed here aim in their rhetoric of national dissent to express alternative, post-national identities relevant for the new multi-cultural configuration of Europe.

# 1

# *Consensus and Dissent in Contemporary Austrian Literature*

## Introduction

THIS STUDY EXAMINES critical aspects of Austrian culture and their representation in contemporary Austrian literature. While there is a wide variety of authors one could use to substantiate such a study, I have narrowed my analysis to three Austrian writers who share similar thematic concerns and display similar public profiles. Thomas Bernhard, Peter Handke and Elfriede Jelinek, established writers on the German literary market, have had an impact that reaches far beyond the confines of Austria's small alpine republic. Their work is thus not only relevant for specific regional issues of Austrian culture, but indirectly affects the cultural debate in other German-speaking areas as well as in other European and Western countries. All three writers, for instance, enjoy high regard in France, Italy, England and the United States and have assumed a solid footing in a loosely defined group of transnational writers whose work is not exclusively marked by national or regional concerns.

From within German literature and its reading audience, these three writers bear resemblance to one another in their provocative styles and unorthodox literary visions that defy ready assignment to any contained and established discourse of literature. Compared to Heinrich Böll or Günther Grass, for example, these writers appear to have a standing or position in the literary and cultural market that is both more and less successful. All three writers have secured a high visibility in the German cultural sphere through their activities as playwrights and their provocative intervention in the public arena. On the other hand, Bernhard's histrionically invoked social pathology, Handke's insistent evasions of the official public domains and Jelinek's flaunted cultural irreverence betray more intense estrangements than usually displayed in Germany's or Switzerland's enlightened and didactic literatures which aim more directly at social transformation and emancipation.

As a result, Bernhard, Handke and Jelinek curiously find themselves both at the presumed centers and at the borders of the cultural public sphere whose attention they command but whose function they reject. A forceful dissenting autonomy characterizes the core of these writers' works, one that Adorno described for modern art in the following terms: "By congealing into an entity unto itself — rather than obeying existing social norms and thus proving itself to be 'socially useful' — art criticizes society just by being there."[1] In Adorno's sense of a critical avant-garde, our three writers appear to practice an art of negation by locating themselves both within society and at its antithetical periphery. Unlike the avant-garde, however, they have not withdrawn into remote, hermetic and self-enclosed experiments that no longer reach a wider public. Their apparent autonomy is not divorced from the heteronomy of society but achieved from within it.

The reception of Bernhard, Handke and Jelinek's works on the literary market is as controversial and puzzling as their literary stance. While all three writers have enjoyed great success, surpassing that of many other prominent writers, their works are rarely welcomed with unanimous approval. Indeed, their high artistic standards have annoyed politically engaged writers who see no use in aesthetic criteria as well as avant-garde aesthetes who scorn any petty-bourgeois conception of culture. Conversely, Bernhard's, Handke's and Jelinek's non-conformity with the expectations of high culture, their breaches of style, tact and tradition, have made them equally suspicious to culturally conservative circles. In addition, as writers skillfully manipulating a mass market, their successes are too uneven and too artistically belabored to fit the label of outright commercial writers. And yet, while their work is criticized and rejected for one reason or another by almost every segment of the reading public, their public image steadily grows.

This puzzling public status of the three writers invites further reflection on their significance from within contemporary German literature and its sphere of reception. Stubbornly occupying a position of difference from within a largely homogeneous cultural sphere with its predictable ideological boundaries, these writers have managed to avoid facile labels. While their works offer exemplary, but by no means innocent, critiques of consumerist standardization, cultural homogeneity and its concomitant ideology of consensus, they do so from within a post-ideological perspective and avoid reducing the complex issues under analysis to any one-dimensional level of discourse. In this sense, they are profoundly literary writers who pay close attention to the multi-coded and multi-directed orientation of social communication.

In spite of this openness in style and ideology, their works take shape in a specific and delimited historical context. A general estimate of the transnational significance of their works can only be reached by means of a detour through Austria's post-World War II cultural landscape. In the increasingly standardized landscape of postwar Europe, this differentiation may at first not appear to be very productive or meaningful. However, the formation and consolidation of the welfare-state democracy typical of postwar European history has perhaps found a more intense realization in Austria because of the manageable dimensions of its geo-political territory. In this respect, Austria highlights the systemic and cultural features underlying many Western post-industrial societies in a more easily discernible manner. My analysis, focusing on issues such as nationalism, the technological standardization of personal domains, historical amnesia and revisionism with regard to the Nazi genocide, will lay bare crisis points that contemporary Austrian society holds in common with other Western welfare states. In trying to give more adequate attention to the narrative constructions of a particular culture, I will explore these issues indirectly through their critical representations in recent Austrian literature.

Bernhard, Handke and Jelinek alert us to the fact that the complexity of many central issues in contemporary Austrian society is exacerbated by their linguistic expression, which does not receive substantial consideration and reflection in the sphere of practical politics. In their respective efforts to enlarge the temporal and self-reflective horizons of their society, the three writers situate their readers in distinct narratives and scenarios that play out the linguistic, cultural and ethical choices of a society's self-understanding. Specifically, by challenging the myth of a cultural or national center, the three Austrian writers explore, as I show, various avenues of critique in reconfiguring the symbolic and self-reflective grammar of their culture. This critical self-representation of a society from within as the object of its own observation, as the sociologist Niklas Luhmann has observed, is paradoxical from the very outset since the empirical ground of description is already distorted by representation. Self-description and self-observation, the tools of classic social phenomenology, as Luhmann claims, become increasingly problematic in postmodernism: "Es gibt keinen métarécit [meta-narrative], weil es keinen externen Beobachter gibt. Wenn wir Kommunikation benutzen, und wie sollte es sonst gehen, operieren wir immer schon in der Gesellschaft."[2]

Questioning in a similar and more radical vein a primordial belonging to a society, region or culture and any of its discourses, the three authors unmask the cultural deceptions of identity that support stable notions of *Heimat* and nation. Handke's novel *Slow Homecoming*, for instance, depicts this tenuous identity both visually and temporally through its steadily shifting topography and the narrator's protracted return to Austria. The works of all three writers expose in differing ways residual notions of fascism and its biological concepts of race and nationhood. They take on particular importance in light of the current revisionism and resurgent nationalism in Europe.

From within their common project of a critical self-portrayal of a society, each writer varies in focus and accentuates different aspects of Austrian culture. The problematic public sphere and the construction of culturally hermetic and complacent myths are at the center of Bernhard's later works, which unsparingly question the remaining value of art and the author's own investment in it. Handke pays particular attention to the narratives of "silenced minorities" against the background of powerful official versions of culture that mute differentiated experience. Invoking a subjectivity with seemingly unremarkable insights and situated in settings of equally peripheral relevance, Handke hopes to undermine his and the reader's sense of a collective national, regional, cultural or social identity by means of rediscovering idiosyncratic modes of perception and articulation. Through her critical textual montages, in which language is meant to expose its latent ideologies, Jelinek brings persistent ethnic, gender and social prejudices in the commodity discourses of Austria's leisure and high culture industry to the foreground. Her critique of consumer culture as an almost inescapable maze of culturally engendered illusions aims, as an initial cure, for a more sobered acknowledgment of our cultural self-inflation including that of literature. All three writers create a critical distance towards not only their culture but, more importantly, their own mode of representation.

## Refocusing Austrian Literature and its Politics

Although contemporary Austrian literature has left an indelible and path-breaking impact on postwar German literature — one need only think of Celan, Bachmann, Handke, Bernhard and Jelinek — it has also suffered in its reception from its equation and association with the literature of fin-de-siècle and Habsburg Vienna. Too often the continuity of this rich cultural heritage is overstressed at the expense of understanding the entirely new configurations of recent Austrian literature. To prepare the ground for such a reception, I will begin by critically reviewing stereotyped representations of contemporary Austrian literature and challenge them with regard to their contextual and historical fidelity. This initial study of the receptive field will allow us to sharpen the focus on contemporary issues that are buried beneath these commonplaces of Austrian literature. In particular, I will question the relevance of analogies between contemporary literature and a cliched post-

Habsburg legacy of a melancholic spirit of dissolution and political immobility.

In his *Der Tod des Nachsommers* (1979; The Demise of the Indian Summer), the first comprehensive assessment of recent Austrian writing, Ulrich Greiner locates its artistic, intellectual and cultural roots rather conventionally in the era of Austria's protracted imperial decline marked by the rise of German and Slavic nationalism. This era, claims Greiner, is embodied by the work of the neo-Romantic Adalbert Stifter who, withdrawn from active political life, devotes his literary ambition to the aesthetic contemplation of self and nature. In following this tradition-oriented and pre-modern approach, Greiner ultimately ignores the politically innovative and rebellious strains in recent Austrian writing, comparable to Germany's own modern liberal tradition of the life and social sciences (Simmel, Weber, Scheler, Frankfurt School). What he discerns so tellingly in Handke as a "neugierige, sehnsüchtige Hingabe an das, was man im Deutschen 'Leben' nennt" is ultimately dismissed as melancholic abstention from political participation.[3] In this fashion, Greiner attributes to recent Austrian literature the same ahistorical mythos of immobility that Claudio Magris had already discerned in the literature written during the decline of the Habsburg empire. Greiner speaks of a literature,

> ob bei Stifter oder Handke, die antirealistisch und apolitisch ist, die gleichwohl ein großes menschliches Paradigma darstellt für die Not des Nichthandelnkönnens und ihrer Transformationen in ein Reich der Sehnsüchte und Hoffnungen.[4]

It remains doubtful whether Greiner's assessment can be substantiated in any manner other than by reading recent Austrian writing through the eyes of the Habsburg tradition. Yet, as Christoph Bartmann rightly argues, in order to recover the contemporary aspects of literature one must go beyond the premises of a *Wirkungsgeschichte* or effective tradition that supposedly frames the present from the past:

> Eine Interpretation, die den Schwerpunkt auf die in einem Werk enthaltenen Traditionsbezüge legt, stärkt unweigerlich die ästhetische Norm gegen die das Neue, das nie harmonisch in die Tradition eingebettet ist, rebelliert.[5]

The apparent ahistorical aloofness of recent Austrian writing cannot be explained in terms of the supra-historical temporality — Austria as the unchanging thousand-year empire — that was favored during the declining Habsburg era for the specific purpose of keeping alive a decaying imperial tradition. The ahistorical quality of recent fiction must be understood instead from within its contemporary situation: it emerges from within a society of democratic consensus with its own peculiar cultural impasses and pervasive ideological, administrative and consumerist standardization. Recent Austrian writing, in its critical strategy to resist wholesale ideological and social co-optation (*Vereinnahmung*), aims to suspend any conventional order of discourse, including political discourse. Greiner at one point speaks of the choice of *Anpassung* (adaptation) and *Verweigerung* (refusal) that emerges in an Austrian climate of planned and tacitly enforced political consensus.[6] This relevant insight, however, ultimately remains buried beneath Greiner's culturally biased judgment that

> Westdeutsche Autoren wie Alfred Andersch, Heinrich Böll, Nicolas Born, Hans Magnus Enzensberger, Günter Grass, Wolfgang Koeppen, Siegfried Lenz, Martin Walser und Peter Weiss beschäftigen sich nahezu unausgesetzt kritisch mit der bundesdeutschen Wirklichkeit. Wo wäre ein österreichischer Schriftsteller, der ähnliches für Österreich unternommen hätte.[7]

Judging Austrian literature solely by the standard of West Germany, Greiner ignores the idiosyncrasy of Austria's political and economic infrastructure, the background necessary for an assessment of its cultural production. His portrayal of Austrian literature elevates its purported decadence while condemning its lack of political initiative. Greiner's argument may therefore be seen as serving the protective interest of Germany's own shaken political conscience in the era of the *Tendenzwende* (change of ideological climate) during the 1970s with its emerging neo-conservatism.

This *Tendenzwende*, following the 1968 student uprising in Germany, indicates an increasing frustration with political reform that quickly becomes ossified in the unwieldy administrative apparatus of the universities and other educational institutions:

> Die Initiierung von Reformen im Schul- und Hochschulbereich beispielsweise, die auf die Kritik der Schüler und Studenten an den verkrusteten gesellschaftlichen Einrichtungen zurückging, führte nur in geringem Umfang zu Veränderungen struktureller und inhaltlicher Art. Zum überwiegenden Teil sind solche Reformimpulse lediglich nach technokratischen Gesichtspunkt der Effektivität aufgenommen und in Reglementierungen umgesetzt worden (Punktesystem in der reformierten Oberstufe, Rahmenpläne, Regelstudienzeit).[8]

Excessive political disputes on the part of the left further led to disenchantment among writers and intellectuals with the entire discourse of politics:

> Am Ende des Politisierungsprozesses, so läßt sich resümieren, steht eine Entpolitisierung, die gleichwohl nicht unpolitisch ist. Denn sie deutet vor allem auf eine Abkehr von gesellschaftlichen Institutionen, auf Mißtrauen gegenüber Parteien und sozialen Hierarchien.[9]

Greiner's work, which deplores but does not fully grasp this new tendency of depoliticization, is a culturally defensive dismissal of Austrian writing that by the late 1970s had soared to unprecedented popularity in Germany. Peter Härtling accounts for the rise of this seemingly depoliticized autobiographical literature in the following terms:

> Je mehr Technokraten auf allen Gebieten zu Scheinobjektivierungen zwingen, je nachdrücklicher sich Ideologien polarisieren, desto subjektiver wird die Literatur sein.[10]

Austrian literature, due to its radically nonconformist style and expression, brought a breath of fresh air into Germany's stifling and ideologically over-determined political climate.[11]

In his *Die sozialpartnerschaftliche Ästhetik* (1990; The Aesthetics of Social Cooperation), Robert Menasse approaches contemporary Austrian literature from a more narrowly defined contextual perspective of considering the specific socio-economic conditions of the Austrian writer. The unique character of recent Austrian literature, as Menasse suggests, is the result of the economically isolated position of the writer, who, unlike his or her German colleagues cannot rely on a network of subsidiary industries (media, radio, film, advertising) that support, albeit commercially, the literary market. Any Austrian who decided to become a writer, notes Menasse,

> hatte keine Möglichkeit, in Tätigkeitsbereiche auszuweichen, wo er als Wortproduzent Anstellung und Absicherung erreichen konnte. Er mußte seine künstlerische Produktion weitertreiben und darauf hoffen, einen Verlag zu finden. Das ist sicherlich ein Grund dafür, daß Österreich ein solch überproportionales Autorenreservoir für das bundesdeutsche Verlagskapital darstellen konnte, eine Vorraussetzung für die österreichische "Literaturexplosion" der sechziger Jahre auf dem bundesdeutschen Markt.[12]

Due to limited reception and opportunities of economic support in her or his native country, the Austrian writer is forced to establish a network of communication that reaches beyond the confines of Austria. This circumstance explains Austria's strong presence on foreign literary markets. Moreover, Menasse compares the remarkable sophistication of Austrian writing, emerging against the background of an absent reading audience, to Austria's sophisticated administrative apparatus, including the virtual elimination of open labor conflict through an instituted system of balanced social partnership, that emerged as a compensation for a backward capitalist economy. Austrian literature, for Menasse, reduplicates this systematic implementation of a social consensus in its aesthetic harmonization of conflicting cultural issues.

The concept of social partnership, according to Menasse, lies at the root of Austria's political and cultural infrastructure. The principle agency of this political institution rests with a parity commission consisting of representatives from all the major interest groups of Austria's labor forces (workers, farmers, employees, employer). The parity commission controls and settles wage and price negotiations in advance of conflicts and has been extremely successful in preventing strikes and other forms of labor unrest. Because this commission is central to Austria's economic and social structure, it has often been considered by critics a shadow government operating behind the scenes of the political public sphere. From an official point of view, social partnership is seen as the major achievement of Austrian government. For instance, a federal press service circulation boasts that "labor and industry in Austria have indeed settled their differences with more understanding and consideration for the common good than has been shown anywhere else in the world."[13]

It is this peculiar co-existence of an instituted avoidance of social conflict and an anarchic and experimental cultural freedom that has often baffled critics in their assessment of recent Austrian writing. While being appreciative of the aesthetic innovations in Austrian writing, many critics tend to overlook the fact that Austria's idiosyncratic apolitical writings are also a strategic response to a social system that devours everything through pre-arranged consensus. Sigrid Schmid Bortenschlager, for instance, points to the more responsible engagement with the reader in Swiss literature, which she believes to be a product of Enlightenment culture and its practical appeal to morality. Austrian literature, conversely, is said to resemble a romantic poetics in its appeal to an abstract universality. The ensuing abstinence from any concrete political action is seen as the outcome of the subservient mentality of the civil servant.[14] This assessment is reminiscent of Greiner's claim that Austrian writing is overwhelmed by an authoritarian tradition and reduced to immobility and imaginative compensation. Bortenschlager convincingly outlines the regional politics that underlies the production of Swiss literature, but she fails to do the same for Austrian writing and relapses into the stereotype of its purported Kafkaesque servitude, absurdity and impotence.

The discourse of social mediation is typical of much of German and Swiss literature and adheres to didactic models of political enlightenment; Bertold Brecht serves as its modern prototype. This discourse of social mediation, however, is a solution already over-determined in Austria's political landscape. To refuse to participate in such a discourse therefore amounts to a political act of its own, one that repudiates a climate of administrative regulation and standardization in all spheres of social interaction. As Menasse notes in the case of Peter Handke:

> Der radikalen, immer umfassenderen Harmonisierung des Systems hat er eine immer radikalere Sensibilität gegenübergestellt, hat jene in dieser immer radikaler aufgehoben.[15]

According to Menasse, the politics of Austrian writing increased in subtlety in proportion to the achievements of Austria's bureaucratic vanguard and its "organisatorischen Avantgardismus." Paralleling Austria's sophisticated administrative harmonization of political affairs, the political import of Austrian literature has become so subtle and diffused that it can no longer be discretely discerned as such:

> Es mag erstaunen, daß Dichter, die die avancierteste Form zur Beschreibung und Kritik von Herrschaftsverhältnissen entwickelt haben, gleichzeitig völlig unpolitisch erscheinen.[16]

This sophistication or over-refinement in cultural critique is negatively and symptomatically linked to Austria's state ideology of social partnership, an apparent harmonization of all social contradictions.

Even Menasse, then, still understands Austrian writing as a reactive response to the socio-economic or cultural situation in which the writer remains entirely trapped. Menasse, who subscribes to Marx's notion of an ideological supra-structure that articulates and conceals the conditions of society's basis, ultimately concedes to the Austrian writer no genuine possibility for social transformation:

> Diese anti-demokratische, anti-öffentliche Struktur im österreichischen Überbau (die vor allem aus der wachsenden Funktionslosigkeit des Parlaments unter sozialpartnerschaftlichen Voraussetzungen entsteht) legt der österreichischen Literatur nicht nur Entpolitisierung bzw. expliziten Konservatismus nahe, sondern drückt sich auch in einer *Apotheose des Ich* aus, die ein ästhetisches Strukturmerkmal der österreichischen Literatur und unter dem Begriff "Innerlichkeit" zum literarischen Markenzeichen wurde.[17]

According to Menasse, every articulation on the part of the writer remains ultimately enmeshed in the state ideology and its ongoing formation of a cultural supra-structure. It may at best point to this malaise symptomatically with a cultivated interiority and withdrawal from active political life. Greiner has similarly described a state-sanctioned interiority in East German literature that is said to erect literary ivory towers. Condemning the alleged political opportunism of Christa Wolf, Greiner writes: "Es ist die alte machtgeschützte Innerlichkeit, die sich literarische Fluchtburgen baut."[18] At the time of Greiner's remarks, the literature of interiority had become what Menasse calls a *literarische Welle* (literary fashion) and therefore an easy target for quick and undifferentiated criticism.

Menasse likewise imputes to the writer an inescapable complicity with the state ideology. This complicity leaves no positive role for literature such as the task of envisioning social transformation through a suspension of the present order of discourse. Menasse grants that this act of suspension may in postmodernism no longer permit a privileged external perspective on society. Karl Mannheim, a modern sociologist, still defined such a utopian perspective as an extra-societal mentality which "in addition [bursts] the bonds of the existing order."[19] However, our post-Shoah preoccupation with society has made us much more sobered in our expectations to subvert the social order from a point beyond its sphere. Nevertheless, this apparent inability to escape society's discourse must not altogether foreclose the possibility of constructive dissent. Contemporary literature may offer no ultimate escape from the existing social order but it still manages to expose its discourse as a negotiable configuration through its peculiar double reflexivity with which it critically comments both on society and on its own act of description. Simultaneously exposing and re-imagining the entire landscape of social discourse, contemporary literature still suspends the existing order of discourse from within. Here, as I will show, skeptical post-structuralists and neo-Marxists may have underestimated the important inroads of literature in their overly rigid adherence to a social determinism linked exclusively to power and ideology.

For the present discussion, it will have to suffice to point beyond Greiner's and Menasse's *métarécits* towards a more central tension determining the discourse of Austrian literature. This tension has been delineated by Klaus Zeyringer's study *Innerlichkeit und Öffentlichkeit: Österreichische Literatur der achtziger Jahre* (1992; Interiority and the Public Sphere: Austrian Literature of the 1980s) in which he places the hidden political dimension among the writers of the New Subjectivity from the 1970s in the foreground, a political dimension that by the 1980s is more visibly displayed in the public arena: "Aus der Innerlichkeit wurde der Schritt in die Öffentlichkeit getan."[20] Zeyringer refers specifically to the end of the liberal Kreisky era (1985) as the turning point in a previously less burdened consensus shared by politicians and writers. As Handke put it in 1983: "Nach Kreisky bin ich bereit zuzuschlagen."[21] Political corruption (*Verfilzung*), neo-conservatism and the election of Waldheim, according to Zeyringer, contributed to a more outspoken engagement by writers and the re-definition of their task in terms of openly expressed cultural resistance. Joint public statements by writers, artists and intellectuals opposing Waldheim and public appearances such as a *Mahnwache* (silent protest) in front of Vienna's St. Stephen's Cathedral (1987) indeed attest to a more direct political involvement.

However, it is too simplistic to reduce this spirit of resistance among Austrian artists to a mere *Gegentendenzwende* (ideological counter-tendency). As Zeyringer correctly points out, the refashioning of the public image of the writer had already begun in the early 1970s as the advances of the New Subjectivity undertook a critical re-evaluation of socialization in postwar and post-fascist Austria.[22] Here Zeyringer's proposed field of tension between the conflicting demands of the private and public spheres needs further clarification with regard to the discourse models that organize participation in society. It is not enough to point to the democratic option of resistance from within society, since this maneuver merely repeats the mechanical structure of democratic decision-making with its majority-enforced consensus. This functional feature of Western democracy, although inevitable in practical politics, is more thoroughly questioned by Austrian writers as a coercive mode of cultural legitimization and indoctrination that belittles the demands of silenced minorities. As we will see in the next section, it is the very dynamics of consensus agreement/disagreement that they critique in its structural predominance in Austria's social and cultural discourses.

## The Politics of Consensus and Dissent

The political climate of postwar Austrian history is one characterized by the reconstruction of its short-lived democratic experiment in the post-Habsburg-era and the consolidation of a broader political consensus meant to prevent the internal civil strife that led to totalitarian rule in 1934. This advance and promotion of a more harmonized political climate found its first rewards when Austria regained its sovereignty in 1955, after having proven itself as an operable democracy to the occupational powers. Since then, this conciliatory climate has been enhanced by Austria's institutionalized policy of social partnership

(1957). While these seemingly peaceful and re-constructive efforts have contributed greatly to Austria's economic recovery and ascent to the status of an affluent welfare state, they have not adamantly confronted the deeper social divisions that led Austria into complicity with the Nazi genocide.

Austria's contemporary writers are critical of precisely this mentality of facile compromise and harmonization of politics. Their critique of Austria's consensus ideology does not restrict itself to the actual political sphere. It extends into culture at large where this ideology is latently present in its concepts of nationhood and its ethnic demarcation of its population, its sense of cultural achievement and identity, its view of the individual's position within society and its clouded sense of historical responsibility. Above all, I would like to show how Bernhard, Handke and Jelinek have begun to initiate a politics of difference by challenging cultural commonplaces and traditional expectations (be they Marxist or conservative) that have been placed upon the function of art and its representation of society.

Commenting on the death and literary legacy of Thomas Bernhard, Austria's president Kurt Waldheim showed little sympathy for what he considered pathological and dangerously subversive tendencies in the author's work. In particular, Waldheim blames Bernhard's "Österreichbeschimpfungen" (invectives against Austria) for having had a corrosive influence upon Austria's youth: "Nicht wenigen unserer Jugend hat er dadurch ohne Zweifel eine negative Sicht unseres Landes vermittelt, die der Wirklichkeit nicht gerecht wird."[23] Recollecting the efforts of his own presumably innocent generation in rebuilding the foundation for Austria's postwar democracy, Waldheim portrays Bernhard as non-patriotic and undemocratic in spirit:

> Dieses festzuhalten, fühle ich mich im Gedenken an die bewunderndswerten Menschen meiner Generation, die mit dem Wort "Österreich" auf den Lippen in den Tod gingen, sowie in Erinnerung an die ungezählten Männer und Frauen, die unter großen Opfern dieses Land aus Schutt und Trümmern zu einem freien demokratischen Staatswesen wieder aufgebaut haben, verpflichtet.[24]

These remarks in their obvious revisions and distortions corroborate Waldheim's own dubious loyalty to Austria: in fact, during the *Anschluß* (annexation) Waldheim was a member of Vienna's National Socialist Student Union and welcomed Austria's integration into the larger German Reich.[25] More importantly, they acknowledge, however negatively, the potentially subversive power of Bernhard's writings with regard to the state and its authority.

Bernhard's generation of writers, like Peter Handke and Elfriede Jelinek, who were infants during the fascist era, displays little of the reconstructive and revisionist fervor of the previous generation. Raised during an interim period in which Austria's national identity found itself dissolved and not yet resurrected, these writers have little use for the concept of the state that was suspended and strongly questioned during their formative years. For Bernhard, as he provocatively and offensively phrased it in his *Staatspreisrede* (acceptance speech of Austria's National Book Award) from 1968, the state "ist ein Gebilde, das fortwährend zum Scheitern, das Volk ein solches, das ununterbrochen zur Infamie und zur Geistesschwäche verurteilt ist."[26] The state, in Bernhard's invective, is a defunct construct condemning its citizens to apathy and mental weakness.

Austria's cultural identity, relatively stable for centuries, has never fully recovered from the collapse of the Habsburg Empire and its aftermath. In his *Die Welt von Gestern* (1944; *The World of Yesterday*), Stefan Zweig nostalgically remembers this unshakable stability of the Austrian empire at the turn of the century: "Alles in unserer fast tausendjährigen Monarchie schien auf die Dauer gegründet und der Staat selbst als der oberste Garant dieser Beständigkeit."[27] The collapse of this tenuous but lasting stability, Zweig believes, led Austria into an irreversible decline, causing its descent into fascism and German nationalism. Peter Demetz would agree with Zweig when similarly pointing to the severe doubt that overshadowed Austria's post-Habsburg confidence in its state sovereignty and shattered its belief in democratic principles: "Die erste österreichische Republik (1918–1938) war von einem zerstörerischen Selbstzweifel geschwächt, der ihre mächtigen Feinde unaufhaltsam stärkte."[28] The loss of a seemingly solid national identity, it appears, helped bring about an increasingly hostile reaction against any form of democratically mediated national consensus.

Zweig's and Demetz's analyses reflect the commonly problematic transition from a dynastic and nascently parliamentary form of government to a fully functioning democracy. Austria's transition, with its detour through a descent into totalitarianism, characterizes the historical challenges of the post-Habsburg era. This transition, however, by no means describes the current challenge of Austria's post World War II society, which has been firmly grounded in a democratic tradition lasting over three decades. The view that any critical opposition to the democratic institution of the state inevitably runs the danger of inviting totalitarian rule is historically limited and not applicable in the present political climate.

Writing against the background of a more firmly established democracy, Peter Handke, for example, questions the self-sufficiency of the democratic state that apparently shelters one from any totalitarian abuse and deprivation of freedom. In an essay written at the early age of seventeen, Handke precociously mocks the sovereignty Austria regained in 1955 and unmasks its phantom nature:

> Der Staat: Ich sang alle Strophen der Bundeshymne. Ich liebte meine Eltern als die Keimzelle des Staates, ich liebte meinen Heimatort, ich liebte das Bundesland, in dem ich geboren war, ich liebte mein geliebtes Vaterland. Ich lernte Sätze über den Staat. Nicht der Staat, sondern die Worte über den Staat reizten mich zum Gebrauchen. Dadurch, daß es einen Staat gab, gehörten wir alle zusammen. Zwei Jahre davor war verkündet worden, daß wir durch einen Staatsvertrag mit den Besatzungsmächten endlich FREI seien: Als sich aber nichts geändert hatte, außer daß ein Staatsfeiertag eingeführt worden war, man aber noch immer hörte, daß wir jetzt FREI seien, hielt ich allmählich die Wörter "frei" und "unfrei" nur für Sprachspiele. Ich sah den Staat in den Wasserzeichen der Zeugnisse. Gerade weil ich mir unter dem Wort "Staat" nichts vorstellen konnte, war ich begeistert für ihn. Ich wollte allem, was ich mir nicht vorstellen konnte, auf die Spur kommen. Ich war für alles begeistert was beSUNGEN werden konnte.[29]

For Handke, the state exists above all as a linguistic convention pliable to the demands of its users. While engendering promises of collective belonging and freedom, the state ultimately remains an indeterminate concept or word game. Handke anticipates here an estrangement from the state characterized by Jürgen Habermas as the phenomenon of the clientele-state in which the state is seen as a service rather than a participatory structure. The recent political apathy in Germany and Western Europe, Habermas notes, reflects this transformation in the profound discrepancy that exists between the promise of democracy at the level of state and administration and the experience of democracy at the base of society and in everyday interactions.[30]

Austrian writers such as Handke, Bernhard or Jelinek would certainly concur with Habermas' view of a social and cultural complacency that has taken hold of Germany's and Western Europe's post-industrial consumer societies. Elfriede Jelinek points in her work *Wolken, Heim* (1990; Clouds, Home) to unquestioned ontologies of nativism and collective belonging that at this late stage of what Habermas calls enlightenment society still form the latent basis of cultural self-understanding and identity. The governing tautology of cultural identity — "Nur bei uns sind wir zuhaus" — reflects, according to Jelinek, not only a cultural narcissism but also a retreat from the burden of having to confront history:

> Das Ende der Geschichte ist uns mißlungen. Sie kommt wieder auf uns zu, rasend auf ihren Schienen. Warum stirbt sie nicht? Was haben wir getan? Warum wächst ihre Hand aus dem Grab? Und zeigt auf uns? Wir wollen vergessen werden. Nur bei uns sind wir zuhaus.[31]

In contrast to Habermas, then, Austria's writers object more strongly to ideologies underlying the procedural nature of the state and its democratic institutions than to its practical political legitimacy and the deficiencies of its democratic formation of public opinion. Doron Rabinovici, a young Jewish Austrian writer, captures the disenchantment with democracy not merely as a passive apathy but also as an active consensus ideology which has come to dominate and subvert the spirit of democratic decision making:

> Meine Probleme sollen nicht an die Öffentlichkeit dringen, aber meine Teilnahme hier Ihrer Harmonie den passenden Kontrapunkt verleihen. Sie wollen meine Absolution? Sie wollen einen Konsens mit mir? Sie wollen alle Widersprüche ausräumen? Nicht mit mir. Ich lasse mich nicht ausräumen. Es ist Zeit das Trennende über das Gemeinsame zu stellen.[32]

Rabinovici touches here upon a problematic aspect of a democratic tradition that, while promoting egalitarian principles, still withholds full recognition from selected groups or members of its community. In the American and Canadian multiculturalism debate, Charles Taylor points to the inherent deficiency of the democratic project founded in the politics of the equal and universal dignity of man. This politics and its "principle of equal respect," Taylor claims, "requires that we treat people in a difference-blind fashion."[33] Bernhard, Handke and Jelinek revolt against this difference-blind ethos of social communication, one aggravated by the large-scale standardization of consumer society. They have purposely chosen to act as an uncomfortable presence within the Austrian cultural sphere.

In the case of Peter Handke, this type of unorthodox intervention has recently come under strong attack due to his controversial stances on Serbia. Interestingly enough, Handke, as we will see, has of late reverted to a more difference-blind ethos, showing little sympathy for the plight of persecuted ethnic minorities. To this extent, he has departed from his original aesthetics that paid special attention to those subjects who are violently silenced within the state. While justifiably resisting an increasing national and ethnic fragmentation of the Balkans, Handke stubbornly chooses to ignore the political reality of ethnic cleansing perpetrated against a Muslim cultural minority. His critique of the NATO war involvement appears one-sided and refuses to acknowledge the urgency of intervention in the face of mass killings.

By not offering a combined critique of NATO imperialism and Serbian atrocities, Handke himself comes under the suspicion of defending the hegemonic powers of his Western Christian heritage and of exploiting a serious political and humanitarian crisis for dubious aesthetic and self-promoting goals. In this respect, his work alerts us to the potential of writers' subscribing to ideologies even when they proclaim to have embraced post-ideological stances. Handke's case does not weaken the undertaking of this study, but rather re-asserts the sober truth that no special and privileged perspective is possible in contemporary society. Presenting new forms of authorship, all three authors develop complex but by no means uncontestable approaches to a variety of social and cultural discourses.

## The Rhetoric of National Dissent in Recent Austrian Writing

In his study *Imagined Communities* (1983), Benedict Anderson highlights among other issues the literary construction of nationhood and national consensus. Citing the example of José Rizal, "the Father of Filipino Nationalism," he shows how the writer skillfully construes in his *Noli me Tangere* (1887) a narrative of continuity in which disjointed and anonymous events in society are given an artificial co-simultaneity and a common vortex:

> It should suffice to note that right from the start the image (wholly new to Filipino writing) of a dinner party being discussed by hundreds of unnamed people, who do not know each other, in quite different parts of Manila, in a particular month of a particular decade, immediately conjures up the imagined community. And in the phrase "a house on Anloague Street" which "we shall describe in such a way that it may still be recognized," the would-be recognizers are we-Filipino-readers. The casual progression of this house from the "interior" time of the novel to the "exterior" time of the [Manila] reader's everyday life gives a hypnotic confirmation of the solidity of a single community, embracing characters, authors and readers, moving onwards through calendrical time.[34]

This continuity established across diverse topographies, biographies and temporal horizons offers a classic example of fictive nation-building in its most rudimentary sense. In the context of Austrian literature, this imagination of a solid community has taken on its own problematic nature due to the multi-national and multi-lingual diversity of its dynastic empire. Its national literature, eventually defined by the condensed German of its official administrative language, developed fairly late and more as a weak response to keep up with the growing national culture of Prussian Germany. German, as the predominant print-language replacing Latin, initially did not, as Anderson points out, inspire a German national sentiment: "German's nineteenth century elevation by the Habsburg court, German as some might think it, had nothing whatever to do with German nationalism."[35] Indeed, the hegemonic range of German was challenged in every non-German area outside the major administrative centers of the empire such as Vienna, Prague and Budapest.

A diversely defined dynastic rather than homogeneous national sentiment can similarly be found in many of the Habsburg writers. Hofmannsthal's "Die Briefe des Zurückgekehrten" (1907; Letters of One Who Returned), informed by the author's cosmopolitan outlook, recoils from what is perceived as a new German spirit of provincial nationalism. Written from the perspective of an international merchant returning to Germany, the letters point to a cultural disunion and dissonance beneath the pretensions of German unity and sovereignty:

> So liegen die Deutschen da und haben ein "Einerseits" und ein "Andrerseits," ihre Geschäfte und ihr Gemüt, ihren Fortschritt und ihre Treue, ihren Idealismus und Realismus, ihre Standpunkte und ihren Standpunkt, ihre Bierhäuser und ihre Hermannsdenkmäler, und ihre Ehrfurcht und ihre Deutschheit und ihre Humanität und stören in den Kaisergrüften herum, als wären es Laden voll alten Trödels, und zerren Karl den Großen aus seinem Sarg und photographieren den Stoff, der um seine Knochen gewickelt ist, und restaurieren ihre ehrwürdigen Dome zu Bierhäusern und treten halberschlagenen Chinesenweibern mit den Absätzen die Gesichter ein.[36]

While engulfed in his own illusions about the imperial tradition of Austria, Hofmannsthal manages to draw a sharp portrait of the violence that dwells beneath Germany's enlightenment culture. Its modern "democratic" urbanity that allows for multiple points of view ultimately falls short of such a freedom when meeting the demands of other cultures. Referring to the punitive reprisals against the Boxer uprising in China which involved the death of a German minister, the letter reveals how relentlessly German culture is defended against any perceived threat from the outside. Within Germany, Hofmannsthal's narrator observes a similar violent tendency towards national consolidation. By means of advancing standardization and mass mobilization, cathedrals are converted into beerhalls, making over the image of Germany in a manner described as "einheitlich."[37]

Writing from the perspective of a post-Habsburg world, Robert Musil sharpens Hofmannsthal's observations by humorously pointing to Austria's structural and cultural inability to become a nation. His famous passage on *Kakania* in his *Mann ohne Eigenschaften* (1930; *The Man Without Qualities*) unmasks thus not only the illusion of nationalism but also the half-heartedness and mediocrity of Austria's imperial ambitions in the face of modernity:

> Natürlich rollten auf diesen Straßen auch Automobile; aber nicht zuviele Automobile! Man bereitete die Eroberung der Luft vor, auch hier; aber nicht zu intensiv. Man ließ hie und da ein Schiff nach Südamerika oder Ostasien fahren; aber nicht zu oft. Man hatte keinen Weltwirtschaft- und Weltmachtsehrgeiz; man saß im Mittelpunkt Europas, wo die alten Weltachsen sich schneiden; die Worte Kolonie und Übersee hörte man wie etwas gänzlich Unerprobtes und Fernes an. Man entfaltete Luxus; aber beileibe nicht so überfeinert wie die Franzosen. Man trieb Sport; aber nicht so närrisch wie die Angelsachsen. Man gab Unsummen für das Heer aus; aber doch nur gerade soviel, daß man sicher die zweitschwächste der Großmächte blieb.[38]

In spite of his humorous and ironic voice here, Musil remains faithful to the historical facts. Austria's only extra-territorial possession in an era of colonial expansion, for instance, consisted of a group of uninhabited arctic icebergs named *Franz-Joseph-Land*. The inability to form a cohesive and efficiently assertive national culture is embodied in Musil's main character Ulrich, the man without qualities. This character, suffering from a lack of a clearly defined identity, has his precursor in Grillparzer's pathetic artist-dilettante, *Der arme Spielmann* and Hofmannsthal's evasive *Schwierige*, misfits in what appears to be a bottomless society. He finds his successors in Bernhard's *Untergeher*, Handke's *Tormann* and Jelinek's *Klavierspielerin* who likewise display serious signs of social maladjustment in a society whose cultural codes have become both too complex and elusive. As William M. Johnston suggests, Austria's second republic, taking up in part the post-Habsburg heritage, still constitutes today what is in essence a "Nation without Qualities."[39]

In Austria's modern literature, we see a particular variation of the breakdown of the national continuity narrative which became the trademark of modern European and American literature. This breakdown was first noticeable in the substitution of universalistic tendencies of historical narrative (such as the nineteenth-century *Bildungsroman* and the social realist novel) through modern phenomenological narratives of radical epiphany (Joyce, Proust, Musil, Stein). In spite of its limited focus on the dramatic present, modernism still betrayed universalistic and essentialist assumptions about the perceptual structure of human consciousness. It is only in the post-Shoah era that representations of the human subject, the existential, and the realm in which the subject lives have become thoroughly problematic as direct phenomena. Hermeneutics and structuralism have made us acutely aware that any phenomenon, because it is embedded in arbitrary social and cultural conventions, is at best only indirectly accessible.

While it is correct to say that such an epistemic upheaval was already apparent in the experiments of the modernist avant-garde, their relativization of culture, with the arguable exception of Dadaism, still bore the mark of a Eurocentric emphasis. The uncritical assertion of culturally identical and collectively shared forms of consciousness in surrealism, expressionism, and abstractionism aided the persistence of Western anthropology in spite of modernist iconoclasm. With the Nazi genocide, the myth of human anthropology and its self-regulating cultural activities had reached its most drastic consequence, engulfing an entire culture in a tacit consensus on the necessity of the mass extermination of an other, so-called "foreign" people. How could one begin thereafter to define human agency responsibly without reverting to all the anomalies of everyday fascism — the desk murders, the enforced consensus on cultural values, and the ostracism of cultural "aliens" — that had so pervasively marked fascism?

After an initial attempt at restoring its less burdened Habsburg memory in the 1950s (Doderer, Weigel), Austrian literature responded eventually more severely with a critical recovery of avant-garde initiatives that had been considered *entartet* (degenerate) during the Nazi era. This critical response allowed initially for a preliminary opening of an ideologically closed and provincial climate that presumed to know the difference between "healthy" and "unhealthy" art. Subsequently, however, the revolt of Austria's postwar Dadaists (Wiener Gruppe) proved weak in resisting the pervasive co-option by the cultural mass market that even found use for their absurd and purposeless works. H. C. Artmann, Wolfgang Bauer and Ernst Jandl soon became standard items on high school reading lists and thus flattered a culture's vanity of entertaining a peripheral and exotically absurd, though ultimately harmless, opposition from within. By the end of the cultural revolution of the 1960s and its ensuing consensus on the left, the ideological confrontation of a culture had become less and less effective and increasingly a ritual of correct political affiliation.

What is significant in the rhetorical and political positions of Bernhard, Handke and Jelinek is their refusal to promote merely a critique from the margin of culture and to espouse a consensual political perspective or ideology. All three writers have undertaken major efforts to situate themselves visibly at the center of Austria and Germany's cultural institutions, while not fulfilling their traditional representational functions. Bernhard, ever since his *Staatspreisrede* in 1968, became a serious embarrassment for Austrian culture regardless of its political outlook at any given time. He made sure to offend Austria's political right (Waldheim) and left (Kreisky), and to Austria's consternation, made his critical concerns internationally known. Peter Handke likewise offended Germany's writers' association, the *Gruppe 47*, and attacked what he considered its smug self-laudatory political attitude. At an international conference in Princeton (1966), he challenged Germany's then best-known writers and their left wing consensus on conventional forms of social representation by alerting them to a symptomatic *Beschreibungsimpotenz* (impotence of description) which overshadowed their literary efforts. On several occasions, he has also critically intervened in Austria's public sphere (over the issues of police harassment and Waldheim's election) even though he is not usually acquainted with the commonplaces of *Alltagspolitik*. His *Versuch über die Jukebox* (1991), for instance, consciously situates its action remote from any contemporary historical context (the breakdown of the East bloc). Handke considers such publicized historical events for the most part the result of controlled opinion markets that allow little flexibility for genuine reflection about anything other than agreements or disagreements based on a conventional structure of social and political consensus.

Finally, Elfriede Jelinek, who is probably closest to Austria's avantgarde, has repeatedly curbed her experimental prose (*Die Ausgesperrten, Die Klavierspielerin, Lust*) so as to reach a larger audience and install herself more powerfully within Austria's and Germany's cultural public sphere. Her plays, now performed at Austria's prestigious Burgtheater (Austria's National Theater), have offended many if not all of its spectators and seriously undermined the Burgtheater's function as a cultural institution of high canonical art. Her play *Burgtheater* (1982), for example, implicates its former star actors (Wessely, the Hörbiger brothers) in cooperating with Nazi propaganda efforts. *Wolken, Heim* (1990) similarly casts a dark shadow on the literary heritage of German romanticism and its essentialist ontologies (Kleist, Fichte, Hegel, Hölderlin) that persistently haunt Germany's Nazi (Heidegger) and post-Nazi thinkers (*Rote Armee Fraktion*).

Apart from this strategy of positioning themselves simultaneously as in- and outsiders, three related stylistic features can be said to characterize the works of our three authors: a radical non-affiliation or nonconformity with any collective interest; a nonredemptive vision of the function of art; and the histrionic exposure of art as a practice that serves purposes of cultural edification and emancipation. All of these challenge the enlightenment precepts of traditional art and avant-garde. This revolt against traditional expectations placed upon art (from both right and left) has led to an aesthetics of dissent that does not spare the writer's own authorial position. Bernhard's self-dissecting narrative subjects are notoriously unreliable and often afflicted by the same pathological symptoms they seek to expose in society. Handke's texts, in their carefully constructed self-referential nature, suspend any facile use of any concept or narrative strategy and continually confront the author with his own subjective mappings of culture. Finally, Jelinek's textual collages create an uncomfortable co-existence of high and low culture that make her entire textual world ripe with contradictions and sobering cacophonies.

While it is correct to identify in Hofmannsthal and Musil forebears of aesthetics without affiliation, one must not overlook their more traditional assumption concerning the didactic relation that links an author to his or her reading audience. Hofmannsthal never fully abandoned the cultic notion of art as a ritual of communal belonging, as seen, for example, in his morality play *Jedermann* (Everyman). Musil never fully doubted the revelatory and universal structure of poetic consciousness as given in his *Heilige Gespräche* (Sacred Conversations), the culmination of his grand modern prose work. Eventually, a generation of writers — arguably because of the doubt raised about their ethnic identity — developed more acutely a critical cultural double vision and challenged this persistent catholicity within Austrian modernism. Karl Kraus, Ludwig Wittgenstein and Franz Kafka, who figure as the acknowledged precursors of Bernhard, Handke and Jelinek, betray a more sobered sense of entrapment in the social discourses of their time. Their critical double vision entailed not only a direct attack on society but also the double exposure of ideological discourses and their own operations from within these same discourses.

This deflation of critic, thinker and artist strongly informs the ironic stances of Bernhard, Handke and Jelinek. In addition, they have carried forward the linguistic critiques of their precursors by challenging inherited forms of social discourse even more strongly with regard to their feigned collective consent. In an era in which Western democracies take pride in their relative stability, their living standard and their democratic outlook, these authors challenge not only the vanity of these assumptions but refuse to place art at the service of representing such a presumably civilizing accomplishment. Even the avant-garde, in its opposition to society, can still be seen as a reflection of a society's innovative potential. Here, in contrast, a staged attack on an inflated sense of culture puts us more in touch with an era in which poetry may no longer be possible in any form other than in the corrupted models of discourse provided by society itself.

## Notes

[1] Theodor Adorno, *Aesthetic Theory*, trans. C. Lenhardt (London: Routledge, 1970) 321.

[2] Luhmann, *Beobachtungen der Moderne* (Opladen: Westdeutscher Verlag, 1992) 8.

[3] Ulrich Greiner, *Der Tod des Nachsommers: Aufsätze, Porträts, Kritiken zur österreichischen Gegenwartsliteratur* (Vienna: Carl Hanser Verlag, 1979) 100.

[4] Greiner, 13.

[5] Christoph Bartmann, *Suche nach dem Zusammenhang: Handkes Werk als Prozess* (Vienna: Wilhelm Braumüller, 1984) 6.

[6] Greiner, 43.

[7] Greiner, 52.

[8] Wolfgang Beutin et al., *Deutsche Literaturgeschichte von den Anfängen bis zur Gegenwart* (Stuttgart: J.B. Metzler, 1984) 558.

[9] Beutin, 558.

[10] Quoted in Beutin, 559.

[11] See, for example, Heinrich Böll's *Berichte zur Gesinnungslage der Nation* (Köln: Kiepenheuer and Witsch, 1975), a satire exposing *Gesinnungsschnüffelei* (ideological spying) after Germany's *Radikalenerlass* (emergency laws passed in 1972 in the wake of terrorist attacks). Böll's satire highlights in particular the highly ideological jargon among various political groups.

[12] Robert Menasse, *Die sozialpartnerschaftliche Aesthetik: Essays zum österreichischen Geist* (Vienna: Sonderzahl, 1990) 47.

[13] *Austria: Facts and Figures* (Vienna: Federal Press Service, 1987) 52–53.

[14] Sigrid Schmid Bortenschlager, "Literatur(en) in Österreich und in der Schweiz," in *Für und wider eine österreichische Literatur*, ed. Gerhard Melzer (Königstein: Athenäum, 1982) 124–125.

[15] Menasse, 40.

[16] Menasse, 42.

[17] Menasse, 42–43.

[18] Ulrich Greiner, "Mangel an Feingefühl," *Die Zeit* (June 1, 1990) 13.

[19] Karl Mannheim, *Ideology and Utopia*, trans. Louis Wirth and Edward Shils (New York: Harcourt Brace Jovanovich, 1985) 193.

[20] Klaus Zeyringer, *Innerlichkeit und Öffentlichkeit: Österreichische Literatur der achtziger Jahre* (Tübingen: A. Francke, 1992) 94.

[21] Quoted in Zeyringer, 95.

[22] Zeyringer, 91–92.

[23] Quoted in Jens Dittmar, ed. *Sehr gescherte Reaktion. Leserbrief-Schlachten um Thomas Bernhard* (Vienna: Edition S., 1993) 218.

[24] Dittmar, 218.

[25] Waldheim's dissertation (1944, University of Vienna) explored "Die Reichsidee bei Konstantin Frantz," a nineteenth century proponent of the notion of a "Greater Germany." The work emphasized Frantz's relevance as a political visionary for Nazi Germany and its expansionist politics. For further reference, see The International Commission of Historians, *The Waldheim Report* (Copenhagen: Museum Tusculanum Press, 1993) 35–37.

[26] Quoted in Wendelin Schmidt-Dengler, *Der Übertreibungskünstler. Studien zu Thomas Bernhard* (Vienna: Sonderzahl, 1986) 96.

[27] Stefan Zweig, *Die Welt von Gestern* (Hamburg: Fischer Verlag, 1970) 14.

[28] Peter Demetz, *Die süße Anarchie* (Berlin: Ullstein Verlag, 1970) 27.

[29] Peter Handke, "Ein autobiographischer Essay," in *Ich bin ein Bewohner des Elfenbeinturms* (Frankfurt: Suhrkamp, 1972) 14.

[30] See Jürgen Habermas, *The Past as Future,* ed. and trans. Max Pensky (Lincoln: U of Nebraska P, 1994) 150–52. Also, Jürgen Habermas, "Further Reflections on the Public Sphere," in *Habermas and the Public Sphere*, ed. Craig Calhoun (Cambridge: The MIT Press, 1992) 432, 436–39.

[31] Elfriede Jelinek, *Wolken. Heim.* (Köln: Steidl Verlag, 1990) 24.

[32] Doron Rabinovici, "Über die Säure des Regens," in *Papirnik. Stories* (Frankfurt: Suhrkamp, 1994) 93–94.

[33] Charles Taylor, "The Politics of Recognition," in *Multiculturalism: Examining the Politics of Recognition*, ed. Amy Gutman (Princeton: Princeton UP, 1994) 43.

[34] Benedict Anderson, *Imagined Communities* (London: Verso, 1991) 27.

[35] Anderson, 78.

[36] Hugo von Hofmannsthal, *Gesammelte Werke, Prosa II* (Frankfurt: Fischer, 1951) 335–336.

[37] Hofmannsthal, 332.

[38] Robert Musil, *Der Mann ohne Eigenschaften* (Hamburg: Rowohlt, 1988) 33.

[39] William M. Johnston, "A Nation without Qualities: Austria and Its Quest for a National Identity," in *Concepts of National Identity. An Interdisciplinary Dialogue*, ed. Dieter Boerner (Baden-Baden: Nomos, 1986) 177.

# 2

# Publikumsbeschimpfung: *Thomas Bernhard's Provocations of the Austrian Public Sphere*

## Introduction

IN THIS CHAPTER, I will explore a new direction in the criticism of Thomas Bernhard's work by examining the relationship of the author's public voice to the public sphere as a potential space for political critique and provocation. Much of the criticism on Bernhard has been preoccupied with his philosophical aesthetics, focusing predominantly on the pathological and epistemological destabilization of Bernhard's narrative subjects, neglecting the work's immediate impact upon the Austrian public sphere. The continued critical approach toward Bernhard's work in terms of its critical epistemology is evident, for example, in Christian Klug's recent study *Theaterstücke*, a study examining Bernhard's poetic absorption and reception of Pascal and Kierkegaard. Manfred Mittermayer's *Ich werden* similarly explores a variety of recent critical epistemes given in Sartre, Lacan and Foucault.[1] Aesthetically, the destabilization of the narrative subject has been analyzed as the discourse of modern pathology or as the deliberate staging of social neurosis.[2] This latter type of inquiry extends the formal analysis of epistemes into the cultural domain by pointing to the problematic socialization undergone by Bernhard's narrative subjects. However, this type of analysis still lacks specificity with regard to the public sphere, the tangible sphere of action and engagement for Bernhard's subjects. Moreover, it ignores the prominent portrayal of Austria's cultural public sphere in Bernhard's later works.

While the study of Bernhard's impact upon the public sphere has received some attention in works examining Bernhard's reception, it has not been fully developed. Its analysis has been left largely in the hands of the public media and its insatiable, though hardly penetrating, appetite for scandal and provocation. Ulrich Weinzierl's remark, for example, is indicative of an academically complacent dismissal of Bernhard's public role. Weinzierl writes: "Die medien-, ja vaterlanderschütternden Skandale — etwa rund um *Holzfällen* anno 84 und Peymanns Burgtheaterpremiere von Heldenplatz — können wir getrost beiseite lassen, denn hier handelte es sich um eine fast hundertprozentig außerliterarische Erregung."[3] In an attempt to avoid such a facile dismissal of Bernhard's public interventions, I propose a new perspective of Bernhard as a politically involved writer and thereby hope to correct some of the received notions pertaining to his work. The political involvement that I wish to attribute to Bernhard here is reducible neither to a partisan politics of left or right nor to fashionable nihilistic gestures reflecting a postmodern frustration with the political realm. Bernhard's political stance, in my understanding, is post-ideological in attributing social responsibility or irresponsibility to society as a whole thereby avoiding complacent projections of ideological deficiency onto limited and clearly defined adversarial groups.[4] In this light, then, I shall explore Bernhard's work as a cultural politics promoted in his critical dramatizations of Austria's public sphere that expose society's dubious expressions of cultural narcissism, amnesia and revisionism.

Peter Handke's *Publikumsbeschimpfung* (1966; Offending the Audience) comes immediately to mind when one attempts to give a description of Bernhard's literary activity within the Austrian public sphere. This analogy, while misleading with regard to the strongly differing literary projects of the two authors, provides a productive point of departure for a more precise differentiation between them and their respective positions within Austrian culture. As Manfred Durzak points out, Handke's play reflects not only a critique of theatrical conventions but also the author's unease with the institution of the theater: "Handke [ist] in der Kärntner Provinz groß geworden und damit ohne eigentliche Bildungserfahrung, was das Theater betrifft."[5] Handke's initial ventures into drama and theater, Durzak explains, were the result of economic necessity rather than preference. The commodified public sphere of the theater, as Handke's *Publikumsbeschimpfung* makes clear, points to the emergence of consensus society and its totalitarian and assimilative powers of socialization.

On the other hand, Thomas Bernhard's exposure to the theater was much more direct and does not reflect Handke's immediate skepticism about public institutions of culture. Bernhard, in fact, received musical and theatrical training at the prestigious music conservatory Mozarteum in Salzburg and was more at ease with the established conventions of the theater. Bernhard's proximity to theatrical space undoubtedly informs his confident perception of the public sphere as an arena where public opinion, in spite of its apparent dilettantism, can be negotiated and subjected to scrutiny. He understands at least implicitly its potentially liberating function as an arena of mutual enlightenment. While Handke's more removed literary aesthetics speaks poetically from beyond the artificial opposition of public and private spheres, Bernhard embraces the populist climate of the public sphere. Indeed, beneath his invoked cynicism and display of public outrage, one detects a stubborn belief in the role of the cultural critic — Karl Kraus being Austria's most prominent model — and an indulgent complicity with the public whom the critic at once entertains and enlightens.

In his *The Structural Transformation of the Public Sphere* (1962, 1989), Jürgen Habermas similarly describes the task of the *Kunstrichter* (art critic), whose occupation became an institution during the Enlightenment era, as that of "the public's mandatary and as its educator."[6] "The Kunstrichter," writes Habermas,

> retained something of the amateur; his expertise only held good until countermanded; lay judgment was organized in it without becoming, by way of specialization, anything else than the judgment of one private person among all others who were ultimately not to be obliged by any judgment except their own. This was precisely where the art critic differed from the judge. At the same time, however, he had to be able to find a hearing before the entire public, which grew well beyond the narrow circles of the salons, coffeehouses, and societies, even in their golden age. Soon the periodical . . . became the publicist instrument of this criticism.[7]

This double function of the lay critic's private and public voice, of an unpredictable wavering between subjective sentiment and objective reasoning, has found a peculiar and belated appropriation in the works of Bernhard. At a time when the public sphere, as Miriam Hansen writes, "can be conceived of only in terms of disintegration and decline"[8] due to its relentless commodification of all areas of public reception and exchange, Bernhard does not entirely desert its democratic stage for opinion formation.

Like Handke, although for different reasons, Bernhard rejects a prevalent German tradition of the social novel that had formed in its exponents — Thomas Mann, Heinrich Böll, Martin Walser and Günther Grass — a sophisticated and coherently argued form of social analysis and critique. Bernhard's prose has abandoned the partially omniscient perspectives typical of such engaged writing and limited the authorial perspective to subjective prejudice and conscious distortion, reflecting the early beginnings of the public sphere grounded in the private autonomy of its citizens. By doing so, his prose has moved into the proximity of what is now fabricated by the media as the remnant of this autonomy, namely a converging consent of public opinion with its impulsive expression and obvious biases. In its deliberate mimicry of this public voice, Bernhard's prose aims at a reflective language that doubles back not so much upon the privileged perspective of the writer or social critic but rather on society itself and its hegemonic discourse of consensus.

In contrast to Habermas, Bernhard does not rely so much on rational as on symbolic and dramatic arbitration of conflicting views and opinions in the public arena. In addition, he rejects Habermas' idealization of the public sphere with its enlightenment telos and its presumed decline in late capitalist consumer society. For Bernhard, the public sphere is always complicit with power and thus inevitably a site for both contention and mediation. This is not to say, however, that the illusions engendered by the public sphere cannot be exposed in a partially emancipatory fashion. Through the dramatic gesture of his subjective appeal, Bernhard as *Kunstrichter* eliminates any distance between himself and his audience, thereby reminding the audience of its own active role in the symbolic clarification and negotiation of its socio-cultural identity. Bernhard addresses in particular a public sphere dominated by consensus or what Robert Menasse calls Austria's "aesthetics of social partnership" which attempts to harmonize and suppress any type of social contradiction. In Bernhard's case, the strategy of staging dissent as a legitimate form of discourse is a mode of criticizing the public sphere from within.

This internal critique is seen especially when Bernhard exposes the inflated consensus on Austria's high cultural tradition of which he himself is a product and when he lays bare his own self-delusions concerning the redemptive role of the artist in society. It would be wrong to assume, however, that Bernhard's project of fracturing Austria's harmonized cultural discourse remains ultimately contained within the immediate artistic public sphere. Rather, it reverberates critically in its political counterpart to the extent that it questions its discourse of institutional authority, one profoundly indebted to the narrative legitimization of cultural and national identity which inform the myths of social consensus and collectivity.

Bernhard follows an idiosyncratic Austrian tradition of the social and cultural critic ranging from Nestroy and Hofmannsthal to Kraus and Musil. Their strength lay in a mixture of histrionic and self-conscious staging of one's public voice against a climate of state censorship (Nestroy), rising German nationalism (Hofmannsthal's "Briefe des Zurückgekehrten"), linguistic and public opportunism (Kraus) and nonreflective and uninspired submission to tradition (Musil).[9] Each of these forebears, while rooted with obvious contradictions in the bourgeois public sphere, questioned prevalent social stereotypes that tended to contain its open and negotiable space. Detecting similar ossifying forces at work in Austria's recent consensus society, Bernhard cast himself as *der Schwierige* (the difficult one) or an unappeasable participant in Austria's public sphere, giving it a new discomforting and provocative range of expression.

My inquiry here will limit itself to the prominent staging of Austria's public sphere as recreated and envisioned in Bernhard's later works. While his earlier work with its irreversibly withdrawn and estranged characters (*Der Kulterer*, *Frost*, *Verstörung*, *Das Kalkwerk*, *Korrektur*, *Gehen*, *Ja*) similarly offered critical case studies of cultural crisis and decline, it did not yet have the power to project this critique forcefully beyond the individual pathology of its depicted characters. It is only in his later works that Bernhard could overcome the resignation, isolation and nihilism afflicting his characters by relocating them as agents in society and its public sphere. Bernhard thus confronts the pathological burden of individuals more directly as one of a culture caught up in the contradictions of its identity. Thus in the 1980s, Bernhard had returned via a detour through his autobiography to the familiar artistic public sphere of his youth. This sphere is embodied by the lay critic (i.e. Paul Wittgenstein) and represented by the ambience of coffeehouses, *künstlerische Abendessen* (artistic dinners reminiscent of the salons). Vienna's reigning cultural institutions such as the Burgtheater (National Theater), the Staatsoper (The State Opera), the Musikverein (the society and concert hall of the Vienna Philharmonic) and the Kunsthistorische Museum (Museum of Art History) serve as a further significant backdrop to Bernhard's public scenarios. In his comic and facetiously nostalgic revival of a bourgeois public sphere that had in essence already disappeared after the collapse of the Habsburg Empire, Bernhard unmasks the residual cultural narcissism that has survived up into the present, particularly in Austria's self-inflated image as a *Kulturlandschaft* (cultural region). My inquiry into Bernhard will attempt to trace this last and ironic stage of the *Kunstrichter* who is compelled to demean publicly the very idea of culture and thereby provocatively offend the public's complacent sense of cultural achievement and identity.

In trying to define more accurately the nature of Bernhard's public provocations, I follow and partially resist Wendelin Schmidt-Dengler's claim that Bernhard's work cannot be measured in terms of a "primärgesellschaftskritischer Literatur."[10] Agreeing with Marcel Reich-Ranicki's observation that Bernhard's writing is an enraged rather than an engaged literature,[11] I wish to demonstrate that it is precisely in this publicly provocative gesture that Bernhard links himself to a concrete socio-cultural situation. Bernhard's fictive or real thesis on Brecht and Artaud, which he claims to have written upon graduating from the

Mozarteum, would likewise point to such a blending of a politically engaged (Brecht) and compulsively enraged style (Artaud's "theater of cruelty"). Through this combination of a simultaneous democratic and agonistic conception of the public sphere,[12] Bernhard has explored pertinent aspects of Austria's society at its cultural and political levels that do not allow one to reduce his works to aesthetic readings alone.

My discussion will focus on four of Bernhard's later works, *Wittgensteins Neffe* (1982; *Wittgensteins Nephew*), *Holzfällen* (1984; *Woodcutters*), *Alte Meister* (1986; *Old Masters*) and *Heldenplatz* (1988; Heroes' Square). I will trace specifically Bernhard's exploration of the artistic public sphere as it increasingly and more directly touches upon the political public sphere. This discussion will exhibit more openly the political motivation that had all along guided the author's literary aesthetics. In my analysis, which attempts to blend a literary with a sociocultural perspective, I will thus concentrate on three predominant aspects which have not yet been given enough attention in Bernhard: 1) the comical unmasking of Austria's highly inflated public image of itself as a *Kulturlandschaft* and its complicit role in national and social mythmaking; 2) the politics of representation underlying this image of Austria's cultural public sphere, concealing a pervasive everyday fascism of cultural homogeneity; 3) the emphasis on dramatic voice and pathos as a form of communicative agency and appeal, challenging the institutional ossification of the public sphere and its normative regulation of public and private discourse.

## *Wittgensteins Neffe*: The Cultural Critic in a Post-Cultural Era

*Wittgensteins Neffe* (1982) can be considered Bernhard's first novel that deals directly with the cultural public sphere. It draws largely on the fame and shadow surrounding the industrialist family of the Wittgensteins with its patronage of the arts (e.g. Klimt), its philosophical genius Ludwig Wittgenstein, and its extreme domestic tragedies (three suicides among Ludwig's siblings). The protagonist of Bernhard's narration, the real-life and widely known Viennese public figure Paul Wittgenstein, a nephew of Ludwig, can be seen as the last embodiment of an elite bourgeois acquisition of culture. For bourgeois society culture served the implicit purpose of legitimating its own economic ascent against the fading feudal order of Habsburg Austria. "As the desire to imitate the aristocracy became more widespread," note Allan Janik and Stephen Toulmin in their analysis of Wittgenstein's Vienna,

> patronage of the arts was transmuted into a symbol of wealth and status, and was pursued with ulterior motives. . . . Viennese of the generation that reached maturity at the turn of the century were raised, indeed, in an atmosphere so saturated with, and devoted to, "aesthetic" values that they were scarcely able to comprehend that any other values existed at all.[13]

As Habermas likewise points out, with the rise of the mercantile classes, the various functions of the court, such as patronage of the arts, were taken over by the emerging institutions of the bourgeois public sphere, now claiming ownership to the cultural heritage.[14] In his novel, Bernhard speaks of the fashion among the *nouveaux riches*, represented by the Wittgensteins, "sich malen zu lassen unter dem Deckmantel des Mäzenatentums."[15]

The confrontation between this aesthetic heritage of bourgeois culture and its modern counterpart in consumer society becomes the central theme of Bernhard's novel that uses real-life characters to make its point unmistakably historical. The autobiographical novel, which recounts Bernhard's (the narrator's) and Wittgenstein's friendship retrospectively up until the death of the latter, is hardly nostalgic in its commemoration. Instead, Bernhard forebodingly casts the first encounter between Paul and the author-narrator in the novel not at the point of their beginning friendship but approximately three years into it, during the Six-Day War of 1967. Bernhard and Wittgenstein meet again in the remote setting of two adjoining lung and mental hospitals, *Baumgartnerhöhe* and *Am Steinhof*, after having suffered respectively a severe physical and mental breakdown. Having caused their own diseases, Bernhard and Wittgenstein oppose everything in their social environment: "Der Paul ist verrückt geworden, weil er sich auf einmal gegen gestellt hat und naturgemäß dadurch umgeworfen worden ist, wie ich umgeworfen bin eines Tages, weil ich mich wie er gegen alles gestellt habe" (WN 35). What unfolds is the story of two social misfits who, because of their misunderstood enthusiasm for the arts and their own unsparing preoccupation with it, suffer periodically from mental and physical exhaustion. This fateful encounter and the friendship eventually contribute to the partial recovery of the author-narrator, for whom Wittgenstein's colorful life, its relation to the arts and its tragic end carry the significance of his own emerging critical perspective of culture.

In this critical retrospective, however, Paul Wittgenstein is not merely presented as another example of Bernhard's severely estranged and irredeemable self-destructive characters that became the trademark of his earlier novels. Rather, by examining Paul Wittgenstein's life and its relation to the concrete social setting of the artistic public sphere, Bernhard undertakes a more extensive critical case study of the consumptive relation between the arts and its consumer audience. In this respect Wittgenstein initially embodies the decline of the bourgeois public sphere and its dubious self-legitimation through the conspicuous consumption of art. However, his dissenting spirit, especially as practiced in his later life, also recalls the initial revolutionary stages of the public sphere ideally envisioned as an alternative and open social space grounded in the idiosyncratic autonomy of individuals and their impassioned and democratic exchange of culture and ideas. In the novel, which constitutes a major departure from his earlier work, Bernhard also recasts his own position as a writer within the Austrian public sphere in Wittgenstein. By confronting himself critically in his double, Bernhard breaks with the alienated bourgeois cultural heritage which had haunted his earlier work and takes on the constructive traits of his mentor-friend Wittgenstein, namely his role of the idiosyncratic *Kunstrichter* in Austria's public arena.

After the transition from bourgeois to consumer culture, the role of the *Kunstrichter* may at first appear to be a throwback to an earlier era. The *Kunstrichter*, however, as Bernhard shows, can still be partially recovered as a subversive and enlightening agency within culture once the bourgeois public sphere and its reactionary social assumptions pertaining to art have been subjected to a thorough critique. It is understood, however, that this resurrection of the *Kunstrichter* remains limited. Ultimately, his persona reflects the perspective of an individual who is the product of the condition he seeks to expose. Bernhard's novel entails not only the critique of his friend Wittgenstein but also the narrator's own self-exposure who, for example, fails to show up for Wittgenstein's funeral and only belatedly acknowledges moral guilt.

Wittgenstein's initial appearance in the role of the *Kunstrichter*, as the model for Bernhard's own critical self-definition, is marked by both an uncritical genius and social complacence. Here, Wittgenstein's unshaken confidence and vitality reign supreme in his pursuit of culture. Possessing a vulgar form of what Kant defined as the genius's apodictic judgment, Paul Wittgenstein elevates himself, for instance, to an unchallenged critical authority at Vienna's State Opera where he becomes a feared "Premieremacher":

> Er riß mit seiner Begeisterung, weil er damit ein paar Sekunden früher als die anderen eingesetzt hatte, die ganze Oper mit. Andererseits landeten mit seinen Erstpfiffen die größten und die teuersten Inszenierungen, weil er es wollte, weil er dazu gerade aufgelegt war, in der Versenkung. Ich kann einen Erfolg machen, wenn ich will und wenn

> die Voraussetzungen dafür gegeben sind und sie sind immer dafür gegeben, sagte er, und ich kann einen totalen Mißerfolg genauso machen, wenn die Voraussetzungen dafür gegeben sind, und sie sind immer dafür gegeben. (WN 47–48)

The subjective arbitrariness of the genius' judgment that eluded a rational definition by Kant is here carried comically to the absurd extreme of a willful mood or *Laune* in which accomplishment and failure become a matter of pure chance. Wittgenstein, in fact, is not so much a genius here as a dandy/comedian who through provocative and gratuitously self-referential gestures in the public sphere mocks and unmasks society's cultural pretensions.

The dandy, however, as Sartre has shown in his analysis of the poet Baudelaire, has a dubious critical relation to society. "Life," wrote Baudelaire, "has only one real attraction — the attraction of a gamble."[16] As a person who parades cynically his indifference to social conventions, the dandy does so in order to secretly reaffirm the attacked social orthodoxy through an ambivalent rhetoric of inversion and negation: "He applies his will to the negation of the established order, but at the same time preserves this order."[17] In Sartre's description, Baudelaire was "a man who felt most deeply his condition as man, but who tried most passionately to hide it from himself."[18] Similarly, Paul Wittgenstein becomes an idiosyncratic cultural fanatic who remains nevertheless enslaved to the institutions surrounding culture. Compulsively traveling around the world to visit all the Opera houses, he returns to Vienna's conservative establishment, embracing it all the more in his typical idiosyncratic fashion: "Die Met ist nichts. Coventgarden ist nichts. Alle waren sie nichts gegen Wien. Aber natürlich, sagte er, ist die Wiener Oper auch nur einmal im Jahr wirklich gut" (WN 50). Wittgenstein, whose willful judgment of taste appears to sway an audience temporarily, remains ultimately ineffective in subverting the social order dominating the arts. He cannot help but return submissively to the cultural establishment of which he claims to be a critic. Even within his domain as a *Kunstrichter*, his idiosyncratic judgment faces strong opposition. In the impeccable judgment of the unerring musical and self-promoting genius of Herbert von Karajan, he finally meets his match and equal: "Viele Kapellmeister, die er nicht leiden konnte, sind in Wien in seine Falle gegangen und er hat sie ausgepfiffen und ausgebrüllt, tatsächlich mit Schaum vor dem Mund. Nur an Karajan, den er haßte, scheiterte er. Das Genie Karajan war zu groß, um von Paul auch nur irritiert werden zu können" (WN 48).

Karajan, as a miracle of Austria's postwar cultural renovation, managed single-handedly to re-establish the international fame of Austria's musical culture. He introduced the now standard multilingual performances at the State Opera, retrieving Austria from its provincialism. He recorded extensively with an international cast and managed to produce heretofore unheard-of sales in classical music. By the time of his death in 1989, he had made over 800 recordings and re-instituted the Salzburg Festival as one of Europe's premiere cultural attractions. Along with this phenomenal success, Karajan enhanced his image as a physically fit sports car driver, sailor and aviator and he complemented these talents with a superb mental discipline: he was the only person who could conduct Wagner's entire *Ring* cycle from memory. If one man embodied the economic and cultural drive of Europe's relentless postwar reconstruction, it was certainly the mythical figure of Karajan who ultimately expanded his enterprise into a global economic force furthered by the advent of laser recording technology. Once a double member of the ethnically exclusive National Socialist party, the genius Karajan eventually transformed himself into an all-inclusive, multicultural sponsor of the arts. At the globally televised New Year's Concert of the Vienna Philharmonic in 1987 he humbly asked for world peace in the conciliatory spirit of Austria's waltz king Johann Strauss.

As the towering figure in the Austrian and international musical culture, Karajan reflects not only the problematic triumph of artistic will but also the transition from the bourgeois artist to the self-promoting genius on the commodity market of mass consumerism. Comparatively, a lesser genius like Paul Wittgenstein, incapable of fully modernizing himself, is reduced to becoming a slave to his own image as a fashionable social singularity and as one of the vanishing executors of Austria's traditional cultural heritage. "Er kam einem immer in hocheleganten Kleidern entgegen, die ihm verstorbene Freunde vermacht oder noch lebende geschenkt hatten," Bernhard recalls:

> Er saß beispielsweise um zehn Uhr vormittags in einem weißen Anzug im Sacher, um halb zwölf in einem graugestreiften im Bräunerhof, um halb zwei im Ambassador in einem schwarzen und um halb vier nachmittags wieder im Sacher in einem semmelgelben. Wo er ging oder stand, intonierte er nicht nur ganze Wagnerarien, sondern sehr oft auch den halben Siegfried oder die halbe Walküre mit seiner brüchigen Stimme, unbekümmert um seine Umgebung. Auf der Straße sprach er ihm gänzlich fremde Leute an, ob sie nicht der Meinung seien, daß es nach Klemperer unerträglich geworden sei Musik zu hören. Die meisten, die er auf diese Weise angesprochen hat, hatten von Klemperer niemals etwas gehört und von Musik überhaupt keine Ahnung, das störte ihn aber nicht. Wenn er Lust hatte, hielt er mitten auf der Straße einen Vortrag über Strawinsky oder Die Frau ohne Schatten und kündigte an er werde Die Frau ohne Schatten demnächst auf

dem Traunsee in Szene setzen, mit den besten Musikern der Welt. (WN 69–70)

Unlike Karajan, whom he partially anticipates, Paul Wittgenstein does not have the artistic will or economic genius to adapt to a cultural public sphere increasingly ruled by the demands of the commodity market. His relation to culture remains more that of the passive consumer reduced to private connoisseurship and to vicarious pleasures of dreaming up scenarios that cannot be realized. Bernhard, who sees in Karajan "den ersten aller Musikarbeiter auf der ganzen Welt" (WN 49), advances here, albeit uncritically, a principle of productivity over the mere apathy of consumption as embodied by Wittgenstein. The novel's beginning, in which Bernhard as narrator lives to see the publication of his novel *Verstörung*, unlike many of his earlier characters whose manuscripts remain unfinished, further stresses the active participation in and contribution to the public sphere as essential for its realization and revitalization. Paul Wittgenstein figures in this sense both as an embodiment of bourgeois decadence and of the decaying ideal of the bourgeois cultivation of the arts which also inform present mass consumerism. As his periodic stays in mental hospitals triggered by his artistic frustrations become increasingly a burden to his family, he is finally disowned and cut off from the economic class he represents. A rebellious dandy and tragicomic hero of this elite culture, he succumbs to his own self-destructive tendencies that merely repeat the voracity and consumptive quality of an alienated and distorted bourgeois thirst for acquisition.

Ultimately, however, it is the economically hindered and severely estranged genius of Paul Wittgenstein that merits the admiration of the narrator: "Denn in den letzten Lebensjahren erst entwickelte er sich zum tatsächlichen Philosophen, nachdem er bis dahin nur ein philosophierender Genießer gewesen war" (WN 58). Up until this later period of his life, Bernhard suggests, Paul Wittgenstein was merely an expert or specialist of culture rather than an authentic voice or embodiment of its spirit. Paralleling what Habermas calls the fragmentation of inquiries into culture into disciplines of specialization, Wittgenstein's initial relation to culture is similarly divorced from any relation to a social whole.[19] Wittgenstein eventually comes into contact with society at large when facing economic necessity. This plight forces him to take on a regular job in an insurance company: "Er sei froh, endlich einmal unter das Volk gegangen zu sein, auf einmal zu sehen, wie es wirklich ist, was es wirklich treibt" (WN 65). Against expectations to the contrary, Wittgenstein punctually shows up for work and maintains his expensive inner city apartment from his own salary. His commitment to culture is thus for once earned rather than inherited, productive rather than merely consumptive. This commitment is also borne out in his attempt, however belated, to write his memoirs.

Wittgenstein's persistence in art at a time when it no longer secures any social privilege for him constitutes, albeit indirectly, a criticism of Karajan as a cultural and economic institution. Surrounded by personal tragedy, the hero in Bernhard's novel matures into a tragic comedian who has learned to endure in the face of adversity. After the death of his life-long companion Edith, Wittgenstein himself is pushed to the brink of death: "Der Todkranke stand sechs Stunden Tristan durch und hatte am Ende noch die Kraft, so laut in Bravorufe oder Pfiffe auszubrechen, wie keiner vor und keiner nach ihm am Ring" (WN 47). The late Wittgenstein thus begins to resemble Walter Benjamin's more positive reconstruction of the dandy, the *flaneur* who meanders among the vestiges of a dying bourgeois culture.[20] And as with Benjamin's *flaneur*, the human ambience is not yet fully withdrawn into the anonymous face of the crowd (as in the myth of Karajan and the anonymous cultural institution he represents) or into the concealed gaze of the secluded *Privatmann* (as in Bernhard's earlier withdrawn characters). This ambience, which offers a profound sense of leisure, is revived in animated everyday and cultural conversations at the Hotel Sacher, in visits to the Opera and the Musikverein, and in the indulgence of the public sphere proper, the city with its cultural vortex. Bernhard's novel resurrects a vision of a *Kulturmensch* for whom life and art naturally intersect.

Bernhard's recuperation of the idiosyncratic educator of the public, the *Kunstrichter*, is neither nostalgic nor blind to the disintegration of the public sphere as an institution. Ulrich Greiner speaks appropriately of the "Liquidation von Geschichte überhaupt" which, as he claims, runs like a leitmotif through Bernhard's works, one indebted to the post-Habsburg heritage of national and cultural dissolution. Bernhard's heroes, notes Greiner, "beschleunigen den Zusammenbruch längst überständiger gesellschaftlicher Verhältnisse."[21]However, this post-Habsburg dissolution myth of protracted decline, which is apparently sped up in Bernhard, does not do full justice to the revitalizing core in the author's work. While it is true that Bernhard does not attempt to recover the institutions representative of Austria's bourgeois public sphere, one cannot ignore the constructive agonistic and democratic forces that inform his work. In *Wittgensteins Neffe*, Bernhard's recuperative efforts lie with the passionate stance that impels individuals to converse about art as a unique realm inspired and sustained by the art of communication. Bernhard's portrait of Wittgenstein as an irresistible conversationalist and the author's own and equally irresistible conversational style of narration with its expressive and performative character of language both highlight this dramatic ambience surrounding art. The emphasis on a conversationally and communicatively shared world is, however, carefully guarded against a reduction to facile consensus and its equivalent in the commodity market of culture. Bernhard at the same time promotes an agonistic conception of discourse whereby social conventions are to be outstripped by compulsive behavior that is transformed into an exuberance or inspiring passion. The excessive nature of both leading characters and their compulsive relation to art is not to be understood exclusively in negative pathological terms. For it is only in their compulsion that Wittgenstein and the narrator can ultimately challenge the commodity sphere of art and restore its experiential quality by breaking with its habitual and instrumentalized modes of interaction. It is this pathological side of Bernhard's heroes that furthermore validates them as credible human characters in a society from which no ultimate escape is possible.

## *Holzfällen*: The Commodified Avant-garde and the Retreat of Art's Critique from the Public Sphere

Bernhard's subsequent novel *Holzfällen* (1984) calls the realm of the *Kulturmensch* or *Kunstmensch* more critically into question, and it harks back to the author's early apprenticeship in the arts under the guidance of the composer Gerhard Lampersberg, a mentor and patron of Austria's avant-garde. Bernhard's novel revisits this scene of instruction twenty-five years later and critically recasts his original sponsors in their now ridiculous and comically absurd effort to uphold a cultural mission exclusively for artists. The suitable occasion for Bernhard's critique of the decadence of the artistic public sphere is that of a *künstlerisches Abendessen* (artistic dinner), whose original function as an alternate public sphere is forgotten and which has become a matter of mere social routine. Bernhard attacks here the privacy of art and its withdrawal from society under the guise of esoteric exclusiveness. Bernhard, it can be said, recasts the last stages of the alienation and gap between artists and their public which, ever since the post-Romantic period, has widened steadily. In addition, and with more critical acuity than in *Wittgensteins Neffe*, Bernhard acknowledges that in the present culture industry all artistic production is likely to suffer the fate of mere reproduction and exhaustion in its marketability and commodification.

The host of the artistic *soirée*, Auersberger, is accordingly a representative of an impotent and commodified avant-garde. His negations are as ambivalent as those of the bourgeois *enfant terrible* Baudelaire, without, however, attaining the latter's artistic accomplishments or his provocative appeal to the public. Auersberger, a composer in the Webern tradition, minimizes his already minor works to significant silences and takes pride in their remoteness from any public. His music, claims Bernhard's narrator from his critical vantage point in the *Ohrensessel* from where he observes the entire dinner, "ist nichts als ein unerträglicher epigonaler Webern, der ja selbst, wie ich jetzt weiß, kein Genie, nur ein plötzlicher, wenn auch genialer Schwächeanfall der Musikgeschichte gewesen ist."[22] The artistic refusal and asceticism of Webern's work to which Bernhard refers bear some resemblance to the declining bourgeois poetic project. In the wake of the growing nihilism and disbelief at the end of the nineteenth century, poetry was no longer capable of legitimating itself as a divinely inspired art and therefore turned to negation as its proper medium. Moreover, the poets of this era began to scorn the "vulgar" and conventional public as their new sphere of reception and thus rejected any possible ground upon which the project of art could be credibly sustained. In his biography of *Mallarmé or the Poet of Nothingness*, Sartre describes a whole generation of such estranged poets who took a curious pride in their esoteric withdrawal from society and their resilience in art:

> Poetry now gives up large scale production and devotes itself to quality. In place of the unbridled abundance of its predecessors who had wound up causing a verbal inflation, it substitutes an aesthetic of scarcity. They now specialize in luxury goods. Constricted to the point of constipation, the newcomers jealously conceal their poems from indifferent crowds. To ward off prying fingers, they put golden clasps on their books: the public is requested not to touch. One writes principally for oneself, then for one's fellow poets, and finally for a few collectors of rare objects. . . . There had, of course, always been misers who wrote; but never before this fin de siècle did one write in order to be a miser.[23]

Bernhard's narrator, following along the lines of Sartre's critique in a more subjective fashion, rails against "Anton von Webern . . ., den ich, wie die stumpfsinnigen Literaten den Paul Celan sozusagen als beinahe wortlosen Dichter, als beinahe tonlosen Komponisten bezeichnen muß" (H 96–97). What Bernhard deplores in Webern or Celan (of whose special situation he shows little understanding) is their abortion of any public discourse that links art vitally to the concerns of a community. Auersberger's compositions, which are said to follow weakly in this miserly tradition, are thus parodied by Bernhard for their sparseness and their retentiveness: "da ein Vierminutenchor, da eine Zwölfminutenoper, dort eine Dreiminutenkantate, da eine Sekundenoper, dort ein Minutenlied, da eine Zwei-, dort eine Vierminutenarie" (H 96). A further more drastic act of this self-erasure is given in the suicide of the dancer and actress Joana that overshadows the dinner, providing the morbid backdrop to Bernhard's account.

In the narrator's account, the dinner is aptly called a "Requiem für Joana" (H 65) denoting a funereal rite for the artistic public sphere that has succumbed to social posturing and pretension. The private reflections of the narrator recall not only his introduction to art through the Auersberger couple in the Carinthian village of Maria Zaal,[24] but also his subsequent infatuation with the Viennese writer Jeannie Billroth (closely resembling the real-life Austrian writer Jeannie Ebner). Also, he recalls his many hours spent in the circle of the deceased Joana and her husband, a famous tapestry artist. The latter couple's studio, which he used to frequent in his youth, still represented a world of art embedded in society and assembled "einen idealen Querschnitt der Stadtmenschheit, die für einen werdenden Künstler . . . notwendig, ja unerläßlich sind" (H 130). Bernhard acknowledges here a public sphere in its ideal and open sense of a democratic mingling of private citizens from different walks of life and backgrounds. Habermas similarly comments on the original notion of the public sphere: "However exclusive the public might be in any given instance, it could never close itself off entirely and become consolidated as a clique; for it always understood and found itself immersed within a more inclusive public of private people."[25] It is ultimately the reduction of this ideal democratic openness to an exclusive and withdrawn circle of artists that Bernhard exposes as a threat to art, affecting not only the commodified avant-garde represented by the Auersbergers but also his artist-narrator. As the narrator notes: "Wir werden schwach und gehen in die Falle, gehen in die Gesellschaftsfalle hinein" (H 140).

In this story of decline and decadence, the Auersbergers remain merely a semblance of their former selves. The husband, who had earlier secured himself socially and financially by marrying into wealthy Austrian nobility, now displays the character of a hopeless drunk and a complacent artist. His wife, a singer, indulges Auersberger's supposed genius by presenting an enlightened and tolerant mien as he throws infantile public tantrums, hurling on several occasions his bowl of gulash against a restaurant wall. His wife willingly entertains these and other staged frustrations by serving as the foil in an equally predictable domestic routine of publicized marital argument. According to the narrator's judgment, both of them have regressed from artists into petty, domestic people. "Gaben sich den Künstleranschein," the narrator notes, "und waren doch nur Kleinbürger" (H 169). Jeannie Billroth, in the narrator's view, has also taken a turn for the worse in pursuing the career of a *Staatskünstler* (state subsidized artist), practicing a dubious "Staatsanbiederungskunst" (H 252) by obsequiously securing state subsidies and literary awards from the cultural administrative apparatus of Vienna. Public and private spheres have thus become completely ossified and dominate the once idiosyncratic and ideally open space of the assembled artists.

The evening's attraction is the grandly announced arrival of the *berühmte Burgschauspieler* (theater celebrity) for whom the entire dinner is stalled much to the dissatisfaction of the already irritated narrator. For Bernhard, the *Burgschauspieler* in his ambivalent role as a public commodity and notoriety points both to the institutionalized and ideal definition of the public sphere. Initially, he is portrayed as the inflated icon of the Burgtheater through which the assembled clique complacently legitimates its artistic and social status. The new Viennese Burgtheater, part of Austria's state-sponsored cultural apparatus, was originally built as part of the Ringstraße project between 1874 and 1888 during Vienna's period of urban expansion. The Ringstraße project, a monument to Vienna's era of bourgeois liberalism, as Carl Schorske points out, represents in its entirety "liberalism's value system: parliamentary government in the Reichsrat building, municipal autonomy in the Rathaus, the higher learning in the University, and dramatic art in the Burgtheater."[26] In the latter institution, Austria linked itself particularly to a German tradition of theater by Lessing, Goethe and Schiller and to the Baroque tradition that brought drama to its first heights in Vienna. This institutional and national authority surrounding the Burgtheater constitutes the false appeal of its actors who are seen as larger than life figures, representing a national culture. However, as Schorske further notes about the origins of Viennese theater, its national mythmaking was preceded by the myth of an open society which still resonates beneath it: "The Baroque style [commemorates] the era in which theater first joined together cleric, courtier, and commoner in a shared aesthetic enthusiasm."[27] The Burgtheater figures in this respect as the quintessential bourgeois public sphere with its audience made up from a variety of social classes and not yet entirely built on exclusionary definitions. The *Burgschauspieler* serves in Bernhard also as a reminder of this public spirit carried by the dramatic and egalitarian voice of the actor who instructs the public in its use of language. As Edward Timms describes the theater's role as a "social paradigm":

> The elevated status of the actors was enhanced by an idealized mode of performance which predominated in Burgtheater performances of the nineteenth century. It seems to have served as a model of social decorum for a bourgeois audience with aspirations to be accepted in polite society. . . . Elias Canetti records that for his parents, living in a small town of Bulgaria, the experience of its productions was so memorable that they spoke together a 'secret language' based on the diction of the Burgtheater.[28]

While the theater, as Timms states, set up the prevalent social standards of discourse, it also extended its model of discourse beyond the exclusive domain of the aristocracy, welcoming the bourgeoisie and the outer provinces of the empire as in the case of Canetti's parents. In Bernhard's novel, the emphasis is ultimately similarly placed on the *Burgschauspieler's* exemplary and potentially democratic power of enunciation and less so on the compromising aspects of providing a model of social decorum.

The *Burgschauspieler* concludes the novel as well as the *soirée* with a pathetic endorsement of the public institution of the theater, one treasured as the most adequate vehicle for Austria's cultural histrionics. His endorsement of his profession is given first negatively by disqualifying German theater — "der letzte Kabarettist in Wien ist besser, als der berühmteste deutsche Schauspieler" (H 290) — and subsequently in a rhapsodic and melodramatic invocation of a natural sphere lying somewhere beyond all the artificiality of the evening:

> In den Wald gehen, tief in den Wald hinein, sagte der Burgschauspieler, sich gänzlich dem Wald überlassen, das ist es immer gewesen, der Gedanke, nichts anderes, als selbst Natur zu sein. Wald, Hochwald, Holzfällen, das ist es immer gewesen, sagte er plötzlich aufgebracht und wollte endgültig gehen. (H 302)

The intensification of "Wald" into "Hochwald" surprisingly finds its superlative not in yet another generic term denoting the forest but in an action, the cutting of wood. The initial desire for a retreat into the forest "sich gänzlich dem Wald überlassen" does not recede into further interiority and passivity as, for instance, in Heidegger's meditative paths or *Holzwege* which allow only for an occasional glimpse of a clearing or *Lichtung*. Instead, through the active gesture of woodcutting, the envisioned agency of man once again appears possible in the baring of the "natural" space for the construction of culture. While Bernhard certainly does not espouse an essentialist view of human agency — the melodramatic and theatrical nature of the monologue clearly qualifies any deeper truth spoken by the actor — the expressed desire for such agency is nevertheless given credibility in the pragmatic sphere of communication. The problematic behavior of the narrator, identified by Gerhard Pail as "die Unfähigkeit des Erzählers, an gesellschaftlichem Leben rollenadäquat teilzunehmen," is momentarily reversed, as he is deeply touched by the profundity of the actor's monologue.[29] For once he overcomes his cynical distance and identifies with the power of the actor's expressed emotions: "Am Ende war ich von dem für mich lange Zeit abstoßenden, mich durch seine Widerwärtigkeit für mich, allein durch sein Gehabe in Erregung und sogar Wut versetzenden Menschen, eingenommen" (H 307). As with *Wittgensteins Neffe*, *Holzfällen* dramatizes the redemptive power of speech and pathos as the pre-reflective condition from which genuine communication emerges. Bernhard ultimately deplores the absence of this affective dimension of language that reduces art to a meaningless commodity. After an effusive and feigned farewell to the hosts of the evening recalling the linguistically depleted rituals of society, the narrator escapes from the "Gesellschaftsfalle" of the dinner into "das mir immer verhaßt gewesene Wien." The once despised city of Vienna is now embraced as the "mir aufeinmal jetzt wieder doch das beste, mein bestes Wien" (H 320–21).

In contrast to Bernhard's endorsement of Paul Wittgenstein as a tragic *Kunstmensch* in his previous novel, the affirmation of *Holzfällen* is concentrated in a short moment of irritation and intoxication. During this epiphany the *Burgschauspieler* utters profundities of which he is usually unaware and which only momentarily assuage the narrator's irritation with the whole social order surrounding art.[30] Still, the contagious nature of impassioned speech persists as a utopian moment immanent in social discourse whose apparently ossified structure can be reversed by it. Unlike Handke, who circumvents social discourse in a revitalizing poetics of the everyday, Bernhard immerses himself in institutional discourse, intensifying its contradictions in order to bring about its eventual breakdown and re-opening. Socio-cultural discourse, placed under enough pressure, as in the case of the *Burgschauspieler* who is insulted and attacked by Jeannie Billroth, may temporarily provoke and give way to a reciprocal level of discourse not yet fully subordinated to calculation and self-interest. Bernhard's strategy, paradoxically, in writing is to descend deeper into the contradictions of art and its establishment in order to achieve an increasing intensification of the power of speech.

## *Alte Meister*: Canonicity and the Nationalization of Art

Compared to *Holzfällen*, Bernhard's subsequent novel *Alte Meister* (1986) ends on an even harsher note, namely not with a dinner saved by a pathos-driven dramatic speech but a performance in the Burgtheater that allows only for the scathing critical comment "Die Vorstellung war entsetzlich."[31] In *Alte Meister*, as we will see, Bernhard applies himself to more extensive woodcutting, demolishing the seemingly timeless icons of high culture through irreverent parody and verbal caricatures of the "fette, stinkende Bach," the "Turteltauben" affectation of Mozart's music and the "Marschmusikstumpfsinn" of Beethoven. After his initial confrontation of the artistic public sphere in a single figure in Wittgenstein, and subsequently in an artistic circle or clique, Bernhard expands his critique here to that of the cultural canon in toto. The suitable location in *Alte Meister* for this inquiry is Vienna's Kunsthistorisches Museum, part of the Ringstraße project and inaugurated in 1891 as the unified site for the Habsburg art treasures collected since the sixteenth century. Bernhard's previously limited condemnation in *Holzfällen* of certain artists for practicing a "Staatsanbiederungskunst" (state sponsored art) is now categorically directed at any art that serves as the representation of the power and glory of the nation. The nationalization or *Verstaatlichung* of all areas of life including art consequently becomes the major concern in Bernhard's critical exposure of the formation of cultural canons.

The critic Reger, his mouthpiece in the novel, resents not only the wholesale nationalization of culture — "Die Menschheit ist ein gigantischer Staat" (AM 60) — but more specifically the complicity of art in this process of cultural standardization: "die sogenannten Alten Meister haben immer nur dem Staate gedient" (AM 62). Tintoretto, whose *Weißbärtiger Mann* becomes the focal point of Reger's habitual and 35-year-long bi-weekly contemplation of this painting in the Bordone-Saal, figures in this respect, like the *Burgschauspieler* and Paul Wittgenstein, as an ambivalent icon of culture with both redemptive and compromising qualities. In his contemplative and critical activities, Reger seeks foremost a sanctuary from the pervasive institutionalization of art. His modest evasion of the overburdening canon lies in the production of short critical pieces on music published abroad in the *Times*. His idiosyncratic relation to art is also shown in his foreshortened readings of books — "zwölf Zeilen eines Buches mit höchster Intensität zu lesen und also zur Gänze zu durchdringen . . . als wir lesen das ganze Buch wie der normale Leser" (AM 39). Finally, Reger's unorthodox or *zweckentfremdet* use of the museum site as a comfortable locale for study and reflection flies in the face of the sanctity of art: "ich gehe wegen dieser Sitzbank in den Bordone-Saal und wegen des idealen Lichteinflusses auf mein Gemütsvermögen, tatsächlich wegen der idealen Temperaturverhältnisse" (AM 37).

Apart from his eccentricity Reger bears some of the more positive traits of a sobered minimalist aesthetician, which Bernhard had still so harshly attacked in *Holzfällen. Alte Meister* ends on a minimal yet significant gesture of friendship in which Reger, in spite of his aversion to the Burgtheater, invites his disciple Atzbacher to attend together what turns out to be one of the Burgtheater's predictably bad performances. The novel's object, announced in the contemplation of the Tintoretto painting, is the partial recovery of the human gaze that escapes us in an art that is forever at the service of the state: "Immer wieder nur ein Antlitz, wie Reger sagt, kein Gesicht" (AM 61). This human approximation is achieved for once in the final visit to the theater, albeit ironically in the presence of Kleist's poorly performed *Zerbrochener Krug*.

Kleist's play, which puts the apparently untouchable authority of a judge on trial, is mirrored in Bernhard's novel where art has to stand a similar trial. The bulk of the novel, made up of Reger's relentless critical dissections of the icons of culture, points to the utilization of these icons in a present era of consumerism and their absurdity as a cultural heritage. Bernhard's parodies of such major figures as Stifter, Bruckner and Heidegger may provoke justified disagreement among their adherents, but deserve more sympathetic understanding with regard to their real target, the culture industry. Bernhard's parody of Stifter, for example, is not solely directed against the author but against Stifter's misappropriation by the publishing industry, that promotes less the author's work than his marketable political ideologies. "Es ist gar nicht so unverständlich," notes Reger, "daß jetzt, wo das Wort Wald und Waldsterben so in Mode gekommen sind und überhaupt der Begriff Wald der am meisten gebrauchte und mißbrauchte ist, der Hochwald von Stifter so viel gekauft wird, wie noch nie" (AM 86). As Reger continues his analysis, he begins to sound uncompromising in the manner of Adorno who espied bourgeois self-deception in every piece of art: "Die Sehnsucht der Menschen ist heute, wie nie zuvor, die Natur und da alle glauben, Stifter habe die Natur beschrieben, laufen sie alle zu Stifter. Stifter aber hat die Natur gar nicht beschrieben, er hat sie nur verkitscht" (AM 86).

Reger's judgment that every piece of art has a serious flaw is close to Adorno who likewise claims that kitsch "lies dormant in art itself, waiting for a chance to leap forward at any moment."[32] Kitsch, according to Adorno, "preys on fictitious feelings, thereby neutralizing real ones" and amounts thus to "a parody of catharsis."[33] Reger dismantles the myth of cultural catharsis through nature, revived by the ecological movement of the 1980s, by characterizing the Romantic symphonies of Bruckner as a "religiös-pubertären Notenrausch," (AM 72), Stifter as the mystification and *Verkitschung* of nature, and finally Heidegger as the sentimentalization of philosophy. Especially with regard to Heidegger, Reger's critique is extremely severe. The target no longer remains Heidegger's thinking but his much more powerful public image documented in a photo series, showing the sage, the "Denkspießer mit der Schwarzwaldhaube auf dem Kopf," (AM 89) at his country residence in Todtnauberg.

Bernhard himself had already once undertaken such a critique of a photo album documenting the private life of Bruno Kreisky, Austria's longtime socialist chancellor. In his scandalous essay "Der pensionierte Salonsozialist," Bernhard took issue with Kreisky and with the way the authors Peter Turrini and Gerhard Roth sentimentally indulge in the politician's domestic sphere, which is paraded as a special private insight granted to the public:

> Der im Klappstuhl auf seinem eigenen Balkon sitzende Kleinbürger in der handgestrickten Kleinbürgerweste, der am späten Nachmittag seine grobbesockten Zehen knapp über den abgelegten Gesundheitspantoffeln (aus Holz!) aneinanderreibt, hat schon immer mehr die Rührung aus dem Betrachter herausgezogen, denn die kalte Verachtung provoziert, denke ich, auch wenn er, wie in dem Buch abgebildet, Bruno Kreisky heißt. Millionen solcher Kleinbürger rühren uns in der Dämmerung, wenn wir zu solcher Rührung aufgelegt sind, und wir gönnen ihnen allen den Sonnenuntergang vor dem Eigenheim. . . . Herr Kreisky, dem das Buch zum 70. Geburtstag gewidmet ist, wird darin schon als Pensionist dargestellt, obwohl der Kanzler, wie jeder weiß, für alle MERKWÜRDIGERWEISE, für viele ENTSETZLICHERWEISE, noch im Amt ist.[34]

Bernhard's attack is directed here against a deceptively harmonious mingling of private and public spheres which makes light of Kreisky's political power and instead creates the harmless and domestic aura of an everyday citizen: "Der Pensionär Kreisky, den das Buch zeigt, hat die gleichen Leidenschaften und Gelüste wie die Millionen seiner frustrierten Kollegen . . . , die man niemals auf dem Ballhausplatz [seat of government] sozusagen als Hausherr antreffen wird."[35] In accordance with Adorno's definition of kitsch, fictitious rather than real aspects of the political figure Kreisky are brought to the foreground in this picture book portrayal, giving the illusion of a proximity between the politician and his subjects.

Bernhard attacks a similar photo-documentation in *Alte Meister* in which Heidegger's ambitious philosophical and political project are made to appear harmless, creating the image of a grounded thinker deeply rooted in his native Swabian soil. This image naturally invites parody by Reger:

> Auf diesen Fotografien steigt Heidegger aus seinem Bett, steigt Heidegger in sein Bett wieder hinein, schläft Heidegger, wacht er auf, zieht er seine Unterhose an, schlüpft er in seine Strümpfe, macht er einen Schluck Most, tritt er aus seinem Blockhaus hinaus und schaut auf den Horizont, schnitzt er seinen Stock, setzt er seine Haube auf, nimmt er seine Haube vom Kopf, hält er seine Haube in den Händen, spreizt er die Beine, hebt er den Kopf, senkt er den Kopf, legt er seine rechte Hand in die linke seiner Frau, legt seine Frau ihre linke Hand in seine rechte, geht er vor dem Haus, geht er hinter dem Haus, geht er auf sein Haus zu, geht er von seinem Haus weg, liest er, ißt er, löffelt er die Suppe, schneidet er sich ein Stück (selbstgebackenes) Brot ab, schlägt er ein (selbstgeschriebenes) Buch auf, macht er ein (selbstgeschriebenes) Buch zu, bückt er sich, streckt er sich und so weiter, sagte Reger. Es ist zum Kotzen. (AM 93–94)

Bernhard's critical parody of Heidegger, like his parody of Kreisky, exposes the illusionary proximity created between a person of society's elite echelon and the common person and further highlights the problematic conflation of *Heimat* and culture, which uncritically promotes Heidegger's philosophy. This strategy of mixing high and low culture, as Adorno has pointed out, fuels the culture industry and makes sociohierarchical structures of elitism more palatable to the mass consumer, thereby reinforcing their continued validity and profitability. Heidegger is no longer questioned in his status as a thinker but instead has become a fetishized icon of culture. Expanding further on this aspect of commodification, Elfriede Jelinek's play *Totenauberg* (1991) reveals how Heidegger provides not only the image of the rustic sage but the conceptual paradigm of *Heimat* and authenticity which Austria markets as its prime commodities of Alpine tourism. As Reger comically remarks on Heidegger as a household brand of Austria's culture:

> Wenn Sie in eine . . . Gesellschaft kommen, wird Ihnen sehr oft schon vor der Vorspeise Heidegger serviert, Sie haben Ihren Mantel noch nicht ausgezogen, wird Ihnen schon ein Stück Heidegger angeboten, Sie haben sich noch nicht hingesetzt, hat die Hausfrau Ihnen schon sozusagen mit dem Sherry Heidegger auf dem Silbertablett hereingebracht. (AM 91).

According to Bernhard, cultural products in their highly commodified form as cultural icons, products of a purportedly free consumer society, ultimately undermine democratic freedom and contribute to the ossification and undifferentiated, mythical omnipresence of the state: "Wir sehen, wohin wir schauen, nur Staatskinder, Staatsschüler, Staatsarbeiter, Staatsbeamte, Staatsgreise, Staatstote" (AM 57). With the advancing standardization of cultural and political discourse, government deteriorates into ceremonious pomp, "seniles Staatsvatergefasel" (AM 120), and becomes a deceptive arena of "Goldene Sitzbänke in der Hofburg [the seat of Austria's presidency]. . . und lauter pseudodemokratische Idioten darauf" (AM 121). These and similar forceful remarks about a mindlessly accepted and seemingly irreversible crisis of the state, mixed in with comical and more banal observations about Vienna's low standards of public hygiene, paint a picture of a new and more grotesque decadence that has taken hold of Vienna. This present-day apocalypse is gaily celebrated together with the economic exploitation of its previous fin-de-siècle decline. "Und Klimt und Schiele, diese Kitschisten," exclaims Reger, "sind ja heute die Allermodernsten" (AM 255) along with Mahler, Loos and Hoffmann who have become the heavily marketed idols of a pseudo-liberal interest in their formerly neglected or reviled art.

Commenting on the socio-historical significance of the recent revival of fin-de-siècle Vienna through major exhibits at Venice, Paris, New York and Vienna, Russell Berman lists among other reasons the "transformation of the bourgeois citizen into the modern consumer" as one of the remaining attractions of this historical period.[36] This past era thus appeals to the cultural narcissism of an effete consumer society that is allowed to revisit its cradle in the beautifully gilded friezes of Klimt, in Schiele's semi-pornographic delights, in Loos' lavish yet critically enlightened department store designs, and in Hoffmann's functional though chic interior decorations. Or more realistically seen, the present consumer society, worried about the limits of its expansion of affluence, finds in Vienna at least the promise of a fabulous decline before the onset of social catastrophe.

Anticipating and already living within such a catastrophic vision of cultural decline, Reger ultimately finds his only sanctuary, corrupted as it may be, in art: "So rettet Unsereinen doch nichts anderes als eben diese verfluchte und verdammte und oft bis zum Erbrechen widerwärtige Kunst, so Reger" (AM 244). This affirmation is seriously called into doubt, however, by Reger's overall estimation that "vierzig Jahre nach Kriegsende haben die österreichischen Verhältnisse wieder ihren finsteren moralischen Tiefpunkt erreicht" (AM 264). Could Reger, a refugee from Nazi persecution, be alluding here to a resurgence of a type of fascism more deep-seated than that administered by the Third Reich? Bernhard's critics tend to belittle this apparently outrageous suggestion, worrying more about the writer's breach of tact. Bernhard Sorg relies specifically on Bernhard's character presentation and finds in Reger's burdened and persecuted psychology — Reger is an 82-year-old widower and a survivor of Nazi persecution — the excuse for his uncontrolled remarks. Given the fact that Bernhard tends to duplicate his tirades in more than just one character, Sorg's criteria of a distinct character psychology to account for the instability of provocative remarks collapses. In *Alte Meister*, Bernhard's sententious judgments are not only spoken by Reger but by Irrsigler and Atzbacher as well. Seriously belittling Bernhard's critical project, Sorg claims that "man ginge Bernhards Pauschalurteilen auf den Leim, oder in die Falle, ließe man sich auf eine ausführliche Diskussion der manchmal witzigen und oft niveaulosen Beschimpfungen ein."[37] Schmidt-Dengler is somewhat more sympathetic and, while dismissing individual remarks by Bernhard as tasteless, acknowledges the merit of his rhetorical strategy of exaggeration: "Er ist der Übertreibungskünstler, denn nur in der Übertreibung wird sichtbar, wie notwendig es ist, die Welt zu entstellen, um sie kenntlich zu machen."[38]

Bernhard's idiosyncratically expressed social criticism, however, needs no psychological or aesthetic apologies. As Sorg himself must admit, Bernhard's works are staged "unter dem dunklen Schatten des Nationalsozialismus."[39] In fact, Bernhard's seemingly tasteless remarks about the visible resurgence of National Socialism have unfortunately been vindicated by the recent history of neo-fascist acts of aggression and the current *Rechtsruck* (move to the far right) in the European political arena. While it is true that Bernhard often gratuitously uses invectives that he does not thoroughly explore and develop, his preoccupation with nationalism and its dangerous Austrian embodiment is consistent. In not taking the discontinuity between fascism and the present political climate for granted, Bernhard has extended the criticism of fascism from its institutional supra-structure to the base of society where it is embodied in various forms of everyday fascist discourse and petty terror. Fascism as a cultural climate lingering over a seemingly rehabilitated Austria, I would agree with Sorg, deserves more than an occasional reference as part of a character's growing irritation with society. Given the consistency with which Bernhard's critique unfolded and widened, however, it was not surprising that this taboo topic would eventually become the final and ultimate provocation of Bernhard's work.

## *Heldenplatz*: Anti-Semitism and Austria's Public Sphere

I would like to close my analysis of Bernhard's later works with a summative perspective of his main contributions to the understanding of the Austrian public sphere by turning to a discussion of Bernhard's controversial *Heldenplatz*. The play, occasioned by the fiftieth anniversary of Austria's annexation by Germany, continues Bernhard's expanding reflection on the public sphere, by finally turning to the political sphere proper. The chosen site, the public square where Hitler was given a jubilant welcome by an estimated 100,000 or more Viennese could not have been a better locale for Bernhard's last provocation of Austria's complacent cultural self-perception. With the help of Austria's media and its denunciation of the play before its premiere, Bernhard's play triggered a scandal of unusual proportion, turning Austria temporarily into a *Staatstheater*. Major politicians from all political camps joined into the hostile chorus of the press, although hardly any of the critics had read the unpublished manuscript and merely relied on brief provocative excerpts chosen by the media. As Sigrid Löffler summarizes the embarrassing calls for censorship: "Schon hat sich ganz Österreich vor der Welt als Bernhardscher Heldenplatz präsentiert."[40] Only Waldheim's election to the post of the president two years prior displayed even more disturbingly Austria's clouded relation to its past.

Bernhard's play, which was eventually performed, disappointed many of its spectators for being merely yet another play in the known style of the author. Sigrid Löffler, Austria's self-appointed cultural critic of the media, dismissed it as a mere public spectacle: "Ich sagte ja schon, daß dieses Stück meiner Ansicht nach diese Brisanz überhaupt nicht hat, die es dann tatsächlich in der Realität bekommen hat. . . . Ich glaube nach wie vor, daß das keineswegs ein bedeutendes Theaterstück ist."[41] Löffler, who had earlier chided Austria's public for its lack of tolerance regarding free speech, endeared herself to the public in the journalistic fashion of advancing and retracting provocative opinions by saying that the play after all did not merit significant attention.

This condescending dismissal of the play by Löffler is symptomatic of a more general and superficial treatment of the work in which little attention is given to its idiosyncratic presentation of the two protagonists, former Jewish exiles resettling in Austria, or to their delineated cultural impasse. In the case of the character of Josef Schuster, the repatriation ends in suicide; his brother Robert Schuster instead chooses assimilation and public concealment of his ethnic heritage. First, it is striking to note that Bernhard does not attempt to give an ethnic or stereotyped cultural portrayal of the Jewish characters in the play. Löffler's charge "daß Peymann [the director of the play] das Judentum aus dem Stück völlig weginszeniert hat" and that "die Juden sind ja, wenn es einem nicht ausdrücklich im Text gesagt wird, als solche nicht zu erkennen,"[42] is particularly symptomatic and disturbing. It reveals more about her own and Austria's lingering racial stereotyping of Jewish culture than Bernhard's purportedly deficient representation of Jews. Bernhard's play remains historically much more faithful in his portrayal of Austria's predominantly assimilated Jewish population. One must bear in mind that it was to a large extent the racial laws of Nürnberg, enforced in Austria after its annexation, that made Jews publicly identifiable and contributed to what Gerhard Botz calls their "begriffliche Ausgrenzung."[43] Bernhard's portrayal of the assimilated Jew underscores the insanity of fascism that persecuted Austrians sharing in and contributing to their culture. His depiction of individualized and complex Jewish characters would further add to this objective treatment by not idealizing or stereotyping them in any specific manner. The Schuster brothers enjoy in Bernhard's literary Austria the same privileges as all its other citizens, that is, they serve Bernhard no less than any other character in exhibiting the author's prototypically tyrannical and acute personality of the cultural critic (Josef Schuster).[44] The conscious reintegration of what the fascists had artificially demonized as a cultural Other is by itself a remarkable feature of Bernhard's play.

In the depiction of the deceased Josef Schuster who never appears on stage and who is presented only indirectly through conversations involving his housemaids and close relatives, Bernhard also gives specificity to the history of Jews in Austria. Jews figure in the present Austria as the empty core or absence of a culture that had first chosen to disembody itself and subsequently refused to acknowledge its loss. Robert Schuster's resignation and withdrawal to the village Neuhaus spells out this death of a culture no longer capable of sustaining itself:

> Jetzt hat alles den Tiefpunkt erreicht
> nicht nur politisch gesehen alles
> die Menschen die Kultur alles
> in ein paar Jahrzehnten ist verspielt worden
> das ist in Jahrhunderten nicht wieder gutzumachen[45]

The catastrophic cultural situation which had previously inspired Bernhard to a wholesale questioning of the literary and artistic canon in *Alte Meister*, ending facetiously in an attendance of Kleist's comedy *Der zer-*

*brochene Krug*, reaches its final destination in *Heldenplatz*, where it amounts to a dismissal of the entire Western culture.

The play sardonically ends on the prospective attendance of yet another comedy, Lessing's *Minna von Barnhelm*: "Vielleicht geh ich mit der Mutter / in die Minna," exclaims her son Lukas, "so ein blödes Stück / hat schon oft Wunder gewirkt" (HP 163–64). This note of cynical resignation pervades the entire play that consists of three fairly subdued scenes. In scene one the deceased Professor Schuster is commemorated by his housemaids, followed by a scene of an after-funeral walk and conversation in the Volksgarten, and ending upon the preparations to move Professor Schuster's widow from her apartment next to the Heldenplatz to Neuhaus, the residence of her brother-in-law. Frau Professor Schuster, suffering from recurring nightmarish hallucinations of the "Massengeschrei" at the Heldenplatz, eventually collapses face downward onto the dining room table upon which the play ends in a mood of an uncannily subdued terror.

Bernhard's critical treatment of the public sphere reaches through its expansion an impasse similar to that of the Schusters in facing the unfulfilling choice between complete self-erasure (as already anticipated in his last novel *Extinction* or *Auslöschung*) and conformist silence. Bernhard's will barred his plays from being performed in Austria up until recently, which had the unfortunate effect of silencing his own critical voice in Austria and which benefited mostly his opponents. Bernhard's original ironic resurrection of the *Kunstrichter* in a post-Kunst era and the progressive extension of his critique to the era's social, cultural and political reifications arrives not at a final saving insight but must return to the crisis point from which it had departed. In reviving critically the significance of the public sphere, Bernhard, as we have seen, increasingly confronts its overextension and commodification and thereby its decline as a space of autonomous agency within a social whole.

The ideal conception of this sphere as an independent and alternative space operating outside institutionalized social forces, as Hansen points out, had from its beginning been blemished by its exclusionary demarcation against women and minorities.[46] This imbalance in the representation of women and laboring classes is the most explicit deficiency of the public sphere dominated by the bourgeois male. Its exclusionary ethnic definition, conversely, appears less obvious. For example, Vienna's public sphere at the turn of the century owed its vivacity and spirit largely to its assimilated Jewish community. However, as Sander Gilman notes, even a prominent figure such as Karl Kraus, Austria's exemplary cultural critic, sustained his position mostly by emphasizing the "distance to his identity as a Jew, his identification with libertarian causes," and by "his condemnation of 'bad' Jews."[47] The decline or impotence of the public sphere can also be attributed to the ethnic regulation of cultural identity, which Bernhard's final work exposes in a powerful way.

With regard to Austria's homogeneous cultural landscape, this negation of cultural difference comes more clearly into focus in Bernhard's later works in their relentless critical revision of an idealized and monolithic cultural heritage. Through the intensification of his cultural critique, Bernhard eventually exposes the practices of exclusion active in this cultural tradition as fascist. Bernhard's austere critical voice echoes the voice of an insidious past denying any legitimate heritage to its heirs. The ending of Bernhard's *Auslöschung* (1985) in which the protagonist offers the inherited property of his fascist parents to the Israelitische Kultusgemeinde in Vienna, however, suggests otherwise. Bernhard, who in his early novels often conjured up protagonists who divested themselves destructively and irresponsibly of their inheritance, has found an ethical perspective that has become increasingly apparent in his late works. Indeed, he has left Austria a legacy, however reluctantly, with which it can begin to re-assemble and reconstruct its ambivalent cultural heritage overshadowed by the narcissistic self-perception of its culture.

Bernhard's commitment to Austria's public sphere as its uncomfortable critical presence, purposely provoking scandal wherever he sensed opportunistic or habitual accommodation in complacent consensus, has thus made him a powerful voice of constructive cultural dissent. The charge of skillfully using the public media in his own interest is beside the point in the case of a writer who operated precisely through his critical presence in the media. Ultimately, Bernhard's public agenda was far from re-assuring and made no attempt to save the institution of culture as embodied in either a national or social ideology. If art is to retain any significance at all in Bernhard's radical universe of dissent and resistance, it is as the realm in which one can articulate forms of communicative agency where an easy consensus is neither presupposed nor desirable.

# Notes

[1] See Christian Klug, *Theaterstücke* (Stuttgart: Metzler, 1991); and Manfred Mittermayer, *Ich werden* (Stuttgart: Akademischer Verlag, 1988).

[2] See, for example, Wendelin Schmidt-Dengler's *Der Übertreibungskünstler* (Vienna: Sonderzahl, 1986) or Willi Huntemann's *Artistik und Rollenspiel* (Würzburg: Königshausen, 1990).

[3] Ulrich Weinzierl, "Bernhard als Erzieher: Thomas Bernhard's *Auslöschung*," in *German Quarterly* (Summer/Fall 1990) 455. A reception study from within academia, such as Schmidt-Dengler's and Huber's *Statt Bernhard* (Vienna: Edition S, 1987) unfortunately does not venture much beyond an account of the media scandals surrounding Bernhard, highlighting the contradictory responses his work receives.

[4] For further reference, turn to my chapter on Handke where I have developed at more length the notion of the post-ideological perspective and its model of self-implication on the part of both author and society.

[5] Manfred Durzak, *Peter Handke und die deutsche Gegenwartsliteratur* (Berlin: Kohlhammer, 1982) 80.

[6] Jürgen Habermas, *The Structural Transformation of the Public Sphere* (Cambridge, Mass: MIT Press, 1989) 41.

[7] Habermas, 41.

[8] Miriam Hansen, *Babel & Babylon: Spectatorship in Silent American Film* (Cambridge: Harvard UP, 1991) 10.

[9] Allan Janik suggests that this type of unconventional social criticism may reach as far back as the theatrical and often comical sermons of Abraham a Sancta Clara directed against a corrupted Viennese public and its growing secularization in the seventeenth century: "Es war die wachsende Besorgnis über dieses Streben nach Luxus, die eine moralische Reaktion in Form einer Art von theatralischer Religiösität in den Predigten Abraham a Sancta Claras auslöste" ("Die Wiener Kultur und die jüdische Selbsthass-Hypothese" in *Eine zerstörte Kultur*, eds. Gerhard Botz, Ivar Oxaal and Michael Pollak (Buchloe: Obermayer, 1990) 105).

[10] See Wendelin Schmidt-Dengler, *Der Übertreibungskünstler: Zu Thomas Bernhard* (Vienna: Sonderzahl, 1986) 8. Schmidt-Dengler, while accurately perceiving the aesthetic significance of Bernhard's style, overlooks the theatrical and public gesture that links his writing both to a critical humanistic tradition (Pascal, Montaigne, Kierkegaard) and to socio-political concerns of Austria's present cultural landscape.

[11] Marcel Reich-Ranicki, *Thomas Bernhard* (Zürich: Ammann Verlag, 1990) 72. Reich-Ranicki calls Bernhard a "radikaler Gesellschaftskritiker, der mit dem vielgepriesenen Engagement nichts gemein hat: Er praktiziert die Revolte um der Revolte willen" (72).

[12] In his discussion of Habermas' *Strukturwandel der Öffentlichkeit*, Peter Uwe Hohendahl raises this distinction between a democratic and an agonistic notion of the public sphere as given in Seyla Benhabib's interpretation of Habermas and Arendt. While the former conception of the public sphere is grounded in the belief of "available procedures that facilitate the democratic process" and rests on the prior assumption of a possible communicative consensus, the latter views the public space more in terms of the contradictory claims of power we bring to its field of contention ("The Public Sphere: Models and Boundaries," *Habermas and the Public Sphere*, ed. Craig Calhoun (Cambridge: MIT Press, 1992) 102). In Bernhard, these two notions overlap and thus privilege neither the progressive nor the regressive side in public discourse.

[13] Allan Janik and Stephen Toulmin, *Wittgenstein's Vienna* (New York: Touchstone, 1973) 44.

[14] Habermas, 32–35.

[15] Thomas Bernhard, *Wittgensteins Neffe. Eine Freundschaft* (Frankfurt: Suhrkamp, 1982) 84; hereafter quoted in text as WN.

[16] Jean-Paul Sartre, *Baudelaire* (New York: New Directions, 1950) 31.

[17] Sartre, 71.

[18] Sartre, 42.

[19] See Jürgen Habermas' discussion of sociology with its integrative approach as opposed to other sciences such as anthropology, economics or political science that deal only with sub-systems of society and therefore tend to specialization. (*The Theory of Communicative Action*, Vol. I, trans. Thomas McCarthy (Boston: Beacon Press, 1984) 1–7).

[20] Benjamin distinguishes the *flaneur* from the *Passant* "welcher sich in der Menge einkeilt" and from the isolated individual or *Privatmann*: "Wo das Privatisieren den Ton angibt, ist für den Flaneur ebensowenig Platz wie im fieberhaften Verkehr der City" ("Über einige Motive bei Baudelaire," in *Illuminationen. Ausgewählte Schriften 1.* (Frankfurt: Suhrkamp, 1977) 205). The *flaneur* takes thus a middle position between private and public person and embodies the social subject proper.

[21] Ulrich Greiner, *Der Tod des Nachsommers* (Munich: Carl Hanser Verlag, 1979) 70.

[22] Thomas Bernhard, *Holzfällen. Eine Erregung* (Frankfurt: Suhrkamp, 1984) 97; hereafter quoted in text as H.

[23] Jean-Paul Sartre, *Mallarmé or the Poet of Nothingness*, trans. Ernest Sturm (University Park: Pennsylvania State UP, 1988) 35.

[24] Maria Saal, as Sigrid Löffler informs us in her review of the public scandal surrounding the publication of *Holzfällen* leading to a temporary confiscation of Bernhard's novel, was the site where Gerhard Lampersberg gathered young talents such as H. C. Artmann, Peter Turrini, Jeannie Ebner and Konrad Bayer at his Tonhof, an estate that had been converted into a small theater. Bernhard himself staged some of his early work at the Tonhof. ("Öfter jemanden umbringen," in *Profil* Nr. 36 (Sept. 3, 1984) 60–64.)

[25] *The Structural Transformation of the Public Sphere*, 37.

[26] Carl E. Schorske, *Fin-de-Siècle Vienna. Politics and Culture* (New York: Random House, 1981) 36.

[27] Schorske, 37.

[28] Edward Timms, *Karl Kraus Apocalyptic Satirist: Culture and Catastrophe in Habsburg Vienna* (New Haven: Yale UP, 1986) 24.

[29] Gerhard Pail, "Perspektivität in Thomas Bernhard's *Holzfällen*," in *Modern Austrian Literature*, Vol. 21 (1988) 58.

[30] In light of this increased critical attitude in Bernhard, I would disagree with Pail's claim that the novel possesses a therapeutic function borne out in the evolving structural dynamics between narrator and the other characters (Pail, 63). Contrary to Pail's assumption, a thematic investigation of the social reality of the artistic public sphere, which I have attempted here, does help us to restore a cultural context to what would appear to be merely a "persönliche Weiterentwicklung infolge einer Auseinandersetzung mit einem entfremdeten sozialen Umfeld" (Pail, 63).

[31] Thomas Bernhard, *Alte Meister* (Frankfurt: Suhrkamp, 1986) 311; hereafter quoted in text as AM.

[32] Theodor Adorno, *Aesthetic Theory*, trans. C. Lenhardt (London: Routledge, 1984) 339–340.

[33] Adorno, 339–340.

[34] Thomas Bernhard, "Der pensionierte Salonsozialist," in *Profil*, Nr.4 (26. Jänner, 1981) 52.

[35] "Der pensionierte Salonsozialist," 52.

[36] Russel A. Berman, "The Vienna Fascination," *Modern Culture and Critical Theory* (Madison: The U of Wisconsin P, 1991) 208.

[37] Bernhard Sorg, *Thomas Bernhard* (Munich: Beck, 1992) 117.

[38] Wendelin Schmidt-Dengler, *Der Übertreibungskünstler*, 104.

[39] Sorg, 112.

[40] Sigrid Löffler, "Farce. Tobsuchtsanfall. Weltblamage," in *Profil*, Nr. 42 (Oct. 17, 1988) 110.

[41] Sigrid Löffler, "Das Werk hat ja auf wunderbare Weise triumphiert," in Maria Fialik's *Der konservative Anarchist. Thomas Bernhard und das Staats-Theater* (Vienna: Löcker, 1991) 21.

[42] Löffler, "Das Werk," 33.

[43] Gerhard Botz, "Die Ausgliederung der Juden aus der Gesellschaft," in *Eine zerstörte Kultur*, eds. Gerhard Botz, Ivar Oxaal and Michael Pollak (Buchloe: Verlag Obermayer, 1990) 291–292.

[44] Countering attacks that Bernhard's outspoken Jewish characters may provoke anti-Semitism, Donald Daviau rightly maintains that "only in a society where prejudice exists could there be any objections" to this type of verbal affront: "Why should not a Jew be allowed to speak his mind like any other citizen?" ("Thomas Bernhard's *Heldenplatz*," *Monatshefte*, Vol. 83, No. 1 (1991) 32).

[45] Thomas Bernhard, *Heldenplatz* (Frankfurt: Suhrkamp, 1988) 96; hereafter quoted in text as HP.

[46] Hansen, 10.

[47] Sander L. Gilman, "Karl Kraus's Oscar Wilde: Race, Sex and Difference," in *Vienna 1900: From Altenberg to Wittgenstein*, eds. Edward Timms and Ritchie Robertson (Edinburgh: Edinburgh UP, 1990) 25.

# 3

# *Cultural Amnesia and the Narration of the Everyday: Peter Handke's Post-Ideological Aesthetics*

## Introduction

When Kurt Waldheim, an alleged accomplice of Nazi genocide, was elected to the post of president in a landslide election in 1986, Austria's denial of historical accountability had once again become apparent as the core of its problematic national identity. Peter Handke provocatively calls Waldheim a "cripple of the spoken word, master of the administrative verb, an amnesiac whose periodic addresses to the population are articulated by the hand which wrote so many 'W's at the bottom of sinister documents." In doing so, he reflects the disenchantment of a critical minority whom he calls "the real people of Austria, those who have so often been discounted, so rarely consulted, almost reduced to silence."[1] This discounted people is most prominently represented by Austrian writers and artists who, since the late 1950s, have repeatedly protested against the stifling spirit of denial and forgetfulness that pervades Austria's socio-cultural landscape.

This inquiry into Handke's literary project will explore the author's particular resistance to this cultural amnesia. This resistance, as I will show, defines itself beyond the clear-cut boundaries of ideology and introduces an entirely new form of cultural self-examination and reflection. In using the concept of ideology, I follow its most basic definition, summarized by Paul Ricoeur, as a "mode of non-congruence" that "designates initially some distorting, dissimulating processes by which an individual or a group expresses its situation but without knowing or recognizing it."[2] Handke's initial reference to a severe amnesia affecting the distorted and dissimulating memory of Waldheim can be seen as an instance of ideological dissemblance. However, the question remains what happens to ideology when it represents the distortion of neither an individual nor a group but that of an entire culture. What if an entire culture suffers from an amnesia in which it hides its own distorted conditions of power from itself? Handke's project of a post-ideological literature begins precisely by asking this question and examines the complacent identification of ideology with clearly defined adversaries.

Of late, this radical post-ideological approach has been exploited by the author for ideological reasons that have baffled readers and critics alike. Handke's problematic stance on Serbia shows little sympathy for the persecution of an ethnic minority and seems to negate his earlier anti-fascist stance as well as his solidarity with those silenced by state authority. More soberly seen, Handke has joined other well-known liberal writers such as Christa Wolf, Botho Strauss and Martin Walser in their revisionist claims concerning the legacy of liberalism. All of them display dubious and embarrassing reactionary tendencies and seem to have fallen out of synchrony with the progressive political tenor of their times. Handke's case is not as singular as it may presently appear but reflects the problematic undertaking of occupying a space beyond ideology. His example illustrates how quickly a post-ideological platform collapses if it does not resist its own generated deception of a value-neutral stance.

Literature, in Handke's early understanding, amounts to a critical revision of a sedimented everyday reality that has the appearance of a pervasive and all-encompassing cultural ideology. It is here that Handke's task becomes akin to what Foucault calls "the tracking down of all varieties of fascism, from the enormous ones that surround and crush us to the petty ones that constitute the tyrannical bitterness of our everyday life."[3] Handke's progressive political preoccupation, as I will attempt to show in this chapter, lies especially with the realm of the everyday and its elusive yet tyrannic symbolic order. Handke is reluctant to apply so-called objective labels to fascism and speaks instead only from within the verifiable experience and tensions of everyday communication.

Focusing on Handke's early works *Die Angst des Tormanns beim Elfmeter* (1970; *The Goalie's Anxiety at the Penality Kick*) and *Wunschloses Unglück* (1973; *A Sorrow Beyond Dreams*), I will begin with an analysis of Handke's initial formation of a post-ideological literary project. This analysis will examine Handke's critique of communicative and cultural commonplaces that are used to construct and maintain ideologies. Turning to Handke's recent prose, I will trace the latest modifications of Handke's post-ideological project, focusing on his subtle reconstructions of open and non-occupied spaces in a culture saturated with conventional meanings. Attention will be given here to Handke's recent incorporation of a *Bildsprache* (visual language) into his writings and to the problems associated with such attempts to create a more unmediated iconography. My goal here is to show how Handke carefully and subtly distinguishes between entirely value-free conceptions of communication (communication as mere semiotic play informing social cynicism) and value-determined conceptions of communication (ideology with its identifiable distortions informing social dogmatism). In an overall estimation of Handke's work, I wish to show that his post-ideological literature does not avoid pressing social concerns as one would surmise from its more critical reception. However, as a final discussion of Handke's stance on Serbia will clearly show, a post-ideological stance also does not immunize writers against political misjudgments.

## Handke's Post-Ideological Aesthetics

Handke's refusal to address ideology directly has earned him criticism from many German critics who favor social realism over an escapist utopianism said to be inherent in Austrian writing. Manfred Durzak, for instance, judges the author severely when polemically asking "Deutet das nicht zudem im Grunde darauf hin, daß der gesamte Kunstanspruch, der hinter den Überlegungen Handkes steht, auf eine äußerst subjektive Situation hinausläuft."[4] Durzak's critical dismissal of Handke's work as exhibiting a "narzißtischer Zirkel" or "Syndrom" is unfortunate, since he does acknowledge a specific cultural setting for Austrian literature in the language critique of Ludwig Wittgenstein and Karl Kraus.[5] This tradition, advancing critical readings of culture in terms of its textual and rhetorical construction, strongly influenced the *Grazer Literaturforum*, Austria's most prominent association of avant-garde writers during the 1960s and seventies, which produced writers like Handke or Jelinek. Its structuralist cultural critique of Austrian society, which departed from the German model of social realism, represents a break with any naive versions of social and cultural representation. Durzak ignores that such a semiotic analysis of social and cultural discourse ultimately aims beyond the safe and privileged perspective of ideology. Handke's subjectivity, in this respect, reveals the author's own implication in whatever he or she constructs as the site of a particular culture. Such misunderstandings concerning the critical self-reflection in Handke's work and its consciously and strategically invoked subjectivity are commonly found in the reception of Handke, particularly among the older ideological schools of German social criticism which have set the tenor for later critical evaluations:

> Handkes Prosa, seine Theaterexperimente, seine irritierte Abwehr gegen Relevanzforderungen setzten ihn so dem Verdikt einer neuen Innerlichkeit von seiten der linken Kritik aus, und manche sprachen ihm dementsprechend jede literarische und politische Relevanz ab. Für

> viele mag hier Peter Hamms 1969 in 'konkret' erschienene Kritk stehen: "Handkes zwanghafte Artistik und sein Versuch, stets up to date zu sein, lassen sich logisch nur erklären aus einem totalen Disinteresse an allem Gesellschaftlichen — soweit es nicht mit der Sprache zu tun hat."[6]

Rainer Nägele and Renate Voris, who point to Handke's proximity to Adorno's critique of consumer culture, ultimately correct some of these common misconceptions surrounding Handke's work by alerting us to a "Verunsicherung der Ichidentität" ("nicht narzißtischer Genuß") that underlies his writing.[7] Nevertheless, even Nägele and Voris safely return to the fold of ideology when claiming that Handke does not reflect upon the objective conditions ("objektiven Bedingungen") that allow literature to fulfill its function in society. In short, Handke supposedly fails to take a critical view of his own privileged social position as a writer engaged in the project of literature ("sich mit der Literatur beschäftigen zu können").[8] Nägele and Voris ultimately still hold a purportedly more legitimate German tradition of normative social criticism over Handke's own peculiar form of inquiry, which they implicitly accuse of political shortcomings.

Ulrich Greiner, as yet another example, correctly identifies Handke's literary strategy but is reluctant to lend what he calls "Handke's subjectivity" any political credibility:

> Handke scheint also gerade jener Konstituierung von Sinn entgegenzuwirken, die Gewalt im Sinn Horkheimers verhindern helfen könnte. Denn auch dies wäre für ihn wieder eine Flucht ins Allgemeine. Nur von der unmittelbaren, authentischen Erfahrung des Subjekts spricht er.[9]

Referring to the critical and conceptual scrutiny of the public sphere undertaken by Horkheimer and the Frankfurt School, Greiner does not see how Handke's subjectivity touches upon an objective social reality. His literature is instead seen as following a tradition of Austrian literature that is "antirealistisch und apolitisch" and said to constitute a paradigm "für die Not des Nichthandelnkönnens und ihrer Transformation in ein Reich der Sehnsüchte und Hoffnungen."[10]

Handke, however, to describe his position more sympathetically, points to the pathology of everyday speech with its normative patterns by which a social discourse is dominated and thereby restrained as a dialogue. Karl Menges takes up for Handke's writing by linking his poetic project to the realism of "komplexer Zeichen- und Kommunikationsysteme"[11] said to be represented and explored in the writer's work. I will follow here Menges' corrective suggestion that subjectivity and engagement share a common origin in the literature of the 1970s, a notion that challenges the reservations of his German colleagues about the so-called apolitical nature of the writers of the "new subjectivity." Indeed, I wish to place the common origin of subjectivity and engagement in Handke altogether outside the loaded terms of the empirical subject and that of an engagement linked to an objective social reality. Handke's literary project, I would like to claim, critically explores the conditions of language and communication as systems that in their capacity to stifle different ways of thinking allow for ideologies such as fascism and that in their conversely constructive and open sense create narrated lifeworld as the possible setting for responsible social action.

In an essay responding to Sartre's influential work *Qu'est-ce que c'est la littérature?* (1948; *What Is Literature?*), Handke asked himself early on in his career whether a writer can ever be politically engaged in the manner Sartre had envisioned. It appeared to Handke that a conventional political engagement as advocated by Sartre presupposed a single-minded and purpose-oriented rationality that was foreign to art — "diese ist weder eindeutig noch mehrdeutig" — and the complex organization of a literary text.[12] "Die literarische Form," claims Handke, "je komplizierter sie ist, verfremdet umso mehr das ihr eingeordnete engagement."[13] Handke concludes that no literature, even social realism, has an immediate and direct access to reality: "Die Literatur ist unwirklich, unrealistisch, auch die sogenannte engagierte Literatur."[14] This hermeneutic insistence on the mediation of all reality in art removes not only literature but also an engaged literature, which appears to appeal directly to social reality, from the sphere of actuality. Consequently, social reality itself is seen as a construction. Its reconfiguration in the political arena differs not in quality but only in the degree of its sedimentation of meaning.

Conventional political discourse raises factuality, the ossified patterns of social discourse, to the level of social reality itself, thereby ignoring its arbitrary formation. Foucault, for instance, refers to the rigid standardization of the political discourse of the left during the years 1945–1965: "there was a certain way of thinking correctly, a certain style of political discourse, a certain ethics of the intellectual. One had to be on familiar terms with Marx, not let one's dreams stray too far from Freud."[15] Conventional political praxis adhering to these strictures strove to correct from within this discourse its apparent imbalances while leaving, however, its structure untouched and intact. Foucault terms this the strategy of the "political ascetics, the sad militants, the theorists of theory, those who would preserve the pure order of politics and political discourse."[16] This one-dimensional approach towards social reality, however, is repudiated by a new generation of post-ideological thinkers like Foucault or Handke who reject authoritarian regulation of the complexity of everyday experience. While Handke may not share the exact agenda of his French contemporaries, who for the most part seek an opening from within academic institutions,[17] he is similarly engaged in overcoming "the old categories of the Negative."[18] This reduction on the part of the instituted discourse of the left is challenged by Handke's search for a more complex narrative that governs social interaction at its roots in everyday discourse.

Handke's goal, as it can be reconstructed from his earlier theoretical remarks, is to demonstrate that literary politics is in principle a politics of language that must critically deal with social reality via the use of language and not merely via social events, the domain of politics proper. Social narratives, he insists, cannot be naively seen as unmediated descriptions of social reality:

> Man glaubt also naiv, durch die Sprache auf die Gegenstände durchschauen zu können wie durch das sprichwörtliche Glas. Dabei denkt man aber nicht daran, daß es möglich ist, mit der Sprache buchstäblich jedes Ding zu drehen. . . . Es wird vernachlässigt, wie sehr die Sprache manipulierbar ist für alle gesellschaftlichen und individuellen Zwecke. Es wird vernachlässigt, daß die Welt nicht nur aus Gegenständen besteht, sondern auch aus der Sprache für diese Gegenstände. Indem man Sprache nur benützt und nicht in ihr und mit ihr beschreibt, zeigt man nicht auf die Fehlerquellen der Sprache hin, sondern fällt ihnen selbst zum Opfer.[19]

Handke rejects the naive instrumental use of language, found in much of conventional political writing, that subordinates language to the objects it describes. For instance, he mentions the description of a trip to Poland that casually drops the name "A." [Auschwitz] and by this predictable maneuver already earns the quality of "political" writing.[20] This facile description, according to Handke, does not reach beyond the rhetoric of everyday political discourse. Handke wishes instead to engage language critically and aesthetically by exploring both its layers of sedimentation and its potential for liberating narratives. Individual perception in particular, which is often labeled and dismissed as the "new subjectivity," is a quality through which Handke seeks to break beyond the predictability of conventional social discourse and its ideological perspectives.

## *Die Angst des Tormanns beim Elfmeter*: The Emerging Praxis of Handke's Post-ideological Perspective

In his first major novel *Die Angst des Tormanns beim Elfmeter* (1970), Handke portrays the fate of a disoriented individual in an equally disorienting reality of social interaction. Handke's earlier treatment of social indoctrination through language, as given for instance in *Kaspar* (1967), reflected this distortion — *Sprechfolterung* (torture by speech) — still with a clear identification of the victim (individual) and the victimizer (society and its imposed order of discourse). However, in the case of his protagonist Joseph Bloch, Handke's goalkeeper, this separation has become blurred. Bloch, while committing a murder, does so gratuitously and without any clear motive. He is as much a victimizer as he is a victim of circumstances. Unlike Sartre's hero in *La nausée* (1938; *Nausea*), a historian who keeps a fastidious diary account of his disintegrating sense of reality, Bloch is hardly aware of his own fragmented existence. His flight is just as erratic as his crime and points to the absence of any integrative or controlling consciousness. Bloch's schizoid reality is a confusion of signs and actions that have lost their rationally motivated links. Moreover, the world of Bloch is one of banality and the everyday. Little in it is of any real significance or would ultimately seem to matter. In an equally alienated social environment where communication has become a matter of routine, his act of murder becomes simply a part of this repetition.

In giving us a semiotic presentation of an exteriorized subjectivity, *Angst des Tormanns* has abandoned Sartre's existential-psychoanalytic description of alienation. The collapse of reflectiveness and significance is no longer determined by a single skeptical subject (Sartre's Roquentin) but seen in relation to society as a whole. Psychology, the interior world (*Innenwelt*), is held inseparable from the exterior world (*Aussenwelt*), as Handke stressed poignantly in his *Die Innenwelt der Aussenwelt der Innenwelt*. The communicative world and its publicly displayed semiotic structure now constitute the tangible psychology of Bloch's social reality. His social pathology is not depicted as a concealed psychological syndrome but presented openly through banal misunderstandings, formulaic linguistic reductions and ritualized gestures of the everyday. All of these socio-semiotic gestures make the pervasive reality of the service industry (ticket operator obliviously spinning the tickets, waitresses mindlessly pursuing their routine, etc.) and the growing instrumentalization of society explicit. The outcome of any social interaction in this strongly objectified environment thus remains in frozen suspense and resembles the limbo of the goalie's anxiety at the penalty kick. Anxiety, which for Heidegger or Sartre still had the quality of a conclusive sensibility foreboding resolute or responsible action, reverts in Handke's novel to a mood of helpless abeyance.

Through its re-absorption of the extraordinary into the ordinary, *Die Angst des Tormanns* expresses a pervasive conformism with which only Bloch seems to be uncomfortable but which affects his entire social environment. As Rainer Nägele und Renate Voris point out with respect to the other characters in the novel:

> Was diese Figuren und ihre Verhaltensweisen von Bloch unterscheidet, ist, daß sie in ihrer Realität und im Gebrauch ihrer Sprache zu Hause sind, negativ ausgedrückt, daß sie sich von den Spielregeln der Signifikanten spielen und leben lassen. Zwar ist auch Bloch darin gefangen, aber er ist nicht darin zu Hause, er leidet darunter, die Sprache wird ihm unnatürlich, so daß er nur noch "stockend" (S. 46) aus der Zeitung vorlesen kann und oft mitten im Satz "stockte und nicht weiter wußte und schließlich nach Sätzen suchte" (S. 59). Die Ordnung der Sprache, die den andern die Welt ordnet, ist ihm nicht mehr geheuer: "es kam ihm nicht geheuer vor, wie man zu reden anfangen und dabei schon wissen konnte, was man am Ende des Satzes sagen würde"(S. 79).[21]

Bloch's skepticism towards the conventional order of discourse and the extreme sedimentation of its linguistic repertoire is one deeply shared by Handke himself. This skepticism strongly shaped Handke's early experimental writings and his search for alternative forms of expression. Handke revolts against the increasing social sedimentation of language that can no longer produce "living metaphors," as Ricoeur calls the innovative function of poetic language.[22] Handke's novel is for the most part a metonymic text, exposing the social contiguity of meaning and its exhaustion through repetition.

Bloch remains a temporary personification in Handke's growing awareness of the complexity of social disenfranchisement. Bloch, while expressing radical doubt about the reification of social discourse, does so still from within the conventional empowerment of a male discourse. His social frustration involves the seemingly negligible and empty sacrifice of the life of a female ticket operator without ever questioning her inscribed social predisposition towards victimization. Though not focusing specifically on the aspect of gender, Gustav Zürcher criticizes more generally the remaining schematization in Handke's narration: "Die Geschichte, die der Leser erfährt, bleibt geschichtslos, Befreiung wird eher modellhaft an Bloch vorgeführt, als von diesem befreiend erlebt."[23] Like much didactic literature, claims Zürcher, Handke's novel has narcissistically fashioned its hero in the idealistic form of the unencumbered social rebel. His portrayal of Bloch acknowledges the social bond to others only defiantly, leaving little space for a more sympathetic depiction of the impasses of social interaction. Ignoring those who are permanently silenced from within the ruling social discourse, Handke's *Angst des Tormanns*, obscures the quality of living discourse that it decries as absent.

By the time of Handke's *Wunschloses Unglück* (1973), the author had suffered the tragedy of his mother's suicide. This incisive event made him recast his poetic skepticism more radically from the point of view of a silenced and excluded voice that had no significant part in the shaping of the dominant social discourse. This intersection of personal tragedy and a stylistic maturity has led to a turning point in Handke's career. It enabled him to leave behind the cultivated image of the *enfant terrible* of German literature as he had been labeled after his initial confrontation with the German writer's association *Gruppe 47* at its Princeton conference in 1966. Handke's literary fame, as some claim, was launched by his irreverent response to what he termed the "Beschreibungsimpotenz" of Germany's prestigious writers and their new realism. "Es wird nämlich verkannt," Handke contested against the narrative norms embraced by the *Gruppe 47*, "daß die Literatur mit der Sprache gemacht wird und nicht mit den Dingen, die mit der Sprache beschrieben werden."[24]

Abandoning this overtly polemic position that he also displayed in his *Publikumsbeschimpfung* (1966; Offending the Audience) and his experimental novels doing away with plot movement (*Die Hornissen*, *Angst des Tormanns*), Handke eventually returned to the story as a narrational form enframing the fate of silenced individuals. This recovery of narration, as his *Der kurze Brief zum langen Abschied* (1972; *Short Letter to a Long Farewell*) made clear, did not have to remain restricted to the linear logic of the *Bildungsroman* or the recuperative and psychological nostalgia of autobiographical accounts, typical novelistic genres playfully parodied by Handke. Handke instead began to combine his earlier formal analysis of social discourse with a critical form of narration in which individuals are examined with regard to strategies of narrative emplotment in their everyday social reality.

## *Wunschloses Unglück* and the Narration of the Everyday

Turning to Handke's *Wunschloses Unglück* (1973), an account of his mother's suicide, I will explore the blending of individual and social narrative as expressed in his politics and aesthetics of language. The discussion will investigate the banal fate of a single tragic life that escapes the quantifiable analysis of social narratives and yet paradoxically remains a product of such social narratives. Handke's narration of the life and suicide of his mother who had lived through Austria's fascist era follows a path akin to Hannah Arendt's famous analysis of the banality of evil. It is a narrative preoccupied with an everyday fascism that persists up to the present day in its rationalization of the value or lack of value that can be attributed to a single human life. Handke's account amounts to a strong critique of the anonymity of this type of instrumental reason which, as a substitute for an individually motivated narrative reason, depersonalizes life and pushes it to the border of meaningless despair. The implicit accusation against a form of reason that dominates the era of late capitalism is directed at its overweening sense of calculation, utilization and disposability of all human affairs. This form of rational domination of human experience predicates and sterilizes the very novelty that lies at the source of every significant human encounter. In so doing, it makes human values banal by transforming them into pre-set categories and thus reducing human tragedy beyond its apparent loss into one that is devoid of wishes and desire, into a "wunschloses Unglück."[25]

In contrast to Arendt's analysis, Handke's narrative exploration avoids any explicit political and ethical treatment of the question of banality other than in the form of a narrative critique itself. The author's narrative strategy is divided between a reconstruction and analysis of the impasse of his mother's life and an accompanying critical analysis of his own hopes and illusions in retelling her story. The emerging structure of communicative repression, the false sense of *Zugehörigkeit* (belonging), a subjective correlative of Austria's consensus ideology, and the abortive attempts at self-understanding will be traced in Handke's account as a belated narrative for an individual life that was never coherently framed as a story. Handke's narration fulfills the double task of 1) shifting the focus of attention from an objective analysis of society to a limited subjective and narrative point of view and 2) insisting on the objective relevance of this limited perspective. Nägele and Voris speak here of the paradox "daß einer aus den scheinbar entlegenen Provinzerfahrungen seiner Kindheit jene Erfahrungsweisen freilegt, die zentral für die spätkapitalistische Industriewelt sind."[26] Bernd Hüppauf calls this pursuit in Handke "[ein] monomanisches Insistieren auf der Frage, wie die Menschen mit Hilfe von Kommunikation ihre Alltagswirkichkeit einrichten."[27] Arguably, it is both communication and the lack thereof that determine everyday reality for the novel's characters.

The critique of society's self-alienation that governs Handke's inquiry reaches as far back as Marx who attributed it largely to the monopolizing of the realm of production by a privileged class. Marx viewed the dispossession of a large segment of society principally in terms of lack of ownership and the divorce from authentic work. Handke's account of his mother's ancestral history similarly begins with a critical review of her father's first efforts to assert his independence from a lingering feudal order. This independence meant foremost property, "Eigentum" as "verdinglichte Freiheit."[28] This stride towards self-emancipation, however, as Handke describes it, is accompanied by a necessary postponement of pleasure and instills an austere sense of *Bedürfnislosigkeit* (asceticism) in the life of the father and is eventually passed on to his children. Handke partially follows Marx's socio-economic critique in illustrating fundamental economic discrepancies at the root of his family history, though not without critically complementing this analysis with a psychology of an internalized worship of property, an ethics of saving money (*Sparen*) and a repressive avoidance of pleasure.

As in the critique of the Frankfurt School, Marx's critical heirs, Handke establishes an inherent connection between objective socio-economic conditions and their subjective counterpart in the consciousness of the rising classes. The Frankfurt School has widened the scope of Marxist analysis by pointing to the enslavement of consciousness through the use of mass media and their enforced consensus of opinion that underlies the maintenance of the capitalist system. "The need which might resist central control," as Horkheimer and Adorno point out, "has already been suppressed by the control of the individual consciousness."[29] Indeed, the effectiveness of mass culture is given in its formation of structures of consciousness that imprison and inhibit its very ability to act independently.

Handke's account prominently demonstrates the use of mass media in two instances. Initially, the account opens with the detached newspaper report of the mother's suicide. Here Handke highlights mostly the euphemistic structure of media language that belittles the loss of an individual life in its factually cold and remote language:

> Unter der Rubrik VERMISCHTES stand in der Sonntagsausgabe der Kärntner "Volkszeitung" folgendes: "In der Nacht zum Samstag verübte eine 51 jährige Hausfrau aus A. (Gemeinde G.) Selbstmord durch Einnehmen einer Überdosis von Schlaftabletten." (WÜ 7)

Horkheimer and Adorno, particularly in their analysis of film and radio, have pointed to a standardization of response among its audiences:

"The culture industry as a whole has molded man as a type unfailingly reproduced in every product."[30] This stereotyping of response leaves no space for imaginative completion and ultimately entirely saturates the content presented. The newspaper clip cited not only relegates a human tragedy to a miscellaneous report but also depersonalizes its account entirely through the elimination of any individually identifiable circumstances. The medical and technical explanation of the overdose sterilizes the event through a clinically objective diagnosis, thus avoiding an investigation of this incomprehensible act of human despair. The concealment of the victim's identity further reduces the tragedy to that of an anonymous mass subject. The overall intended effect of mass media lies with what Horkheimer and Adorno identify as the reduction of the individual's response to inertia, passivity and automatism, a response similar to the "stumpfsinnige Sprachlosigkeit" (numb speechlessness) of the narrator upon hearing the report of his mother's suicide.

A further instance of media control is drawn from the biography of Handke's mother herself whose historical ambience the author evokes. Handke explains his method of procedure as the attempt to link the general linguistic repertoire of society with the particular fate and story of his mother:

> Nun ging ich von den bereits verfügbaren Formulierungen, dem gesamtgesellschaftlichen Sprachfundus aus statt von den Tatsachen und sortierte dazu aus dem Leben meiner Mutter die Vorkommnisse, die in diesen Formeln schon vorgesehen war. (WÜ 45)

Unlike the Frankfurt School, Handke does not locate the social commonplaces in the institutional structures and their engendered mass psychology. Instead, this psychology of conformity is made more concrete in Handke's analysis of the social discourse that prefigures the fate of the individual. His account of the fascist scenario of "Gemeinschaftserlebnisse" (communal experiences) accordingly pays attention to both the institutional level of propaganda and to the narrative framing of an institutionalized mythology meant to substitute for the individual's. This subtle difference in social analysis places more emphasis on the narrative need of individuals rather than a coercive system of mass manipulation. Critics like Adorno had virtually closed off this avenue of investigation with their severe condemnation of the "jargon of authenticity"[31] which, in their view, could only produce pseudo-individuals and totalitarian forms of thinking. The need for a narrative framing of one's life is dismissed by the Frankfurt School and placed under a critique of totalitarianism, mass culture and kitsch.

Handke, however, shows that beneath the kitsch of these conventional forms of self-expression lies a deeper and distorted need for a community that had been exploited by the fascist propaganda. His mother, for example, recollects nostalgically the general excitement and sense of orientation that the fascist scenario of communal loyalty had facilitated:

> Zum ersten Mal gab es Gemeinschaftserlebnisse. Selbst die werktägliche Langeweile wurde festtäglich stimmungsvoll, "bis in die späten Nachtstunden hinein." Endlich einmal zeigte sich für alles bis dahin Unbegreifliche und Fremde ein großer Zusammenhang: es ordnete sich in eine Beziehung zueinander, und selbst das befremdend automatische Arbeiten wurde sinnvoll, als Fest. (WÜ 23)

As with the workings of a narrative, the discordant and random elements of everyday reality are integrated into a whole of seemingly significant relations. This narrative framing, as Handke's mother states, makes banal reality bearable. Indeed, much of the fascination with a mythology of the community can be seen as result of the technological elimination of all experience mediated through narrative. In a return of the repressed, this elimination of imaginative and non-objective experience leads to an excessive aestheticization of the public sphere that may be seen not only as an expression of kitsch but more importantly as that of despair. Handke's description of the war as the experience of a "sagenhafte Welt" (epic world) corroborates this point:

> Der Krieg, eine Serie mit gewaltiger Musik angekündigter Erfolgsmeldungen aus dem stoffbespannten Lautsprecherkreis der in den düsteren "Herrgottswinkeln" geheimnisvoll leuchtenden Volksempfänger, steigerte noch das Selbstgefühl, indem er die "Ungewissheit aller Umstände vermehrte" (Clausewitz) und das früher täglich Selbstverständliche spannend zufällig werden liess. (WÜ 27)

War, as this description makes unmistakably clear, suspends the everyday order of life and restores to it a primeval excitement of unpredictability, danger and adventure. It is this lack of genuine human experience which Handke sees foremost at the root of the political and ideological distortions of reality. Handke ultimately transcends the critique of the Frankfurt School that had originally so forcefully demonstrated that the masses were enslaved to an anonymous and self-governing system rather than to a privileged class as in Marx. But, as Handke's further analysis shows, the Frankfurt School had only displaced the class stereotyping in Marx's analysis onto that of an omnipotent system which left the individual in passive abeyance.

More recently, Hannah Arendt has similarly drawn attention to the systematic control of mass consciousness in her study on the banality of evil. Like the Frankfurt School, she views its origin in the uncritical stereotypes that serve as the frame of reference in a society dominated by repetitive practices of mass coercion and mass consensus. Unquestioned generalizations and social norms, as Arendt points out, deprive the individual of her or his own motivation to think, rendering one incapable of communication. The Nazi culprit Eichmann, as her analysis illustrates,

> repeated word for word the same stock phrases and self-invented clichés. . . . The longer one listened to him, the more obvious it became that his inability to speak was closely connected with an inability to think, namely, to think from a standpoint of somebody else.[32]

The ensuing banalization and reduction of human values to a set of pre-established conventions alerts one to the danger of hollowing out a community so that it becomes virtually incapable of renewing its self-understanding and thus also deaf to the plight of others. Unlike the Frankfurt School, then, who attributed mass alienation exclusively to a self-consuming system of technological exploitation, Arendt seeks the ultimate cause of such alienation in the prior breakdown of interpersonal communication and the individual's reluctance to assume responsibility for others.

In Handke's account, the danger of society's communal forgetfulness appears more elusive than in Arendt's portrayal of the Nazi genocide. Because of the much less drastic debt incurred by society in its loss of a single person who willed her own death, the entire problem appears inevitable and therefore tolerable. Handke, it can be said, radicalizes the critique of mass alienation even further and places it strictly into a subjective framework. Arendt may have indicated the direction for such a critique by depicting Eichmann as the banal anti-hero of the fascist state rather than a Machiavellian culprit. In Handke, the struggle between oppressor and oppressed that is echoed throughout Marxist analysis and still residually present in Arendt is now entirely abandoned. Handke's mother figures instead as a non-heroine or non-victim and is unaware of her disposability within society. The absence of any dimension of loss in her death reveals the persistent impersonality of a community founded solely on regulative principles without a complementary individual dimension of the human face-to-face encounter.

Handke's subjectivist account should not be understood as an escapist withdrawal from society's pressing needs but as a partial and necessary attempt to personalize and humanize its suffering so as to make it real. As the narrator himself admits at the end of his account, the act of writing offers no escape from the human tragedy it attempts to portray but simply realizes it at a tolerable distance:

> Es stimmt nicht, daß mir das Schreiben genützt hat. In den Wochen, in denen ich mich mit der Geschichte beschäftigte, hörte auch die Geschichte nicht auf, mich zu beschäftigen. Das Schreiben war nicht, wie ich am Anfang noch glaubte, eine Erinnerung an eine abgeschlossene Periode meines Lebens, sondern nur ein ständiges Gehabe von Erinnerung in der Form von Sätzen, die ein Abstandnehmen bloß behaupteten. . . . Natürlich ist das Beschreiben ein bloßer Erinnerungsvorgang; aber es bannt andrerseits auch nichts für das nächste Mal, gewinnt nur aus den Angstzuständen durch den Versuch einer Annäherung mit möglichstentsprechenden Formulierungen eine kleine Lust, produziert aus der Schreckens- eine Erinnerungsseligkeit. (WÜ 99)

Even though Handke may approach here the darker implications of what Maurice Blanchot calls the "writing of disaster," the experience of human disaster so extreme that it can no longer be expressed fully in writing, he does not succumb to its melancholy logic. Handke's critique of alienation does not entirely resign itself to Blanchot's pursuit of "the unknown name for that in thought itself which dissuades us from thinking of it, leaving us, but its proximity, alone."[33] In Handke, this limit of meaning in human experiences does not become the exclusive focus of his account. The pursuit of moments of aporia in the narration is merely incidental and subordinated to the interpersonal drama which first makes the human subject possible as a socially constructed subject. Manfred Durzak rightly discerns in Handke's narration a moment of artistic distance "die es ihm zum ersten Mal konsequent möglich macht, Wirklichkeit nicht nur als Reflex der Innerlichkeit des Autors, sondern in bestimmten historischen Bezügen einzubringen."[34] The subject of Handke's narration is historically concrete and decentered into a communicative world. Subjectivity, consequently, is not an attempt at a single authoritative account. The author attempts to write a story which affects the narrator as much as he affects its subject matter: "In den Wochen, in denen ich mich mit der Geschichte beschäftigte, hörte auch die Geschichte nicht auf, mich zu beschäftigen" (WÜ 99). The story becomes for Handke in this respect an expression of the communicative drama underlying the definition of subjectivity.

Handke's intersubjective account above all exposes the narrative void in the life of his mother that depletes her relation to her environment, others and ultimately herself. "Es gab nichts von einem selber zu erzählen" (WÜ 51) is the simple and resigned confession of the non-heroine. "Wenn jemand von sich redete und nicht einfach schnurrig etwas erzählte," as the mother recalls, "nannte man ihn 'eigen'" (WÜ 51). Handke, as he does throughout the entire narration, completes and restores the implicit insights of his mother by anchoring them in a more general historical evaluation:

> Das persönliche Schicksal, wenn es sich überhaupt jemals als etwas Eigenes entwickelt hatte, wurde bis auf Traumreste entpersönlicht und ausgezehrt in den Riten der Religion, des Brauchtums und der guten Sitten, so daß von den Individuen kaum etwas Menschliches übrigblieb; "Individuum" war auch nur bekannt als ein Schimpfwort. (WÜ 51)

In spite of changing political constellations, the repression of individuality, as Handke shows, is archaically rooted in forgotten and habitualized ritual. This stereotyping of human interaction is repeatedly illustrated in the engrained linguistic and narrative rituals of the community. Patterns attributing social inferiority and insignificance to the lives of women become already apparent in the role plays of young girls — "Müde / Matt / Krank / Schwerkrank / Tot" (WÜ 17) — which spell out their tragic and curtailed destiny:

> Keine Möglichkeit, alles schon vorgesehen: kleine Schäkereien, ein Kichern, eine kurze Fassunglosigkeit, dann zum ersten Mal die fremde, gefasste Miene, mit der man schon wieder abzuhausen begann, die ersten Kinder, ein bißchen noch Dabeisein nach dem Hantieren in der Küche, von Anfang an Überhörtwerden, selber immer mehr Weghören, Selbstgespräche, dann schlecht auf den Beinen, Krampfadern, nur noch ein Murmeln im Schlaf, Unterleibskrebs, und mit dem Tod ist die Vorsehung schon erfüllt. (WÜ 17)

Handke's analysis of a conventionalized self-understanding that belittles the self parallels the earlier mentioned critique of a socio-economic ethics of *Bedürfnislosigkeit.* This asceticism, as Handke shows, cannot be attributed to socio-economic conditions alone but must be seen as well as a part of the restrictive cultural understanding imposed upon women. The one-sided distribution of gender roles and resulting marginalization of women is exposed by Handke as an even deeper level of cultural indoctrination than that of economic calculation.

More generally, Handke's narrative analysis focuses on the struggle between convention and innovation in narrative and cultural tradition. As Handke's account makes clear, this productive struggle is virtually eliminated in the cultural environment of his non-heroine due to the predominance of a patriarchal tradition over any genuine innovation.

By consequence, the narrative link to tradition itself disintegrates since its original moment of self-legislation can no longer be reactivated. Handke's mother appears profoundly uprooted from her culture that no longer provides any new possibility of role definition.

In a further complication of this analysis, Handke also reveals the unconscious complicity of his mother with the repressive and preordained order of society. Handke points here to a sense of false *Zugehörigkeit*, the subjective expression of Austria's state ideology of social partnership. This ideology dwelling on agreement and commonality in all areas of life masks a fear of intimacy in which the individual foregoes a dialogic encounter with others and instead seeks to be reabsorbed into an anonymous mass or consensus culture. Handke, for example, recalls the "übermütige Wesen" of his mother who hysterically linked herself to others in a pretense of unburdened happiness and ease: "Sie lachte immer und schien gar nicht anders zu können" (WÜ 19). On another occasion, he speaks similarly of her "selbstbewußte Heiterkeit: 'Mir kann nichts mehr passieren!'" as "eine geheimnislose, überschwengliche Lust zur Geselligkeit" (WÜ 21). This false conviviality of "Ausgehen, tanzen, sich unterhalten, lustig sein" is at first merely seen as the expression of adolescent sexual fears: "Die Angst vor der Sexualität wurde so überspielt" (WÜ 21). However, this excessive need to find shelter in an anonymous collective "they" is repeated throughout much of his mother's life in one form or another and attests to a desperate need to conform.

Handke's account, by pointing to the obsession of becoming a type "als Zeichen der Anpassung an eine allgemeine Entschlossenheit" (WÜ 40), ultimately lays open a pervasive consensus ideology that facilitated Austria's uncritical cultural reconstruction in the postwar era. Through this recourse to the general, the individual was relieved of his or her own history and partook in the events of history without any burden of responsibility: "In einer solchen Beschreibung als Typ fühlte man sich auch von seiner eigenen Geschichte befreit" (WÜ 40). In addition, this identification with a mass standard allowed for the construction of a pseudo-identity taking pride in merely meeting the cultural norm without ever questioning its anonymous constellation. As a type, writes Handke, "trat ein Menschlein aus seiner beschämenden Einsamkeit und Beziehungslosigkeit hervor und wurde doch einmal wer, wenn auch nur im Vorübergehen" (WÜ 41–42).

These pseudo-expressions of the individual — and Handke's account contains many more than can be analyzed here — point indirectly to aborted narrative attempts in which a discordant reality is made cohesive through the individual's creative and critical reasoning.

Handke's mother comes closest to this realization of an individual narrative when she begins to read. "Sie las jedes Buch," as the narrator recounts,

> als Beschreibung des eigenen Lebens, lebte dabei auf; rückte mit dem Lesen zum ersten Mal mit sich selber heraus; lernte, von sich zu reden; mit jedem Buch fiel ihr mehr dazu ein. So erfuhr ich allmählich etwas von ihr. (WÜ 67)

Handke stresses in reading not so much a political *Mündigkeit* (maturity), as Adorno desired of the enlightened citizen, but a *Mündigkeit zur Kommunikation*, maturity for communication. Reading can be understood here more in Ricoeur's sense as the reconfiguration of a life by way of the narrative. A literary text, writes Ricoeur,

> is not an entity closed in upon itself, it is the projection of a new universe, different from the one in which we live. Appropriating a work through reading it is to unfold the implicit horizon of the world which embraces the action, the personages, the events of the story told. The result is that the reader belongs both to the experiential horizon of the work imaginatively, and the horizon of his action concretely.[35]

To simplify Ricoeur's somewhat abstract formulation, one can say that in the act of reading the reader recovers a sense of individual agency in the envisioning of his or her own self-definition in a new and yet undetermined manner. Wolfgang Iser similarly refers to this imaginative rehearsal and testing of different personae as an act of "anthropological staging" whereby literature permits the patterning of human plasticity.[36] But even more importantly, as Handke has pointed out, literature allows us to hear from one another as enigmatic agents on the stage of human drama.

A critical reservation may be advanced that Handke himself has deprived his non-heroine of any sense of agency only to restore it auctorially and in a belated fashion. This objection, however, must be deemed too suspicious of the author's intentions, for it overlooks the genesis of the story in the mother's suicide. Rather, Handke unfolds the history of his mother from this resigned ending point and recounts it backward so as to question its inevitability. Again and again, he stresses the banality of the events leading up to the culminating human tragedy and not their historical or psychological determinacy. In other words, from within the closed narrative of his mother, the author reopens a negotiable space by which this tragedy could have been altered, averted or at least significantly redeemed. This revisionary effort may be seen largely as the work of the author himself who in the work of mourning extricates himself from the fate that binds him to his mother. And yet, from a dialogic point of view, it represents merely the spoken part of the significant silences that are already inherent in the mother's own repressed history of communication. Ultimately, Handke does not want to give us a case history of his mother. Neither does he hope to save himself by writing this narration — "Es stimmt nicht, daß mir das Schreiben genützt hat" — since it actually heightens the dread into an "objektives Entsetzen" (WÜ 99). In its most simple intent, the narration merely completes a dialogue that did not occur and thereby only redeems the potential communicative value of writing in the face of the banality of all human tragedy.

In Handke's account, the tragic fate of his mother is restored to an individuality and uniqueness that would stand in contradiction to this all too common occurrence in Austria which is among the world's leading countries in its rate of suicide. Thomas Bernhard, for instance, has remarked in this respect: "Ich wundere mich hier überhaupt nicht, wenn einer durch Selbstmord stirbt, ich wundere mich nur, wenn er nicht durch Selbstmord stirbt."[37] Indeed, Austria's popular psychoanalyst Erwin Ringel finds suicide as endemic to Austria's "diseased soul." Ringel speaks of a self-destructive climate that has governed Austria's cultural landscape in the prototype of the self-denying state servant embodied by the emperor Franz Joseph II.[38] And yet, this psychological model of an emulated prototype does not place us directly in the complex communicative field that Handke explores. Handke's account is one of implication in which the seemingly negligible individual fate is once again directly linked to an everyday communicative praxis in the frame of a narrative.

## Return to Experimentation: Handke's Iconography

The visual mode that Handke has begun to explore since his *Lehre der Sainte-Victoire* (1980; Teachings of St. Victoire) brings his overall project of a post-ideological literature to a new height, though not without some problems, as we will see, of inadvertently reconstituting ideology. Handke's attempt to dissolve conceptual and ideological worlds is intended foremost as a subtle self-critique of writing checking itself against its own obtrusive narrative reason, allowing the writing to become more tangibly embodied in the image. The image becomes in this context the dynamic and open site of a narrated lifeworld. However, this transformation of narration into an iconographic *écriture* trying to avoid reduction in language is not by itself a safeguard against ideology and continues to pose a challenge for Handke's work.[39]

In his recent *Versuch* trilogy (1992; *The Jukebox and Other Essays on Storytelling*) Handke has returned to his early cautious beginnings, namely to the concern with the experiment of writing. This experiment, however, is now undertaken from within the proximity of writing to living experience and not the formal experimentation and free-floating semiotic play in Handke's early work of *Die Hornissen* and *Angst des Tormanns*. Handke's work has since become the self-criticism of its own potentially reifying activity in bringing to the fore increasingly the significant silences which make literature the domain between (*Zwischenbereich*) writing and life, articulation and praxis. In line with this self-emancipation of writing from writing, Handke's recent work has taken a new direction by paying more attention to narrative as a partially self-emerging vision or reconstruction of open cultural spaces.[40] Embedding this narrative concretely in the image, a realm that stands between experience and articulation, Handke's recent aesthetics assumes a visionary quality wherein writing becomes visible both as an auctorial act and an event beyond auctorial control.

Handke's trilogy opens with the explorative "essay" (*Versuch*) concerning "tiredness" (*Müdigkeit*)[41] which we will discuss at some length here. This essay superficially appears to give expression to a pervasive historical mood or *Zeitgeist*, namely to a sense of apathy and passivity felt as the predominant mentality of the affluent postwar generation in Europe. The state of tiredness, which operates as a self-fulfilling prophecy, attests to the sense of exhaustion and decline that is felt in a culture that has become increasingly dominated by practices of repetition and mass coercion in all aspects of life. By means of a narrative understanding of this affliction the author attempts to move the sense of apathy to reverse itself into an emotional state (*Empfindung*) without apathy, one with options still remaining. "Wenn ich mir für die Fortsetzung des Versuch von der Müdigkeit etwas wünschen dürfte," writes Handke, "so wäre es eher eine Empfindung."[42] The work sets the stage for a subtle transformation of the exhausted cultural climate from its imprisonment in derivative *Weltbilder* (world hypotheses) towards new and liberating representations of a culture still in its making.

The essay begins with an emptying out of images reflecting tiredness as an emotional state truncated of meaning. Among recollections of subjective failures, all too familiar from many of Handke's protagonists not at ease with their everyday surroundings, Handke also offers accounts of collective experiences that similarly attest to the deficiency of communal practices. One recollection, for example, nostalgically looks back to the partially pre-industrial past of Austria's postwar era, its "heilige Zeit" (VM 36). The narrator remembers here — and uncritically so — the communal work of harvesting as a rite of communication fraught with meaning. Upon the completion of this communal task, one attuned to the natural rhythm of a social whole, the narrator recalls, "genossen [wir] redend oder schweigend die gemeinsame Müdigkeit" (VM 27).

Communication, remembered in this idyllic fashion, emerges from within the immediate silence that follows the noisy thrashing:

> Aber war das Dreschen wieder einmal glücklich vorbei, die allesübertönende Maschine . . . abgeschaltet: Was für eine Stille, nicht nur in der Scheune, sondern im ganzen Land; was für ein Licht, das, statt zu blenden, einen nun umfing. (VM 27)

The intensified aural image of rhythmical thrashing gives way to the even more powerful visual and synaesthetic image that blends silence and light, thus illuminating the practice of the community, lending the sense of exhaustion a quality of meaningful satisfaction. This image foreshadows some of the pitfalls of Handke's recent visual aesthetics that occasionally has the ring of nostalgia or salvation, thus turning Handke's project into an undesired ideology.

In opposition to this self-illuminating or quasi-ritualistic seasonal activity, Handke places the degraded experience of work in the practical and bourgeois pursuit of building an "Einfamilienhaus," a senseless and non-reciprocal type of labor that can only be seen as a drudgery or "Schinderei" (VM 37). This decline in the communal realm of labor finds its parallel in the historical decline of Austria which, in the wake of its promising postwar renovation, failed to bring about a true reversal of its own cultural destiny. "Unser Volk," writes Handke with a contempt reminiscent of Bernhard, "ist das erste unabänderlich verkommene, das erste unverbesserliche, das erste für alle Zukunft zur Sühne unfähige, umkehrunfähige Volk der Geschichte" (VM 32). The omnipresence of utilitarian pursuits, the total lack of cultural memory and historical responsibility create a threatening climate in which *Müdigkeit* divorces the individual irrevocably from the collective. Commenting on his various work experiences, the author writes: "Obwohl ich in einer wachen Müdigkeit dahinging, ohne Schläfrigkeit, ohne Eingeschlossenheit in mich selbst, fand ich mich von der Gesellschaft ausgesperrt" (VM 41). The sense of accomplished *Müdigkeit* has, according to the author, been replaced by a bourgeois industriousness that is barely able to mask its latent apathy and cynical resignation.

A comparable sense of tiredness that divests the individual of self and social identity, Handke writes, is also experienced in the act of writing. However, its sense of expropriation is curiously reversed: “Nicht die Gesellschaft war unzugänglich für mich, sondern ich war es für sie” (VM 44). In introducing for the first time this alternative mode of tiredness, Handke speaks of a “Schaffensmüdigkeit” (creative tiredness) that had induced in his early efforts of writing a comforting sense of self-sufficiency:

> Was gingen mich eure Lustbarkeiten, Feste, Umarmungen an — ich hatte ja die Bäume da, das Gras, die Kinoleinwand, wo Robert Mitchum nur für mich seine unergründliche Miene spielen ließ, die Jukebox, wo Bob Dylan allein für mich sein “Sad-Eyed Lady of the Lowlands” sang, oder Ray Davies sein und mein “I'm Not Like Everybody Else.” (VM 45)

Handke recalls here the initially liberating momentum of popular culture that allowed the individual to recover his lost privacy away from the coercive climate of society. Careless enjoyment of non-productive activities, such as the contemplation of nature, the indulgence in escapist fantasies of cinema and popular songs celebrating narcissism, reflect the artist's youthful efforts. Handke, however, is aware that this socially rebellious stance of the 1960s was mixed with a considerable portion of complacency and had not yet achieved the level of an accomplished sensibility. “Eine Müdigkeit als ein Zugänglichwerden,” he writes, “ja als die Erfüllung des Berührtwerdens und selber Berührenkönnens, erlebte ich erst viel später” (VM 46).

Successive images that leave Handke's biographical recollections and the locale of Austria behind eventually bring us closer to the site of writing, Linares, where Handke writes the present essay. The topology of the narration thus moves gradually from the periphery (Austria) to the central site of action (Spain),[43] from the story as recapitulated memory to the story in its making where it allows also for the reader's immediate contact with its unfolding drama. In his *Versuch über die Jukebox*, Handke further complicates this imparted sense of proximity by simultaneously exposing the historical marginality of his account that takes place in the world-removed — “weltentlegene” — location of Soria. In this town near Linares, Handke undertakes his equally paradoxical search for old jukeboxes that bear the stamp of idiosyncratic human rather than commercially standardized musical selections. In doing so, the author seeks to retrieve the more innocent beginnings of consumer culture where technology could apparently co-exist with human originality. Akin to Heidegger in his reflections on technology, Handke points here to a common origin of *techne* and *poesis* without, however, erecting a primordial ontology. The jukebox is after all merely a man-made and temporary machine, a desire machine, to use a term by Deleuze and Guattari.

Handke's narration performs a double-movement in removing itself at once from seemingly overdetermined sites (Austria, replaced by Spain) and in seeking the proximity of places that appear underdetermined (open squares; old jukeboxes). Handke, in this ambivalent search for freedom, thus both escapes and accepts the contingency of a particular site. A juxtaposition of freedom and contingency is evoked, for instance, in the recollection of a lengthy and exhausting trip that takes the author-narrator to New York. Upon his arrival, the narrator, in spite of his *Müdigkeit*, chooses to leave the hotel room so as to join the vivid scene near Central Park from the spectator's position of a sidewalk café. Overwhelmed by tiredness, he finds himself more receptive to his surroundings because his burdened self-consciousness vanishes in the wake of his weariness: "Die Müdigkeit war jetzt mein Freund. Ich war wieder da, in der Welt, und sogar — nicht etwa, weil es Manhattan war — in ihrer Mitte" (VM 51). The sense of belonging to a site or world is experienced in the form of a silent participation so that events, in the absence of willful interference, come to acquire a significance that is not already attributed to them.

As if by their own logic, as the narrator has us believe, events begin to take the shape of a "wunderbar feingliedrigen, leichtgefügten — Erzählung" (VM 55). "Die Vorgänge," writes Handke, "erzählten sich selbst, ohne Vermittlung über die Wörter. Dank meiner Müdigkeit wurde die Welt ihre Namen los und groß" (VM 56). The writer functions here merely as the invisible consciousness or medium of the spectacle to which he listens and gives voice: "Ich sah, spürbar für den anderen, mit ihm zugleich seine Sache mit" (VM 54). This return to the open space with its free and unhindered movement is reminiscent of *Die Stunde der wahren Empfindung* where Gregor Keuschnig at the end of the novel finds himself partially restored to life in the bustling Parisian Place de l'Opéra. In Handke's *Versuch*, this fascination with open squares is now translated back into the structure of narrative, arranging itself loosely like a sharpening impression — "es genügt das Schauen,"[44] as Samuel Moser puts it in his review of the *Versuch* — and without the author's interference.

Handke's "weltvertrauende Müdigkeit" becomes the utopian figure of a resurrected confidence overcoming alienation, distance and apathy by accepting local contingencies. The result of such a conscious surrender or release from subjectivity, as Handke conjectures, would be that of the final *Müdigkeit* by means of which one abandons oneself to a communal vision as an event unfolding like a story or narration (*Geschichte*):

> In der Stunde der letzten Müdigkeit gibt es keine philosophischen Fragen mehr. Diese Zeit ist zugleich der Raum, dieser Zeitraum ist zugleich die Geschichte. Was ist, wird zugleich. Das andere wird zugleich ich. Die zwei Kinder da unter meinen müden Augen, das bin jetzt ich. Und wie die ältere Schwester den kleinen Bruder durch das Lokal schleppt, das ergibt zugleich einen Sinn, und hat einen Wert, und nichts ist wertvoller als das andere — der Regen, der dem Müden auf den Puls fällt, ist gleich wert wie der Anblick der Gehenden jenseits des Flusses —, und es ist so gut wie schön, und es gehört sich so, und so soll es weiter sein, und es ist, vor allem, wahr. Wie die Schwester, ich, den Bruder, mich, um die Hüften packt, das ist wahr. (VM 69)

In this final moment, event and story unroll simultaneously, interpenetrating one another: "Das andere wird zugleich ich." The ideal vision of plain reality — "es ist so gut wie schön" — becomes the story where the world revolves in its simultaneity of potency and act, narration and event. Accordingly, the narrative arrangements of images transform themselves from the initially hesitant dragging into the open — "aus dem Lokal schleppen" — into the more natural and fluid movement of walking alongside a river. They culminate in a final arresting embrace — "an den Hüften packen" and its accompanying human gaze — "unter meinen müden Augen."

It is with such a seemingly timeless and enduring vision that Handke ends the first part of his trilogy. With the image of an Easter procession in the region of Andalusia, the resurrection from the dead is more than just conventionally indicated. Handke's narration comes full circle in reintegrating the present, past and future. The celebratory display of "Leidens- und Trauerstatuen" (VM 71) stands next to the memory of a walk with a grandfather at dawn and the image of raindrops wetting the desiccated earth, "den Einschlägen der Sommerregentropfen, meinem ersten, sich immer neu wiederholenlassenden Bild" (VM 72). The narration, however, while reaching this total point of integration, can be said to slip back into uncritical iconic worship. Catholicism is after all also an ideology with a violent history of oppression and subjugation.[45] Handke betrays here to some the degree the despair of his impatient character Sorger in *Langsame Heimkehr* who "empfand keine Sehnsucht mehr" but a "Bedürfnis nach Heil," hoping thereby to be redeemed by destiny.[46] Moser refers similarly to a "Beteiligung" that has turned into a "sich beteiligen lassen," one which he already detects in Handke's Tormann Bloch who "saß so still, bis er sich selber nicht mehr auffiel."[47]

While Handke's attempt to let images "naturally" accumulate into a story promises a new departure reminiscent of his early experimental style, it cannot be accepted uncritically. Handke's new advance may constitute a liberating aesthetic redefinition of writing as a complex structured iconography, but it cannot thereby avoid the question of ideology in images that are uncritically contemplated as icons, even if only for aesthetic stimulation. Christoph Bartmann points to a diminished critical distance in Handke's turn to vision:

> Die Vision von außen hat offensichtlich nicht dieselbe Absicht wie im Nouveau Roman. Nicht Objektivität und Sprengung anthropozentrischer Klischees, sondern möglichst unscheinbare Subjektivität, die ohne Innensicht auskommt, scheint intendiert.[48]

Handke's visionary turn, at its best, however, can ultimately be seen as a significant departure from the stance of his contemporary Thomas Bernhard who remained in many ways an acutely critical and tragic-comic voice expressing the impasse of cultural history in postmodernism. As Karl-Markus Gauss correctly notes:

> Kaum ein zweiter Schriftsteller unserer Zeit hatte so leidenschaftlich wie Handke auf dem Glück, auf der Suche nach Fülle beharrt. Während Thomas Bernhard das Laufwerk der Verzweiflung immer feiner schliff und die Hölle auf Erden beim ihm naturgemäß immer höllischer wurde, hat Handke über verschiedene Brüche und Wendungen seines Lebens und seiner Literatur hinweg das Glück als den menschlichen Zustand gerühmt.[49]

In his excavation of the utopian possibilities that are still immanent in a seemingly degraded reality (e.g. Jukebox), Handke reaffirms in the wake of the postmodern disintegration of all tradition the minimal possibility of a present and partial history as made possible through literature.

In the trilogy, Handke's narration gradually shifts from an initial idyllic vision of a pre-industrial and folkloric Spain (as depicted in its archaic Easter rituals) to a more realistically modern consumer world. The residual traces of modernity (highways, Jukebox) that have left their mark even in remote villages of Spain are intensified in the final *Versuch* setting, a heavily industrialized suburban area of Paris. The closing work of his trilogy, *Versuch über den geglückten Tag* (1991; Essay on the Successful Day), ends more credibly in a setting of a Parisian suburb metro station. Here the gray of the asphalt contrasts with the blue evening sky, leaving us with Handke, the poet of the everyday.

Handke's attempt to articulate a post-ideological position of resistance attains credibility when he carefully and critically explores the narrative strategies of everyday life and discourse. His recent shift to the image may help to enhance the presence and plasticity of this discourse but does not redeem it from the task of a critique. As Gerhard vom Hofe and Peter Pfaff have noted in more positive terms, Handke displays a messianic tendency in which his narration often takes on the form of "weltliche Heilsgeschichte."[50] Handke exhibits this prophetic tendency, for instance, when he posits an ideal community that he nostalgically retrieves from his rural upbringing, one characterized by ritual, customs and religious images. Such an imagined community, however, must remain a critical one and contain possible contradictions if it is not to revert to an ideology. Thomas Bernhard, for example, adamantly exposes Catholicism as an ideology by linking it to fascism and views the combination of the two as the latent core of Austria's state ideology. What Handke's writing ultimately needs is a continuation of his more successful secular stories like *Versuch über den geglückten Tag* that check themselves by asking "Oder war das schon wieder ein Glaube?"[51] This self-critique would limit Handke's vision more soberly to the imperfect accomplishments of the everyday. It places habitual concepts, ideology and ultimately the narrator/author himself in doubt: "An dem geglückten Tag wird eine Gewohnheit ausbleiben, wird eine Meinung verschwinden, werde ich überrrascht sein von ihm, von dir, von mir selbst" (VT 73).

## Handke's Postmodernism: Beyond Subject and Nation

Handke's work, as his recent *Versuch* trilogy indicates, still explores and advances new possibilities of narration. In spite of apparent changes in Handke's narrative strategies, one should not overlook the continuities that give his work a coherent thematic outlook. For example, his early *Wunschloses Unglück*, in which negligible individual fate is once again directly linked to an everyday communicative praxis, has helped to shape much of his subsequent work. Pertinent examples of Handke's stories about insignificant outsiders recovering their sense of narrative identity are *Die Stunde der wahren Empfindung* (1974) *Die linkshändige Frau* (1976), *Die langsame Heimkehr* (1979) *Der Chinese des Schmerzes* (1983), *Die Wiederholung* (1986) and *Abwesenheit* (1987). The attention given to the silenced, the overlooked and the unremarkable persists in Handke's cultural counter-aesthetics and figures prominently in his most recent novel *Hier in der Niemandsbucht* (1994; *The No-Man's Bay*) set in a remote suburb of Paris.

In light of such continuity it seems advisable not to speak too hastily of a *Kehre* (turn) in Handke's work, one often evoked as parallel to that of the late Martin Heidegger. Rather, it is more correct to view Handke's recent work as a fuller explication of his original post-ideological project. As he has made clear in a recent interview, Handke intentionally deploys the recurring theme of the unremarkable in order to relieve a heavily burdened Western literary canon, that has itself become an ideology of some weight:

> Mir kommt vor, daß ich mit diesem Buch [Hier in der Niemandsbucht] zu der Literatur, die es schon gibt, etwas hinzugefügt habe, was aus dem, was vorher war, zwar kommt, aber es — diese Werke der Weltliteratur — nicht beschwert, eher dafür sorgt, daß sie leichter werden.[52]

Resisting on all levels any borrowings from pre-fabricated official versions of history and social reality, Handke's new novel indeed affirms little more than the sobered banality of a contemplative day centered upon the banal activities of writing and walking. This anti-historical and anti-ideological gesture carried to the length of over 1000 pages reflects Handke's strongest stance so far of cultural and literary self-deflation. The novel is set at the periphery of Paris, which the narrator deems more important than the metropolis. It is cast in the less than utopian year 1997 rather than the predictable millenium, and envisions a civil war in the unlikely territory of West Germany (mentioned first in a brief remark on page 741).

Handke's compendious novel betrays little of the vanity of so-called world literature that presumes to reflect history from a seemingly universal perspective. Nor does Handke echo Heidegger's effort of excavating a radicalized ontology buried beneath poetic speech, as has been suggested by critics. Handke, in spite of superficial aesthetic affinities to Heidegger, has left the latter's vision behind. Handke's recent reception, however, belies this difference and often places the author's work uncritically in the proximity of Heidegger's philosophical reflections on art and poetry. A prominent example of such a one-sided appropriation of Handke is Rolf Günter Renner's which, while revealing suggestive parallels to Heidegger's aesthetic concerns, fails to point out important differences in their approach to language, ideology and culture.[53] Similarly, Gerhard vom Hofe and Peter Pfaff account for Handke's writing exclusively in the terms of an existential ontology (Heidegger, Bachelard). They ignore that Handke's poetics, at its most acute, is directed against any conceptual construction that overarches the narration of the everyday.[54]

This oversight of Handke's ironic stance towards tradition, history and the centrality of cultural claims is finally acknowledged in Renner's more recent evaluation of Handke which places the author into a postmodern context of playful and ironic quotation.[55] Renner, however, refuses to bring the suggested context to bear in Handke's work in the usual post-ontological terms of postmodernism. Instead, he still attributes to Handke's work a "philosophische Selbstreflexion" that is said to entail an "ontologische Ausrichtung."[56] Handke, he believes, incorporates Heidegger's reconstructive existential hermeneutics into his project of a *posthistoire* form of narration, thereby arriving at a peculiar form of postmodernism that checks itself against its destructive momentum.[57]

A critical evaluation of Heidegger's significance for Handke can also be found in the comments of Alfred Kolleritsch, a longtime friend and mentor of Handke. Reading Heidegger's ontology as a critique of subjectivity, Kolleritsch locates the affinity between Heidegger and Handke in their post-metaphysical attempt to arrive at a poetics of the "Ereignis":

> Heidegger und Handke verzichten auf jeden metaphysischen Ansatz der einem allem vorrausliegenden Subjekt die absolute Trägerrolle zuspricht. . . . Sie halten sich im Offenen einer Begegnung, die als unerschöpfliches Ereignis Natur und Mensch in einen Weltbezug stellt.[58]

While both Renner and Kolleritsch appear to make convincing claims that substantiate Handke's indebtedness to Heidegger, both do so by ignoring Heidegger's own problematic affinity to National Socialism and its ideology of *Heimat.*

In his *Of Spirit: Heidegger and the Question* (1989), Derrida has compellingly shown how Heidegger's sophisticated postmetaphysical ontology does not escape a common Western metaphysical preoccupation with a primordial belonging founded in the "spirit" of a particular people and site. Derrida gives the telling example of Heidegger's claim that German is the ultimate philosophical language since it alone can name the essence of the spirit in the German word *Geist*:

> It turns out then that of the two twinned languages, Greek and German, which have in common the greatest spiritual richness, only one of them can name what they have and are in common par excellence: spirit. And to name is to offer for thinking. German is thus the only language, at the end of the day, at the end of the race, to be able to name this maximal or superlative (geistigste) excellence which in short it shares, finally, only up to a certain point with Greek.[59]

Heidegger, in what amounts to a *metalepsis* (reversal of history), installs German culture in a position prior to that of its Greek precursor, presumed to be the Ur-civilization of Western culture but lacking the spiritual word *Geist.* Greek *pneuma* is after all only the reflection of human breath and thus remains an anthropological determination, a term of lesser value because it is a metaphor for a physical act.

In light of these known and controversial positions of Heidegger, one wonders how beneficial the analogies between Heidegger and Handke's works really are. Handke, one should bear in mind, carefully characterizes his relation to *Heimat* in *Langsame Heimkehr* without any recourse to any fundamental ontology that accepts uncritically a unity between particular human practices and the possession of a particular geographic space as self-evident. Given these deep discrepancies between Handke and Heidegger, Klaus Bonn justifiably asks:

> Die Frage wäre, ob die Schriften beider, Handkes und Heideggers, vor dem besagten Wandel (analog zur "Kehre") schon den gleichen Weg gegangen sind oder aus unterschiedlichen Richtungen gekommen sind, sich an einer Gemarkung wie zufällig kreuzten.[60]

Handke, as I would even further maintain, never crosses the path with Heidegger. Handke's entire project of writing consists in showing how both space and agency are constructed concepts of particular and revisable cultural practices that do not add up to a critical and universally extended metaphysics of human *Dasein.*

Handke's shortcomings emerge not from an irreversible and entrenched position but from an occasional lack of rigorous inquiry into the struggles underlying an imagined culture. Here Handke's topographies of culture may at times revert to superficial travelogues revelling in the exotic climate of the poetic imagination. Andalusia, Slovenia and Alaska, for example, often serve Handke only as utopian alternatives to an Austria whose problematic history Handke ultimately cannot escape. While the early Handke had to struggle to liberate himself from the dogmatism of ideology, the late Handke, it appears, must now likewise gain distance from empty utopias where struggle and ideology seem to be completely absent.

Handke's recent novel *Hier in der Niemandsbucht* attempts to do so by linking and intertwining these two aspects from within the topography of Paris. Cultural alternatives are no longer presented as sites of escapes; they are embodied by seven characters engaged in their own problematic investment of sites in Spain, Slovenia, Japan, Mongolia, Bator, Alaska, Scotland and Austria. Handke, known for his restless desire to travel, accepts now the contingency of a specific site and remains a stationary character and only an imaginary fellow traveller in his novel. The balance between freedom and contingency has thus been slightly adjusted to accommodate the latter more credibly. But this acceptance of a particular site of action should not mislead anyone into assuming that Handke's cultural interventions have now taken on a conventional character. Handke's *langsame Heimkehr* has merely taken another turn in an open terrain where arrival and departure seem interchangeable.

In his recent works, as we have seen, Handke has slightly de-emphasized an obtrusive element of subjective agency in his narration and embedded it more within an event structure, a sensation joining spectator and event. Subjective agency is thereby subordinated to a participatory dynamics in which the story as if by its own motion speaks through a community. It silences its discourse for the utopian and emerging present moment of new encounter as Handke's pantomime play, *Die Stunde da wir nichts voneinander wußten* (1992; The Hour In Which We Knew Nothing of One Another), suggests. How far this utopian path can be pursued with this renovative fervor, given the growing commodification of our social environment, remains to be seen. Yet Handke's poetic transformations of the everyday, his recovery of the idiosyncratic story of the individual and his re-awakening of cultural memory as an active remembering forward into the future, can, in spite of their apparent limitations, hardly be dismissed.

## *Justice for Serbia* and Recent Public Interventions

In an attempt to personalize and transcend ideology, Handke has made politics the imaginative initiative of the private citizen who rewrites her or his social history so that its story can be told comprehensively from multiple angles. This post-ideological approach to politics works well when it remains within the limits of literary discourse and its symbolic reconfiguration of culture. However, it produces serious misjudgments when it is brought to bear in pragmatic politics. Handke's recent works, *Gerechtigkeit für Serbien* (1993; *Justice for Serbia*), and particularly his public remarks concerning the most recent war in Yugoslavia have drawn sharp criticism from leading cosmopolitan writers such as Susan Sontag and Salman Rushdie as well as from many liberals with whom Handke formerly shared an alliance. Handke's four-day visit to Belgrade amidst the bombing raids added further to the histrionic nature of the author's protests against NATO imperialism. Moreover, Handke formally quit the Catholic Church in protest against the Pope's silence and returned the Georg Büchner prize but accepted a state decoration by Yugoslavia. To the dismay of Handke's readers, however, the mass killings perpetrated against a Muslim cultural minority were not even addressed in his against-the-grain public intervention.

His most recent play *Die Fahrt im Einbaum oder Das Stück zum Film vom Krieg* (1999; The Script to the Film about the War) similarly displays tendentious content in its assessment of the civil war in Yugoslavia that ended in 1995. The play dwells, for instance, on the plight of Serbia as former victims of Habsburg oppression and Nazi and Allied bombings at the expense of representing the victimization of Bosnian Muslims suffering atrocities at the hands of Yugoslavia. In spite of its biased views, the play does not reduce the question of the civil war to the simplistic (or "idiotic," as Rushdie claims) opinions that inform much of Handke's recent public remarks on the war between NATO and Yugoslavia.[61] Instead, multiple and contradictory positions are voiced by an equally heterogeneous assembly of characters such as a tourist guide, a chronicler, a historian, a former beauty queen, a madman, and three international observers. The play, at its best, produces a productive moment of doubt that reflects a justified ambivalence towards Western intervention. Handke's claim that the Serbian conflict was escalated in the early 1990s by Germany's reckless recognition of Slovenia's and Croatia's (which is a former Nazi ally) national independence would further appear to substantiate his criticism of the diplomatic handling of this conflict.

Handke's insistent and facile dismissal of the plight of persecuted and evicted Albanians in the recent conflict, however, raises ultimately serious doubts about the balance of his political judgments. His play, though not dealing with the most recent war, similarly betrays lapses of critical assessment when it attempts to explain war solely in terms of a degradation of interpersonal communication: "da verloren wir Nachbarn einander mehr und mehr aus dem Gesicht."[62] The human face-to-face encounter cannot be transposed into the realm of conflicting collective claims as much as Handke may want to insist on his simplistic vision of peaceful co-existence. Private and collective worlds are in the end asymmetrical and demand different strategies of politicization. Handke, as we have seen, has been exemplary in politicizing the dimension of private life. It is within this limit that his poetics makes most sense. It becomes tyrannic and despotic when applied to a pragmatic political context in which strategic and rational negotiation are required.

The case of Handke, embarrassing as it may seem to his old admirers, is not a singular incident in recent German literary history. He joins several other authors such as Christa Wolf, Botho Strauss and Martin Walser who have betrayed regressive sides heretofore untypical of liberals or who have abandoned liberalism. Whether a tacit defense of systemic oppression, of nationalism or of historical normalization, the various slips made by these writers point to their inability to adjust successfully to a present post-national and multi-cultural reconfiguration of European culture.[63] Handke, along with these fellow writers, may also feel the pressure of the vastly changing literary market in which representatives of former national literatures must yield to a diversity of traditions and participants. While Handke's literary aesthetics is highly advanced, closer to Benjamin's cosmopolitanism than Heidegger's onto-nationalist aesthetics, his literary reception for the most part still took place within a climate of national literatures and their major canonized exponents. This reception led to early fame and made Handke a star on the German scene of writing. Recently, however, the literary market has lost its elitist boundaries that used to mark it off from entertainment literature and has also become a much wider and diversified field of voices. Handke's star position has gradually eroded over the years and forced him to accommodate to a less hierarchized and diversified cultural landscape that he had actively helped to build.

A further irony that surrounds Handke's case is the present pragmatic mode of decision making in politics. Handke's neo-fascist compatriot Jörg Haider, while advocating xenophobic anti-immigration policies as his party's platform, came out in support of NATO's attack on Yugoslavia. His party is presently on the way to becoming Austria's second largest party. Germany's and Austria's current support of Kosovo Albanians should also not mislead one into believing that their deeply engrained xenophobic attitudes towards Yugoslavians, Turks, Arabs and any person of different race have suddenly abated. In fact, it is quickly becoming a habit in politics to make progressive alliances in international affairs while fiercely clinging to reactionary attitudes at home. Handke's singular voice, going against the grain of this consensus of pragmatism and compromise, could have had a significant impact if only he had taken care to formulate his own alliances more carefully. By not condemning Serbian nationalism and European political hypocrisy at the same time, Handke missed a crucial opportunity to contribute to the critical legacy of postwar European culture of which he was once a main representative.

It is incorrect to account for this discrepancy between Handke's progressive and regressive leanings in his recent works as a turn or reorientation since his aesthetics has not embraced an essentialist position as various critics claim. Rather, it is the praxis of Handke the white

European writer that is increasingly at odds with a multi-cultural reconfiguration of Europe. His pro-Serbian stances, for example, appear facile and condescending given the fact that his acquaintance with this region comprises only various visits amounting to several weeks. Handke does not speak Serbocroatian and relies heavily on friends who accompany him during his trips. And while his aesthetics is extremely cautious about establishing a ground of inquiry beyond doubt, his public actions belie this hesitant and critical approach. Here Handke speaks with the universal tenor of white European culture that demands to be listened to and tolerates no different point of view. This eurocentric attitude has yet to be subjected to the same doubt that the author brings to collective ideologies of state and nation. It requires that Handke view himself for once as the product of a majority culture endowed with the privileges of speaking as a white European rather than posturing as a persecuted Serb in the suburbs of Paris.

## Notes

[1] Essay originally published in the Austrian magazine Profil, added as appendix to Luc Rosenzweig and Bernhard Cohen's *Waldheim*, trans. Josephine Bacon (New York: Adams Books, 1987) 177.

[2] Paul Ricoeur, *Lectures on Ideology and Utopia* (New York: Columbia UP, 1986) 3,1.

[3] Michel Foucault, "Preface" to Gilles Deleuze and Felix Guattari's *Anti-Oedipus: Capitalism and Schizophrenia* (Minneapolis: U of Minnesota P, 1983) xiv.

[4] Manfred Durzak, *Peter Handke und die deutsche Gegenwartsliteratur. Narziß auf Abwegen* (Stuttgart: Kohlhammer, 1982) 46.

[5] Durzak, 48, 67.

[6] Rainer Nägele and Renate Voris, *Peter Handke* (Munich: C.H. Beck, 1978) 115.

[7] Nägele and Voris, 127.

[8] Nägele and Voris, 127.

[9] Ulrich Greiner, *Der Tod des Nachsommers* (Munich: Carl Hanser Verlag, 1979) 90–91.

[10] Greiner, 13.

[11] Karl Menges, *Das Private und das Politische. Bemerkungen zur Studentenliteratur, zu Handke, Celan und Grass* (Stuttgart: Hans-Dieter Heinz Akademischer Verlag, 1987) 106.

[12] Peter Handke, "Die Literatur ist romantisch," *Ich bin ein Bewohner des Elfenbeinturms* (Frankfurt: Suhrkamp, 1972) 43.

[13] Handke, 45.

[14] Handke, 50.

[15] Foucault, "Preface" to *Anti-Oedipus*, xi.

[16] Foucault, xii.

[17] Manfred Frank speaks of a "legitimation crisis of academic philosophy" which is symptomatically expressed in the work of Deleuze and Guattari representing a new generation of French thinkers (*What is Neostructuralism?* (Minneapolis: U of Minnesota P, 1989) 318.

[18] Foucault, "Preface," xiii.

[19] Peter Handke, "Zur Tagung der Gruppe 47 in USA," *Bewohner des Elfenbeinturms*, 30.

[20] Handke, 31.

[21] Nägele and Voris, 50.

[22] See Paul Ricoeur"s "Metaphor and the Central Problem of Hermeneutics," *Hermeneutics and the Human Sciences* (Cambridge: Cambridge UP, 1981). Ricoeur attributes to metaphor the "capacity for letting new worlds shape our understanding of ourselves" by "[raising] language above itself" (181). Literary texts, according to Ricoeur, free "reference from the limits of ostensive reference" and convert a simple "situation" [*Welt*] into a complex "world" [*Umwelt*] (177). Metaphor understood as a conventional "system of associated commonplaces," Ricoeur insists, remains "something dead" or ossified in that it fails to alter radically the entire contextual horizon of meaning (172–173). Ricoeur's notion of metaphor is not restricted to the limited substitution of one word for another as in Aristotle's conventional definition but includes the larger units of sentence and paragraph whereby discourse becomes an inaugurating act of possible meaning.

[23] Gustav Zürcher, "Leben mit Poesie," in *Text und Kritik*, Vol. 24 (1976) 41.

[24] Peter Handke, "Zur Tagung der Gruppe 47 in USA," 29.

[25] Handke inverts here the idiom "wunschlos glücklich" (a happiness fulfilling all wishes) into the neologism "wunschloses Unglück" (a misfortune with nothing to hope for).

[26] Nägele and Voris, 60.

[27] Bernd Hüppauf, "Peter Handkes Stellung im Kulturwandel der sechziger Jahre," *Handke: Ansätze, Analysen, Anmerkungen*, ed. Manfred Jurgensen (Munich: Francke, 1979) 11.

[28] Peter Handke, *Wunschloses Unglück* (Frankfurt: Suhrkamp, 1972) 14; hereafter quoted in text as WÜ.

[29] Max Horkheimer and Theodor Adorno, *Dialectic of Enlightenment* (New York: Continuum, 1972) 121.

[30] Horkheimer and Adorno, 127.

[31] This is not say that Adorno's critique of existential authenticity is not adequate. He is right in saying that the existential self-institution of the subject may lead to the self-delusion that the "individual owns himself" and "no longer has to bother about the societal and natural-historical origin of this title deed" (*The Jargon of Authenticity* (Evanston: Northwestern UP, 1973) 115). However, this criticism, as Jürgen Habermas points out, cannot be carried to an extreme degree if it is not to undermine the possibility for individual social action. With Horkheimer and Adorno, as Habermas observes, "the suspicion of ideology becomes total, but without any change of direction. It is turned not only against the irrational function of bourgeois ideal, but against the rational potential of bourgeois culture itself" (*The Philosophical Discourse of Modernity* (Cambridge: The MIT Press, 1987) 119).

[32] Hannah Arendt, *Eichmann in Jerusalem: A Report on the Banality of Evil* (Harmondsworth: Penguin Books, 1977) 49.

[33] Maurice Blanchot, *The Writing of Disaster*, trans. Ann Smock (Lincoln: U of Nebraska P, 1986) 5.

[34] Manfred Durzak, *Peter Handke und die deutsche Gegenwartsliteratur*, 118.

[35] Paul Ricoeur, "Life: A Story in Search of its Narrator," *Paul Ricoeur: Reflection & Imagination*, ed. Mario J. Valdes (Toronto: U of Toronto P, 1991) 431. Ricoeur distinguishes narrative intelligence from theoretical intelligence as the "field of a constructive activity, deriving from the narrative intelligence through which we attempt to recover (rather than impose from without) the narrative identity which constitutes us" (436). By consequence, the recovered narrative subject is predicated neither empirically nor epistemologically but simply by its own self-interpretation and imaginative role variations: "Subjectivity is neither an incoherent succession of occurrences nor an immutable substance incapable of becoming. It is exactly the kind of identity which the narrative composition alone, by means of its dynamism, can create" (437). This narrative reason, as Ricoeur insists, frees the subject in its imaginative exploration and testing of possible personas and allows it to integrate its biography by means of reinventing the cultural and symbolic repertoire of self-expression.

[36] Wolfgang Iser, "Staging as an Anthropological Category," *New Literary History*, Vol. 23 (1992) 877–888.

[37] Quoted in Erwin Ringel, *Österreichische Seele* (Vienna: Hermann Böhlaus, 1984) 33.

[38] Erwin Ringel, 34–35. The emperor is seen by Ringel as father figure embodying the repressive force of the Oedipal order.

[39] Even Arlette Camion's excellent inquiry *Image et écriture dans l'oeuvre de Peter Handke* (Berne: Peter Lang, 1992) cannot avoid this question. By claiming that "L'acte d'écrire signifie alors faire apparaître la trace. La trace est autant de l'ordre du Visible que de l'Invisible" (198), she does not yet address the question how the visible becomes instead of a trace a sediment or an ideology in Handke.

[40] I take the idea of the *Zwischenbereich* from Herbert Gamper's interviews with Peter Handke, entitled *Aber ich lebe nur von den Zwischenräumen* (Zürich: Ammann Verlag, 1987).

[41] The German term "Müdigkeit" does not limit itself to "tiredness," its literal English translation, but comprises instead a variety of figurative and non-figurative uses such as weariness, fatigue, lethargy and apathy. The German compound "lebensmüde," denoting a weariness of life, is a related expression that further comes to mind when one reflects on the resonances of Handke's title.

[42] Peter Handke, *Versuch über die Müdigkeit* (Frankfurt: Suhrkamp, 1989) 23; hereafter quoted in text as VM.

[43] Handke speaks in this context literally of a "Flucht": "Seine Fluchtgedanken schlossen jede Rückkehr aus. Eine deutschsprachige Umgebung kam jetzt für ihn nicht mehr in Frage" (*Versuch über die Jukebox* (Frankfurt: Suhrkamp, 1990) 23; hereafter quoted in text as VJ.

[44] Samuel Moser, "Das Glück des Erzählens ist das Erzählen des Glücks," *Peter Handke. Die Langsamkeit der Welt*, eds. Gerhard Fuchs and Gerhard Melzer (Graz: Literaturverlag Droschl, 1993) 146.

[45] Handke once commented in an interview: "Lieber noch als marxistisch würde ich katholisch sein. Das kommt daher, daß ich auf dem Land war als Kind, an der österreichisch-jugoslawischen Grenze, und diese slowenischen Litaneien gehört hab' mit ihrer pathetischen Monotonie. Da hab' ich heute noch ein erhabenes Gefühl, wenn ich das höre" (*André Müller im Gespräch mit Peter Handke* (Weitra: Bibliothek der Provinz, 1993) 27). On occasion, Handke may succumb to this nostalgia, but to remain faithful to his own open project of writing, he cannot allow himself to surrender to this nostalgia, especially when it involves a major ideology of Western history.

[46] Peter Handke, *Langsame Heimkehr* (Frankfurt: Suhrkamp, 1979) 9.

[47] Moser, 146.

[48] Christoph Bartmann, *Suche nach dem Zusammenhang* (Vienna: Wilhlem Braumüller, 1984) 220. Though Bartmann's study ranks next to *Image et écriture* by Arlette Camion, mentioned earlier, among the most informed of contemporary receptions of Handke, I would disagree with the teleological structure that he imputes to Handke's work. What Bartmann calls "Handkes Begierde nach Zusammenhang" expresses a greater need for plasticity in writing but not for a "immer deutlicher aus seinen Werken verlautende Universalitätsanspruch" (239). Handke's work, in spite of an occasional prophetic

tone, is still too ironic and mundane to lend itself entirely to such a universal demand.

[49] Karl-Markus Gauss, "Vorort-Vermessung und Reiseroman," *Profil* 46 (Nov. 14, 1994) 88.

[50] Gerhard vom Hofe and Peter Pfaff, "Peter Handke's weltliche Heilsgeschichte," *Das Elend des Polyphem. Zum Thema Subjektivität bei Thomas Bernhard, Peter Handke, Wolfgang Koeppen und Botho Strauss* (Königstein: Athenäum, 1980) 59–92.

[51] Peter Handke, *Versuch über den geglückten Tag* (Frankfurt: Suhrkamp, 1991)15; hereafter quoted in text as VT.

[52] Peter Handke, "Gelassen wär' ich gern," *Der Spiegel* 49 (Dec. 5, 1994) 176.

[53] See Rolf Günter Renner *Peter Handke* (Stuttgart: Poeschel Verlag, 1985). Other works following the Heidegger path too uncritically are Christine Winkelman's *Die Suche nach dem großen Gefühl* (Frankfurt: Peter Lang, 1990) or Peter Laemmle's essay "Gelassenheit zu den Dingen — Peter Handke auf den Spuren Martin Heideggers," *Merkur* (April 1981).

[54] See Gerhard vom Hofe and Peter Pfaff, *Das Elend des Polyphem.*

[55] Rolf Günter Renner, *Die postmoderne Konstellation. Theorie, Text und Kunst im Ausgang der Moderne* (Freiburg: Rombach Verlag, 1988).

[56] Renner, 373.

[57] Renner, 387.

[58] Alfred Kolleritsch, "Die Welt, die sich öffnet. Einige Bemerkungen zu Handke und Heidegger," *Peter Handke: Die Arbeit am Glück*, eds. Gerhard Melzer and Jale Tükel (Königsstein: Athenäum, 1985) 123.

[59] Jacques Derrida, *Of Spirit: Heidegger and the Question*, trans. Geoffrey Bennington and Rachel Bowlby (Chicago: U of Chicago P, 1989) 71.

[60] Klaus Bonn, *Die Idee der Wiederholung in Peter Handkes Schriften* (Würzburg: Königshausen und Neumann, 1994) 13.

[61] Salman Rushdie, "De Pristina à Littleton," Le Monde (May 11, 1999) 17. In a public comment, for instance, Handke compared NATO's stance against Serbia to the Holocaust and later softened this charge to practices resembling anti-Semitism. He also suggested that the Bosnian muslims had staged rather than suffered genocidal war crimes in order to blame them on Serbians. These remarks drew severe criticism from Rushdie who ranked Handke next to Charleton Heston with his ludicrous remarks on gun control as "crétin international de l'année."

[62] Peter Handke, *Die Fahrt im Einbaum oder Das Stück zum Film vom Krieg* (Frankfurt: Suhrkamp, 1999) 29.

[63] See Eva Geulen, "Nationalism: Old, New and German;" Russell Berman "Nationhood and Solidarity;" and David Pan "Myth, Community and Na-

tionalism" *Telos*, Number 105 (Fall 1995) 2–20, 43–56, 57–76. All three essays discuss the recent political reconfiguration of Germany and its problematic revival of nationalism on the supernational (Europe) or regional level.

# 4

# *Elfriede Jelinek's Austria: Simulations of Death*

## Introduction

THE STATUS OF ELFRIEDE JELINEK'S writings has risen in the last decade so that she is now on a par with Handke and Bernhard. Her work has gained a wide German reading audience beyond the boundaries of Austria, and Jelinek has also increasingly been recognized as one of the leading contemporary female writers in the German language. In this chapter, I will try to define her emerging critical position and importance in comparison to Handke and Bernhard, and I will explore her strikingly new version of a post-ideological form of writing. In the previous chapter, I discussed Handke's project of a post-ideological narrative analysis of society. He launched this project in the wake of a pervasive consumer standardization of society that co-opts and contaminates traditional ideological positions, thereby rendering their critiques powerless. Handke therefore directed his post-ideological critique specifically toward the language of consumer society and the cultural and social stereotypes embedded in it. His writing is impelled by a utopian desire to reinvest everyday reality with signs and images that frame it in an individualized narration, which is outside of any prefabricated social identity. This innovative desire is exemplified in Handke's telling titles *Als das Wünschen noch geholfen hat*, *Wunschloses Unglück* and *Die Stunde der wahren Empfindung*.

Thomas Bernhard, as we have seen, is less vigorously innovative with regard to society's discourse. Instead, he chooses to work with cultural stereotypes by holding them up to society as its repressed mirror image. Bernhard's treatment of social icons, such as those emanating from Austria's decadent fin-de-siècle bourgeois tradition, directs our attention to Austria's complacent cultural self-representation, which conceals its latent yet persistent cultural narcissism. While Bernhard does not subscribe to any ideological critique, he still retains, like Handke, at least the hope of a constructive provocation of society, if not the hope of a constructive renewal. Bernhard's discourse is not so much one of desire as of crisis (*Verstörung*, *Korrektur*, *Der Untergeher*), and it seeks to revive a sense of morality and integrity in the social and public spheres through acute critical comment.

It is this latter avenue of post-ideological inquiry that has also partly guided the work of Elfriede Jelinek. Her iconoclasm would superficially resemble Bernhard's, were it not for an additional severity with which Jelinek converts social icons into irreversible simulacra. Yasmin Hoffmann, in her essay "Hier lacht sich die Sprache selbst aus," establishes a connection between Jelinek's work and what she calls the "Krise der Wahrnehmung zur Gesellschaft des Simulakrums."[1] Hoffmann places Jelinek's work in the tradition of Karl Kraus' critique of public media and its "Entleerung und Entehrung aller Begriffe und allen Inhalts."[2] Kraus' critique, however, as Hoffmann claims, was eventually outdone by surrealism, which radically questioned any implied objectivity of language. By creating artifacts with an objective randomness, surrealism instead pointed to the absence of any content of normative truth in language. This insight in turn was subjected to a commercial exploitation by the culture industry and has led, according to Hoffmann, to a blurring of the borders "zwischen Realem and Imaginären zugunsten des Simulakrums," indicating a general cultural shift from image production to reproduction and image consumption.[3]

As Sigrid Berka has noted, Jelinek's style reflects this shift in its use of citations which are liberally distorted and not set off against the writer's own voice.[4] Such a blurring of the borders between the real and the imaginary can further be seen in the multiple overlapping discourses (gender, race, class, high and low brow culture) in Jelinek's portrayal of Austria's simulated cultural landscape. Jelinek's work, as I will show, parallels in many ways Jean Baudrillard's inquiries into the simulacrum said to lie at the root of a postmodern and disembodied social consciousness. If it were not for the pathos of mourning and melancholy that underlies her postmodern discourse fashioned upon the simulacrum, however, Jelinek's work would offer merely yet another version of this type of cultural skepticism.[5]

The simulacrum in Jelinek is not only the site for unmasking post-industrial society and its radical instrumentalization of human practices; it is also a site of mourning for Europe's wholesale cultural disembodiment that culminated in the Shoah. Jelinek finds herself in the ironic position of carrying the memory of this loss while being prevented from reconstructing her cultural origins or identity in any facile manner, due to critical insights emerging from the Shoah. The melancholia underlying Jelinek's discourse appears as both memory and forgetting. Melancholia appears on the one hand as mourning in the Freudian sense, mourning over a loss that remains repressed and cannot be identified concretely. Here Jelinek acknowledges that the practices of an extinguished Jewish culture in Europe cannot be revived, that the dead cannot be brought back from the dead. On the other hand, in the wake of the expropriation and extermination of Jewish culture in Europe, melancholia figures further as a critical self-denial to any legitimate claim of cultural belonging, which after all had informed the ideology of fascism. The genocide of the Jews in Europe is in this respect unique not only as a culmination of centuries of European anti-Semitism, but also in its devastating effects upon the memory of such catastrophic loss.

It is this simultaneously visible and invisible Jewish heritage and memory, one often ignored by her critics, that has shaped Jelinek's distinct and sobered cultural critique. Although she is not perceived as a Jewish writer in the more visible manner of Robert Schindel, Maxim Biller, Barbara Honigmann or Raphael Seligmann, Jelinek insists that her writing is profoundly Jewish in a critical and historical sense:

> Man nimmt deutsche Erde, und sie zerfällt zu Asche in der Hand. Das ist ja mein ewiges Thema. Das ist ganz zwanghaft. Man kann, wenn man hier lebt, habe ich das Gefühl — das ist dieser Adorno Ausspruch — natürlich sind Gedichte nach Auschwitz möglich, aber es ist kein Gedicht ohne Auschwitz möglich. Robert Schindel, den ich sehr gut kenne, ein alter Freund von mir, der hat einen Roman geschrieben, der heißt *Gebürtig*; der hat gesagt, er wollte das einmal abarbeiten, um dann nicht mehr darüber sprechen zu müssen, was sein gutes Recht ist als Opfer; also ich habe das Gefühl, ich muß eigentlich immer darüber sprechen.[6]

The melancholic memory and loss of identity leaves Jelinek with a complex and sobered Jewish identity, one that does not take comfort in the myth of normalization that seems to underlie much of the present attention given to the revival of Jewish ethnic identity in Germany and Austria. Instead, a permanent rift or duplicity of intentions in Jelinek's discourse recalls now with a marked difference the duplicity that, as part of Europe's anti-Semitism, had once been commonly ascribed to the language of Jews.

Jelinek writes under the shadow of what Sander Gilman has identified as the pervasive anti-Semitic view in the history of the Western Christian tradition "that Jews possess a polluted or polluting discourse."[7] Jews, according to this stereotype, form a culture without a proper discourse. The myth of the Jews' contaminated and deficient linguistic identity, as shown in the derogative German terms of *mauscheln* or *jüdeln*, was applied to, among others, Jewish Austrian writers such as Theodor Herzl, Karl Kraus and Hermann Broch and left a deep-seated uncertainty in their discourse. For instance, Karl Kraus' linguistic purism, his loyalty to the high cultural canon (Goethe) and his dissecting citational style reflect not only the ambivalent critical consciousness of an individual but also the pervasive social and cultural pressures placed upon Kraus' ethnic identity. Kraus became at once a critic of and master in the use of *mauscheln*. As Kafka comments on the ambivalent achievement of Kraus: "No one can *mauschel* like Kraus, in spite of the fact that none in this German Jewish world can do anything but *mauschel*."[8] Kraus' bi-cultural perspective, as Kafka makes evident, possesses nothing intrinsically Jewish, as Kraus himself may have feared, but is rather the result of social and cultural stereotypes projected onto what was framed as the alien discourse of the Jews.

For Jelinek, who consciously places herself in the tradition of Kraus (and in the subversive tradition of Kafka's minor literature), the ambivalence towards the so-called uprooted discourse of the Jews no longer exists. In undertaking a critical transvaluation of this linguistic and cultural stereotype, Jelinek projects the longing and melancholia for an originary language buried beneath this stereotype back onto Austrian society at large. In doing so, Jelinek explodes Austria's myth of cultural uniformity and strategically deploys a form of *mauscheln* to introduce an uneasy *heteroglossia* into Austria's hegemonic cultural language. As Jelinek explains her debt to Kraus and the Jewish tradition of language critique: "Das Jüdische ist ja einfach die Arbeit an der Sprache, die Kritik an Zuständen mit Hilfe der Sprache, die sozusagen selbst spricht und sich selbst entlarvt."[9]

In adopting defiantly what was once held as a denigrated discourse, Jelinek opts for a subtle and ironic ethnic identity. She refuses to perform the task of the exemplary Jewish victim in a culture that tends to assign nostalgically great importance to "dead or half-dead Jews."[10] Jelinek has little use or understanding for this permitted role in society, and she instead dons the mask of the stereotype to deflect it back at its perpetrators. In a post-ideological manner, she applies her critique to herself and refuses to construe any sentimental version of her ethnic identity. Of fully assimilated and secularized Jewish background, Jelinek makes no attempt to locate her identity in cultural folklore, religious customs, and any revival of these practices which may give the appearance of cultural "normalization" in present Germany or Austria.

To make Jelinek's Jewish perspective more tangible, I will begin my inquiry in this chapter with her recent play *Totenauberg* (1991), which on the surface lends greater visibility to Jelinek's Jewish identity than previous works. I will explore here her critique of culture as a tangible site (*Heimat*) and of Austria's insistence on its authenticity. The author, it can be said, undertakes in this drama a sober examination of Austria's tourist and cultural landscape which belies an insidious past and an even more insidious marketing of ethnic and cultural identities as its primary commodities. Following my discussion of *Totenauberg*, I will reconstruct the genesis of Jelinek's melancholic cultural perspective in two earlier works. While insisting that a proper language for minorities is absent, Jelinek, as I will show, advances a minority discourse without relying on an identity politics that reifies the position of minorities. In this respect, Jelinek's *Die Klavierspielerin* (1983; *The Piano Player*) reflects her idiosyncratic treatment of gender and feminism as less innocent positions than held by their ideological proponents. Instead, these positions unmask the sadistic and masochistic struggle for identity among a cultural minority. Similarly, *Lust* (1987; *Lust*), exposes through mock-pornographic discourse the ruling patriarchal values in Austria's society. Here Jelinek deploys a polluted discourse in its most visible form to subvert the euphemistic discourses that establish social and cultural distinction. As we will see, the expropriated discourse of minorities has its own resources of resistance, without having to assert minority claims in the traditional form of consensus mediation.

## Beyond Baudrillard's Simulacrum

Since the Frankfurt School, the shift from image production to image consumption has been acknowledged as a characteristic of a modern society increasingly governed by mass media. However, it was not until Jean Baudrillard's *Simulations* (1983) that the epistemological nature of this media world was explored in more depth. Extending Walter Benjamin's sobering reflections on the reproducibility of art and the loss of its aura, Baudrillard alerts us to the irreversibly derivative and prefabricated matrix of social reality in the various media of reproduction that dominate consumer culture. "The real," claims Baudrillard in revising Benjamin, "is not only what can be reproduced, but that which is always already reproduced."[11] The image of social reality in a simulated media and consumer world consequently "bears no relation to any reality whatever: it is its own pure simulacrum."[12] Whereas the Frankfurt School still viewed mass media as a problematic control of individual consciousness through systemic and administrative manipulation, Baudrillard views its role as totally pervasive in the formation of social consciousness. Society is no longer founded on any governing ethical or cognitive principles but consists merely of empty disposable images and reproducible fantasies.

Jelinek's conception of discourse, as Michael Fischer has shown, was influenced in part by Roland Barthes' *Mythologies* (1957), a work anticipating Baudrillard's more critical conception of simulated realities.[13]

Fischer makes an important, though critically still deficient, contribution to our understanding of Jelinek's use of popular culture. In pointing to the many textual borrowings from Barthes's *Mythologies* in Jelinek's prose radio-drama *Die endlose Unschuldigkeit* (1980; Eternal Innocence), he ultimately fails to acknowledge that Jelinek's assemblages aim beyond literary montages of mere stylistic import. While borrowing from Barthes, Jelinek also parodies his pure and seemingly innocent semiotic interest and re-contextualizes his work historically.

For instance, Fischer juxtaposes two passages from Barthes and Jelinek and claims "daß sich [Jelinek's] Leistung in der endlosen Unschuldigkeit auf eine Montage beschränkt."[14] However, Barthes's statement "Der Mythos verbirgt nichts. Seine Funktion ist es, zu deformieren, nicht etwas verschwinden zu lassen"[15] is critically corrected by Jelinek who attacks the remaining ahistoricality in Barthes's semiotic conception of myths:

> die Funktion des mythos ist es zu deformieren nicht etwa ganz verschwinden zu lassen. das heißt die müten des trivialbereichs der werbung der illustrierten der massenkommunikation etc. werden ihrer geschichte beraubt und in reine gesten verwandelt, deformiert.[16]

In subtle difference to Barthes, Jelinek views the work of popular myths as intimately connected with consumerism and its aim of de-historizing myths altogether. Popular myths thus rob images of their power of critique. Likewise, Barthes's exotic and somewhat bizarre examples of "der Löwe und der Neger" as disposable images in our semiotic world, are countered by Jelinek's more acute focus on the woman as a consumer fetish. Substituting woman for Barthes' exotic examples, Jelinek once again sharpens his insights with her critical rewriting and alteration:

> die nackte frau auf dem foto wird ihrer sexualität ihrer geschichte beraubt und in geste verwandelt. sie ist deformiert aber nicht vernichtet sie ist amputiert und ihres gedächtnisses beraubt nicht ihrer existenz.[17]

Jelinek thus aims beyond Barthes' aesthetic and innocent semiotic vision of popular myths (a universe of pleasant distractions, such as in Barthes' exploration of cinema, fashion or strip-tease) and lends it the historical and social critique missing in Barthes.

In fact, it is Jelinek's critical reception of Barthes that likens her project, apart from her explicit feminist and ethnic perspective, to Baudrillard's. The goal of her project reaches beyond the rhetoric of desire and iconicity, that characterize Barthes or Handke, and the rhetoric of crisis and iconoclasm, that characterize in Kraus or Bernhard. She pays close attention to the elusive yet omnipresent social realities of consumerism, gender and race. The simulacrum is ambivalent in Jelinek not merely because it is a disembodied episteme, indicating the failure of signification. Nor is it a mere "Spiel mit dem Signifikanten,"[18] as Hoffmann suggests. Rather, Jelinek's conception of the simulacrum concretely captures the hypnotic and eroticized world of consumer images that devour the consumer as much as he or she devours them. The "pornographic" sense that underlies many of Jelinek's works underscores the overall impression of a pathological society falling prey to its own illusions even while recognizing them as illusions. In this respect, Jelinek's work also parallels Baudrillard's, who claims that pornography as the artificial or ecstatic amplification of desire and consumption has managed to penetrate virtually every aspect of society:

> Obscenity is not confined to sexuality, because today there is a pornography of information and communication, a pornography of circuits and networks, of functions and objects in their legibility, availability, regulation, forced signification, capacity to perform, connection, polyvalence, their free expression . . .[19]

In this pervasive, pornographic consumer reality, every commodity has the appearance of an eroticized woman and every woman the appearance of a commodity. Jelinek's feminist critique of this sense of reality, however, acquires an additional ethnic qualification.

Unlike Baudrillard, Jelinek does not construe the simulacrum as the inevitable and therefore only logical episteme of Western commodity culture and its pervasive consumer fetishization. Disneyland and America, that figure prominently in Baudrillard as the perfect embodiments of the simulacrum, remain for Jelinek still weak analogies. Insisting on greater historical accountability, Jelinek focuses in her conception of simulated realities on a site closer to home than in the distant and mythical techno-dystopia of America. For Jelinek, the simulacrum is not merely a semiotic cultural reflection of deceptive commodity realities; instead, commodity illusions mask more powerful discourses of race, gender and nationhood thought to have been overcome in Europe's postwar society. It is in Austria, as Jelinek suggests, where the Disney theme park of distraction and illusion truly comes undone. For if a natural relation had ever existed between the soil and the inscribed practices of a particular people, if there had ever been a *Heimat*, so to speak, it was in Austria where this significance was annulled, depleted and carried to the utmost level of dehumanization.

## *Totenauberg*: The Theme Park of Genocide

In recent history, Austria's latent and explicit fascism has been closely scrutinized by a critical minority of writers and artists who, in the words of Peter Handke, represent the "real people of Austria, those who have so often been discounted, so rarely consulted, almost reduced to silence."[20] Gerhard Roth's large scale prose cycle *Archive des Schweigens* (*Archives of Silence*) offers in this vein a careful documentation of what has been conveniently forgotten and deleted from Austria's cultural heritage. Austria's persistent and recently intensifying cultural amnesia, as we have mentioned earlier, was directly confronted in Peter Handke's public attack of Kurt Waldheim during his 1986 presidential election campaign. Thomas Bernhard further exposed Austria's entrenched cultural fascism in his drama *Heldenplatz* (1988), earning himself the title *Nestbeschmutzer* (a nest dirtier) from all major political camps. Elfriede Jelinek, as an Austrian writer of Jewish descent, likewise addresses the question of fascism as it arises in the present political reality of revisionism and pan-nationalism in Europe. Asked in an interview with Maxim Biller about her reaction to Germany's increased national awareness since the unification, Jelinek's answer was prompt and direct: "Deswegen will ich ihm [the German] seine Selbstzufriedenheit erst recht vergällen."[21]

Austria's writers, one could argue, are currently attempting to project a form of denigration and internalized resentment experienced by a silenced minority back onto Austria's entire cultural landscape. Austria is consequently forced to confront its own distorted image, its own dirty nest, filled with resentment against anybody challenging its hegemonic social and cultural consensus. Jelinek's recent play *Totenauberg* (1991), following this rhetorical strategy from an intensified Jewish point of view, extends the author's intent of spoiling Germany's revisionist confidence to her own country of origin. As a Jewish Austrian writer, Jelinek is especially sensitive and vulnerable to the dynamics in which margin and center parasitically constitute one another in the struggle for cultural expression and identity. Her recent play *Totenauberg* reflects this dynamics critically by relating fascism and consumerism as historical peripheries and thereby as hidden centers to one another.

In *Totenauberg* and her previous *Burgtheater* (1984), Jelinek carries out her critique of fascism explicitly with regard to the rhetoric of consumerism that makes fascism, as Handke, Roth and Bernhard also argue, a dangerously habitual phenomenon of the everyday. Jelinek's earlier play *Burgtheater*, which was rejected by the Burgtheater (National Theater) and premiered in Bonn, anticipates *Totenauberg* in its analysis of fascism. Jelinek exposes in this play the opportunistic complicity and participation of the Burgtheater's star actors (Paula Wessely, Attila and Paul Hörbiger) in the fascist culture industry and draws attention to their quick political rehabilitation and unquestioned engagements in the highly popular postwar *Heimatfilme*. In these films the fascist rhetoric of *Bodenständigkeit* (nativism) was less overt in tone, but it was never seriously called into doubt. The critique of her play, as Jelinek explains, is ultimately directed at an equivocating discourse that allows for the facile accommodation of fascism in the postwar culture industry: "Ich kritisiere eine Sprache, die in ihrer Pervertierung die faschistische Kulturindustrie und eine nicht erfolgte Entnazifizierung in diesem Unterhaltungsbereich ermöglicht hat."[22]

In her recent play *Totenauberg*, Jelinek views the resurgence of fascism and its dissemination through the discourse of consumerism in a similar light, emphasizing even more strongly the deceptive adaptability of fascism: "Nur wird der neue Faschismus ein verwaschener und unspezifischer Faschismus sein."[23] Jelinek's play specifically confronts the dispersion of fascism into consumerism in the form of cultural and entertainment commodities that sell the illusion of both collective and subjective identity. Staging an imaginary encounter between Martin Heidegger and Hannah Arendt, the play dramatizes the clash between the dominant concepts of *Zugehörigkeit* (belonging)[24] in Heidegger and rootlessness in the work of Arendt.[25] The latter concept, as the play shows, has still not found a positive resonance in the cultural perspectives of contemporary Europe, and it is outweighed by the narcissistic and marketable fantasy of a primordial belonging.

Jelinek's play, like Bernhard's *Heldenplatz*, projects social and cultural internalizations of negative self-perception back onto its source in the culture at large. Differently from Bernhard, however, Jelinek situates the socio-psychological formation of cultural discourse in an evasive consumerist rhetoric that precedes the construction of individuals and social groups. The illusory reference group in the construction of social awareness is no longer solely derived from institutional power and high cultural status. Rather, it is the phantom reality of consumer mobility against which an entire society measures its successful or unsuccessful socialization. Apparently, as Jelinek shows, Austria's society falls short of its desire to approach the imagined and ever receding norm of consumer affluence. As Gilman explains the vicissitude or double bind of self-hatred in any socialization based on negative self-perception: "As one approaches the norms set by the reference group, the approbation of that group recedes."[26]

Rephrasing this phenomenon in terms of Jelinek's more neo-Marxist leanings, one could say the following: As a society attempts to achieve a high consumer standard, and thus to conform to the artificial norms of capitalism, its justification as a socially integrated community paradoxically dwindles. Consumerism in Jelinek's terms becomes an increasingly broadly enforced standard subverting social freedom. The consequence of this disenchantment is the fragmentation of the social whole into class and ethnic margins upon which hatred is projected from the center. Persecution of minorities as perpetrated by fascism becomes an epi-phenomenon of consumerism, and ever more accelerated consumption of collective and subjective identities. What Gilman calls the "fragmentation of identity" forming the "articulation of self-hatred"[27] is in Jelinek's analysis interpreted at an intersection of consumerist and ethnic discourse. *Totenauberg* represents in this respect a synthesis of her earlier prose pieces. Jelinek expands the satirical comment on the marketable ecological aesthetics of the mid-1980s of her novel *Oh Wildnis, oh Schutz vor ihr* (1985), a grotesque *Heimatroman*, in *Wolken, Heim* (1990), a text that unmasks the rhetoric of the "native" from German Romanticism (Hölderlin, Kleist, Fichte, Hegel) through Heidegger.

In her synthetic analysis Jelinek exposes the conflicting claims with which a society construes its dominant and marginal discourses, and the complexity of her analysis is specifically reflected in the language of her play. The principle figures of Heidegger and Arendt appear barely disguised but, according to the author's stage directions, are not meant to be evoked too literally: "Die Person Heideggers bitte mit einem winzigen Zitat nur andeuten, vielleicht der Schnurrbart? Hannah Arendt desgleichen."[28] The presentation of Heidegger and Arendt is by no means intended to be concretely historical or even remotely biographical. As Jelinek explains: "Ich schreibe ja nicht über reale Personen, sondern über Personen, wie sie sich als Sprachschablonen oder Sprachmuster materialisieren."[29] "*Totenauberg*," as the author explains,

> ist im Grunde ein Requiem. Wie der Name sagt: Wir leben auf einem Berg von Leichen und Schmerz. Es ist ein Requiem auch für den jüdischen Teil meiner Familie von dem viele vernichtet worden sind. 51 Personen — das sind nur die, die gezählt wurden.[30]

The genocide of Europe's Jews demands, however, a gesture of mourning that does not belittle their extermination or make it banal. A direct and personal attack on Heidegger as a contributor to fascism would have been too easy and facile given Heidegger's own evasive answers about his past. Jelinek complicates the question of guilt and complicity by locating Heidegger, and thus her audience, in the landscape of a perverse culture and commodity industry, the only one in which we can possibly come to know him these days.

Thomas Bernhard, for example, gives us a hyperbolic and satirical portrait of the cult that surrounds Heidegger and precedes the acquaintance with his thinking:

> Wenn Sie in eine kleinbürgerliche oder aber auch aristokratisch-kleinbürgerliche Gesellschaft kommen, wird Ihnen sehr oft schon vor der Vorspeise Heidegger serviert, Sie haben Ihren Mantel noch nicht ausgezogen, wird Ihnen schon ein Stück Heidegger angeboten, Sie haben sich noch nicht hingesetzt, hat die Hausfrau Ihnen schon sozusagen mit dem Sherry Heidegger auf dem Silbertablett hereingebracht.[31]

Heidegger, as Bernhard's caricature reveals, has become a commodity that confers the status of cultural and intellectual sophistication that Heidegger's own narcissistic fascination with his exemplary personality has partly furthered. In another caricature, Bernhard mimics Heidegger's self-presentation as a natural, self-sufficient and natively grounded thinker:

> Heidegger ist mir immer widerwärtig gewesen, nicht nur die Schlafhaube auf dem Kopf und die selbstgewebte Winterunterhose über seinem von ihm selbst eingeheizten Ofen in Todtnauberg, nicht nur sein selbstgeschnitzter Schwarzwaldstock, eben seine selbstgeschnitzte Schwarzwaldphilosophie.[32]

This caricature, based on a series of pictures taken of Heidegger at his Todtnauberg residence, reveals how Heidegger's thought cannot be separated from his reception. Unlike Bernhard, Jelinek no longer gives Heidegger any personal treatment; she embeds him, and perhaps Arendt to a slightly lesser degree, in the anonymity of mass products that have a life of their own and have become at least in part independent of their creators.

As an example of this style in which characters no longer show personal traits but personify their own language, Heidegger appears in this play strapped into a *Gestell* (a scaffold, skeleton). This grotesque and humorous costume evokes his own concept of "enframing," (*Gestell*) a poetic-ontological ordering that Heidegger posits as the elusive and yet-to-be-recovered essence of modern technology. In the same essay in which Heidegger introduces the notion of *Gestell* "The Question Concerning Technology," he also argues that the prefix "ge" indicates the act of enframing. This enframing appears, for instance, when it "unfolds mountains into mountains, . . . the gathering that we call

"Gebirg" (mountain chain)."[33] *Ge-stell* suggests man's technical control over nature, and it has more deeply poetic roots because existence situates man in the context of nature, thereby calling his independent self-determination into question. For Jelinek, however, who does not attempt to undertake a philosophical inquiry into Heidegger's thinking, the semantic asymmetry between the two terms *Gestell* (skeleton) and *Gebirg* (mountain chain) may have been enough to spawn the entire grotesque scenario of *Totenauberg* in which Heidegger's language paradoxically unveils itself.

Jelinek's title clearly brings conflicting associations to mind: Heidegger's mountain residence Todtnauberg on the one hand and the mountains of the dead on the other, whose linguistic origins cannot be easily explained away with an etymology of the word's roots like the "coming into being" explanation of *Gebirge* (mountain chain). Instead, these mountains of the dead came to haunt Heidegger in his peaceful residence, as, for instance, in the visits paid by the poet and Holocaust survivor Paul Celan. As if Heidegger's two terms *Gestell* (skeleton) and *Gebirge* (mountain chain) had strangely found one another in a fluid and contaminated ambience of language, Jelinek conjures up a surreal landscape in which the memory of the Holocaust remains buried beneath Austria's Alpine tourism. The setting of Jelinek's play revolves around Alpine tourist sites and projected screen images of historical footage with Jews being publicly humiliated and boarding the trains for deportation. Even the Holocaust is present only indirectly in the specter of media reproduction.

Characters in the play resemble floating commodities in that they have no defined boundaries and for the most part interchangeable discourses. The languages of the characters offer an assemblage of loose citations from Heidegger and Arendt and incessantly revolve in their uprooted reflections around the possibility or impossibility of dwelling and *Zugehörigkeit*: "Und immer am selben Ort ankommen, wo man behauen wird und behaust ist: die Heimat" (T 10). Duplication and reproduction are among the main devices Jelinek uses to indicate the simulation of all reality. Commenting on Heidegger and his *Gestell*, Jelinek writes: "Er ist sozusagen doppelt vorhanden" (T 9). Similarly, the stage is doubled through the use of the cinematic screen.

The first scene, ironically titled "im Grünen," opens with Arendt's critique of Heidegger and underscores the omnipresence of technology and commodity in contemporary leisure culture: "Die Sonne fällt durch die Löcher im Gezweig, aber ihre Glut . . . Unschädlich ist sie geworden" (T 9). The aged figure of Heidegger enters the stage in an old rustic skiing outfit and his *Gestell*, appearing impotent and overhauled by time:

> Nachdem Sie einst ein Liebender waren, werfen die Frauen jetzt ihre Stöcke um andre stachlige Früchtchen in den Baumkronen. Es fällt ihnen nichts mehr in den Schoß. Die Bänke dienen den Frauen zum Stricken, Nadeln wohnen in ihren Händen. Sie jedoch, Sie sind ausgestoßen aus diesem Wohnen, das ein Ausruhen ist. Die Jugend, deren Körper vor Mode leuchtet, umsteht die Gebäude. (T 9–10)

Heidegger's once celebrated proximity to nature and his native soil, as *die Frau* (Arendt) puts it, has lost both its charisma and its power over women like herself and women of the younger generation, who once were avid followers of the philosopher.

In an essay honoring Heidegger's 80th birthday, Hannah Arendt recalls how Heidegger had in his early years attracted followers like herself by challenging the academic industry in paying concentrated attention to the "matter of thinking" and not merely to an "object of scholarship."[34] Heidegger's seductive charisma thus offered the promise of a thinking that was to outgrow institutions and move solely in tandem with experience. The character of *die Frau* likewise recalls the deceptive promise of Heidegger's thought but also unmasks its pretensions: "Bitte erinnern, was für ein verführerischer Entwurf Sie waren: Der Mensch, in die Stille gestellt. Und ist er Grund seines Seins, ist er schon Gott, in zehn Lektionen" (T 12).

Heidegger's grand ruminations on *Dasein* and destiny now appear pompous and antiquated, as if providing a technical manual for man's self-determination: "Verlangt es nicht nach kleineren Wörtern als Sie überhaupt besitzen? Sie sind auch so ein Bilderl, eine Abbildung! Passen nicht ins fesche, aber falsche Kleid dieser falschen Landschaft" (T 10). In an era of Alpine tourism and fashionable leisure entertainment, Jelinek's dramatic version of Arendt ultimately does not fully recall Heidegger's once charismatic personality. Instead, it recedes into a cheap and antiquated copy (*Bilderl*) or reproduction (*Abbildung*) that is ironically also out of synchrony with the present order of simulacra with its more deceptively sophisticated tourist landscape.

Heidegger's philosophical attempts at reconciliation between technology and poetic thinking likewise prove to be hopelessly naive and therefore vulnerable to ideological deception: "Schauen Sie, wie die Heutigen ihre Erholungsschlachten austragen! Und da wagen Sie zu sagen, die Natur ruhe sich aus . . . Die Technik läßt sie ja nicht!" (T 11). Arendt's more modern perspective is underscored by her urban dress and contrasts with Heidegger's provincial rustic outlook. He uncritically accepts an idyllic vision of community as represented by the religiously enshrouded images of the holy family, the messianic Hölderlin and the mysterious Black Forest: "Aber das einzige, was Ihnen widerfahren ist: die Eltern. Der heilige Großvater in der Krippe von Hölderlins Stall. Der Schwarzwald!" (T 13).

This mock nativity scene can be construed as a powerful scene of instruction that presumably imprisoned Heidegger's thinking. Günther Neske and Emil Kettering, in their introduction to *Heidegger and National Socialism*, wonder likewise what may have "led Heidegger to look expectantly first to Hitler and, later, to the poet Hölderlin." Their answer is in part congruent with Jelinek's evocation of Heidegger:

> There was also Heidegger's strong Catholic upbringing. Although he outgrew this while a student at Freiburg, he could never quite leave it behind; just as could never leave behind his native Messkirch, where his father had been a sexton at the church of St. Martin.[35]

Heidegger's parochial family and communal narcissism, as Neske and Kettering speculate, may have prevented Heidegger from making a more critical assessment of the technical and political sphere of Germany's culture. From the very beginning, it would appear, Heidegger remained out of touch with a considerable part of his cultural environment in pursuing a project of pure ontological thinking almost religiously, and he was in this respect easy prey for facile ideological manipulation and self-delusion.

Jelinek's play, however, ultimately refrains from drawing such definitive conclusions but merely gives us fragmentary strains of discourses that circumscribe and partially unveil her characters' thinking. Heidegger's presumed family narcissism is not seen separately from the narcissism that has befallen a culture at large. Jelinek conducts her examinations in a broader fashion on the level of a variety of intersecting and evolving discourses. "Mein Stück," as Jelinek explains,

> ist jetzt kein irgendwie hexerischer, kein rachsüchtiger Text. Es geht nur darum, wie es in Totenauberg einmal heißt, ob nach der gigantischen Vernichtung, die passiert ist, jeder einzelne noch einmal umgebracht wird im Denken.[36]

Jelinek's play foregoes a causal reconstruction of what may have ultimately led to the Nazi genocide. Instead, she is more interested in trying to account for a "second death" threatening the victims of Nazism in the current cultural amnesia of Austrian society. Here she traces the partially autonomous displacement of language, typical of the author's own style, from the ideological discourse of fascism, of the unity of soil and being, to that of a more dispersive and ideologically elusive discourse of consumerism with its deceptive and evasive modes of *Zugehörigkeit*. This latter discourse, she believes, threatens the memory of the victims in its pretense of having overcome the symptoms of fascism.

The post-ideological project of cultural self-examination in Jelinek's writing is also apparent in her effort to stage the play's premiere performance in Vienna. The often farcical interweaving of ideology and consumer culture would be understood best in this location, according to the author:

> weil schon die Metaphorik des Skifahrens und die Ideologie des Wintersports, die den Hintergrund des Stückes bildet, nirgendwo so verstanden wird. Als Karl Schranz [famous Austrian skier] 1972 von den olympischen Spielen in Sapporo ausgeschlossen wurde und sich ganz Österreich darüber empörte, hat er — der "Abfahrtskönig" — da hat er bei seinem Einzug in Wien genausoviele Leute auf die Beine gebracht wie Hitler 1938. Es war, wie es Marx im "Achtzehnten Brumaire des Louis Bonaparte" beschrieben hat: daß sich die Weltgeschichte irgendwann noch einmal als Farce wiederholt. Und es ist nicht einmal die Farce eines jüdischen Professors, der sich bei Thomas Bernhard am Heldenplatz aus dem Fenster stürzt, es geschieht nur durch die Erbärmlichkeit eines Skifahrers. Was diese klerikal-alpine Verlogenheit an gesellschaftlichem Sprengstoff hat in Österreich, das könnte man in Frankfurt nicht nachvollziehen.[37]

Jelinek's play addresses such general problematic cultural concepts as *Heimat*, *Gesundheit* and *Unversehrtheit* and locates their distortions specifically in Austria's simulated Alpine culture where they receive their ontological and theological blessing, as it were. Jelinek's observation, taken from Marx, that an unreflected history tends to repeat itself as a farce — consider Hitler's and Schranz's receptions at the Heldenplatz — further points to the strong commercialization that Austria's culture has since undergone. Its new heroes are those who represent foremost its leisure industry and appear more benign than former political leaders.

In this shift from direct to indirect expressions of the fascism that comprises much of the rhetoric of postwar European reconstruction, Jelinek alerts us to the extent of our failure to work through a fascism which permeates the everyday structure of society. The popular and Oscar-winning American film musical *The Sound of Music* (1965), with its partial exculpation of Austria's fascist complicity and its rehabilitation of folklore as a regional force of resistance against the *Anschluss* (annexation), reflected for the first time a significant change in the international perception of Austria after the war. This rehabilitated image was enhanced by Austria's status of neutrality, acquired in 1955. The

Olympic Winter Games of 1964 in Innsbruck eventually paved the way for an entire new era in which Alpine folklore with its once problematic emphasis on *Heimat* was now attached to a leisure culture patterned on the democratic and capitalist principles of the Western world, particularly the United States. The ensuing development of an Alpine tourist industry brought Austria's backward economy up to date and placed it among the leading nations with regard to the sophistication of its service industry (currently amounting to almost 60% of its GNP).[38] A concomitant elimination of strongly marked economic classes was facilitated in Austria by means of its instituted policy of social partnership (1955). Austria's socio-economic cohesion, it can be argued, along with its cultural and religious homogeneity (78% Catholics)[39] has made it not only a country of remarkable consensus but also one of an insidious denial of its fascist past covered up by an administrated harmonization of politics and culture.

As Jelinek dramatically demonstrates in the central scenes of her play, all the dubious concepts inherited from fascism, such as *Heimat*, nature, authenticity and health, persist and have merely been euphemistically adapted to the needs of man, the insatiable consumer of being:

> Diesen absolut egoistischen Anspruch auf eigene Gesundheit, diesen arroganten Anspruch der reichen Ersten Welt auf Unversehrtheit, auf gesundes Trinkwasser und ungefälschte Naturprodukte, den denunziere ich ja!"[40]

The particularly perverse thought that guides the postwar reconstruction of Austria, and to which Jelinek's linguistic assemblages obsessively refer, is the realization of the commodity value of *Heimat* in an age of mass migrations and cultural displacement. *Heimat* is not merely a desired location that shelters an uprooted population in a presumably native territory; it is also an illusion that can be sold to others. The tourist guides, evoked in the character collages of the two natives (*Gamsbärtler*) wearing national costume and feather-decorated Tyrolean hats, summarize this simple yet lucrative insight hidden beneath the Alpine attractions:

> Unsre vorgeschnitzten Balkone verbergen unsre zurechtgestutzten Lebenshecken. Für andre sind wir das Fremde. Sie fahren zu uns, nehmen uns zu sich und werden auf unseren Wegen heimisch. (T 39).

Beneath the simulacrum of the native, the "prefabricated carved balconies" that evoke a weak semblance of folkloric culture, one finds organized economic interests, trimmed hedges that constitute the livelihood of the so-called natives. These economic interests rule the

*Zugehörigkeit* of the contemporary native culture that has been distorted into a commodity. Indeed, this distortion carries the usual distinction between native and foreign to absurdity. Representing itself as foreign to visitors, the host country simultaneously sells the illusion of a homeland or *Heimat.* In this curious contamination of the meaning of foreign and native, their positions appear to be constantly reversible. At the same time, the host country is uprooted from its own territory that is always offered and leased to others: "Wir, die wir hier wohnen, betrachten die Landschaft überhaupt nie, wir erfahren sie durch den Wert, den andere ihr zumessen" (T 46). The market value of the *Heimat* is in turn preserved by not surrendering the illusion of belonging and inclusion: "Wir sind die wahren Fremdenzimmer, uns bewohnt man gut. . . . Nur Geschwisterliches darf nicht ausbrechen. Sie sollen ja fremd bleiben and dafür zahlen" (T 48).

On the surface, Jelinek's play appears to follow Adorno's claim that "the entire practice of culture industry transfers the profit motive naked onto cultural forms."[41] The conversion of fascism into consumerism extends to ethnic and cultural discrimination that is concretely linked to economic motives. Jelinek refers in her play specifically to the new mass migrations from Eastern into Central Europe since the collapse of communism. Ethnic and economic refugees are perceived as used up commodities "ausgespien aus ihren Ländern, für die sie untragbar wurden und die ihnen längst keinen Ertrag mehr einbringen" (T 51). They are not welcome guests in a country that tolerates only profitable visitors: "Sie sollen in ihre armen Zimmer zurückkehren" (T 52), says at one point the old weary character of Heidegger for whom the present reality has become much too complicated for his rural and homely outlook. The resurgence of neo-fascism in Europe may after all have economic motives as well, Jelinek seems to suggest, motives that have inscribed themselves deeply onto the mass psyche and its simulated cultural memory of a native identity.

Hannah Arendt, in her analysis of fascism, has also pointed to economic motives of profitability that in part contributed to the marginalization of Austrian Jews after the collapse of the empire and that even among Jews became a criterion for selection in deportations.[42] And yet, neither Arendt nor Jelinek seeks to reduce fascism to economic motives alone. Jelinek's portrayal of cultural consumerism is a larger category than economy in that it is concerned not only with the marketability of products but of cultural identities as well. "Ja die Fremden haben das Bedürfnis bei uns zu wohnen erst geweckt," (T 65) as one of the characters comments on the mimetic struggle for identity. Adorno was an early and wary critic of this treacherous new form of capitalism that reduced the consumer to a consumer of images, an enlightened pseudo-individual taking pride in taste and consumer refinement. Jelinek's play radicalizes Adorno's critique by pointing to the commodity value of cultural and ethnic identity that lurks beneath enlightened consumerism.

Heidegger's sophisticated critique of humanism and technology as metaphysical instrumentalizations of being, for example, has found in Jelinek's play its seemingly innocent and adulterated version in new commodities such as ecologically safe products and a widespread cultivation of leisure activities substituting for the work of existential reflection: "Im Sport sind wir Schmuck unseres Daseins. . . . Der Sport ist jetzt unsere wirkliche Auslegung, als Werk" (T 72). The innocence of these appropriations of wholesome being, however, begins to disappear once one looks beneath the surface. Derrida's reflection on Heidegger's avoidance in *Sein und Zeit* (1927) and subsequent reconstitution of the metaphysical concept of "spirit" since his infamous "Rectoral Address" (1933) could be applied here.[43] Sports becomes in Jelinek's play the last manifestation of the problematic presence of "spirit" in culture. Sports, the *pneuma* or breath of the competitive rhythms of consumer society, has received, according to Jelinek, cultic significance in the present era. Jelinek's recent play *Ein Sportstück* (1998; A Sport's Play) likewise parodies the ideology and universality of sports and leisure culture as the new metaphysics of the masses, displayed in the ubiquitous use of sports' fashion, the "uniform" of capitalism's global army.[44]

One must also bear in mind the ideological significance of sports during the fascist era, where the fire of this spirit symbolically kindled the Olympic flames in Berlin in 1936, and its constructed rite of sacrifice and ritual purification that soon took on a literal sense in Germany's culture. Sports, as a new "spirituality," is in Jelinek's play unmasked in its reactionary obsession with authentic possession of nature and self-determination that feeds not only consumerism but actively contributes to the cultural alienation of those who do not or cannot share this spirit of leisure, health and fitness. Friedrich Ludwig Jahn, the "father of gymnastics," in the wake of Germany's defeat at the hands of Napoleon, had originally conceived of the *Turnverein* (gymnast's association) in order to boost the physical and moral powers of his fatherland. Sports once again was exploited as a vehicle of promoting national unity under fascism where it signified the racial and biological superiority of the Aryan. Alfred Bäumler, Hitler's chief ideologue of the body, viewed "Leibesübungen" (physical exercise) as part of the political education of the body in the formation of the "Gesamtleib" or collective body of the nation.[45] In addition, the Berlin

Olympic Games of 1936 further served as a deceptive public spectacle to lend credibility to Germany's promotion of itself as a peaceful and internationally compliant nation. This illusion of the universal language of the fit body was aesthetically enhanced by Leni Riefensthal's follow-up documentation *Olympia* (1938).[46] Germany indeed saw it fit to celebrate its unification by making a bid for the Olympic Games in the year 2000 to be held in Berlin.

In the present era of late capitalism, the rhetoric of sports, except in the usual display of overt nationalism in international events, has for the most part lost its militant overtones and become a leisure pursuit. Sports now conforms to economic norms of fitness on the job and promotes release of stress and a generally strong state of health. A latent cultural ideology of the leisure class and of organic and biological health still accompanies the appearance of sports as a healthy diversion, however, and there is an overall cultural amnesia promoted by the cult of distraction surrounding sports. Austria, a nation that once militantly persecuted perceived foreign elements, presents us with the irony of a miraculous transformation of itself into an unburdened leisure site for foreigners. What better way, as Jelinek's play suggests, to forget a bothersome history than by cashing in profitably on the false tourist paradise erected in Austria's winter and sports *Heimat*.

Jelinek's *Totenauberg*, magnifying the latent discourse of *Heimat* and cultural sanitation in present Austrian society, ultimately undoes the latter's false charisma and power by reflecting on the cost of the desire for such a cultural purity. A scenery of scattered casualties of mountain climbers and farcical appearances by various characters (cheerleaders, a *Leistungsportler*, two Tyroleans) spell out the physical and spiritual death of a culture that deludes itself in its leisure identity. The briefly interspersed and understated cinematic footage of deportation and public humiliation of Jews casts a further shadow on this spectacle in which everything has turned into a bizarre simulacrum of narcissistic self-display: "Das Besuchen wird von unsren Film-, Video- und Fotoapparaten ersetzt. Wir gelingen erst durch sie. . . . Was Wald war, wird Bild. Was Berg war, wird Bild" (T 19, 25). The opening and closing reflections of *die Frau*, the character of Arendt, finally place the loosely unfolding center of the play into perspective. It is from this margin that the voice of mourning and memory surfaces.

Initially, this sense of mourning, as we have seen, is expressed in a relentless critique of the recollection of Heidegger in which the peasant philosopher, a synechdochical remnant of the past, now appears in his frail human *Gestell*, hopelessly dwarfed and antiquated. This sense of a disembodied history is taken up again in the final sequence entitled

*Unschuld.* Heidegger's project of a human Dasein that is reflectively accountable for its own death and finality has, according to Arendt's character, forfeited its legitimization at Auschwitz:

> Das Selbst hat sich als Gewissen an die Stelle der Menschheit gesetzt und das Selbstsein an die Stelle des Menschseins. Jetzt fliegen die Hüte. Indem Sie diese Masse an Leuten umgebracht haben, haben Sie sie um den Augenblick betrogen, als einzelner noch einmal vor den Vorhang zu treten im Augenblick des Todes und sich verbeugen zu dürfen. (T 81)

Authenticity or poetry, as Adorno would say, died at Auschwitz. One is left with an uprooted identity whose terrifying quality is concealed in the marketable fantasies of belonging. As the classic study *Die Unfähigkeit zu trauern* (*The Inability to Mourn*) by Alexander and Margarete Mitscherlich has shown, a dimension of shame was curiously not achieved in postwar Germany (nor Austria). This failure was instead quickly compensated by the miracle of economic reconstruction. Jelinek's play makes Austria's inability to mourn explicit by making visible its latent melancholia, which, as Freud explains, expresses the grieving over a repressed loss.[47] The play ultimately suffers from this melancholic presentation of mass marketability of cultural identity. By her own admission, it is the author's most resigned play.[48] Little of Arendt's constructive thinking — her emphasis on political solidarity that penetrates the dehumanizing layers of institutionalized discourse[49] — finds any echo in Jelinek's play. Arendt instead becomes the uprooted mouthpiece for the author's own frustration over what is perceived as an unthinkable crisis in postwar Europe where fascism blooms anew in both a visible but also a more subtle and disguised manner.

Jelinek's critique exposes fascism as an attempt to domesticate the realm of *Zugehörigkeit* in order to repress the sense of rootlessness that afflicts modern cultures. Arendt, for example, attacks Heidegger's "peasant" philosophy as one of a cowardly and sheltered member of the bourgeoisie who never placed his life at risk but advocated others do so: "In Wahrheit waren Sie feig, Sie Freund des Hauses, während die Burschenschaften sich in die Strampelanzüge des Krieges schmissen" (T 16). Later in the play, this hidden petit-bourgeois ideology is once again stressed with regard to Heidegger's idealization of death as the reflective limit of Dasein: "Was für ein Glück, dass andre den Tod für euch haben erfahren müssen! Menschenherden habt ihr aus der Behaglichkeit gerissen, während eure Bergbäche rauschten" (T 80). The result of this repression of rootlessness and its domestication into *Zugehörigkeit* is a fanatic over-legitimization by which a culture installs itself as primordial or, in a more banal sense, erects an ideological landscape of deceptive leisure and distraction.

Jelinek's critique of Austria's "Wintersportideologie" points to the institution of cultural amnesia in a manner akin to Bernhard or Handke while additionally offering a different approach to its conceptualization. With regard to Bernhard, Jelinek has sharpened the farcical irony of his *Heldenplatz* by identifying the impending cultural implosion not in the realm of a despairing elite alone (the Schuster brothers') but in the area of Austria's omnipresent leisure industry and its ideological reductions. With respect to Handke, Jelinek follows in part his critique that sports provides one with a technical vocabulary that relieves one from the burden of self-definition. Handke, for instance, points to the increasing technification of language in various popular sports, particularly automotive sports. As Handke ironically claims:

> Das Bewußtsein, über die Technik und ihre Sprachen zu verfügen, nicht mehr sich als jemand albern Persönlichen, Einmaligen offenbaren zu müssen, sondern sich mittels der Apparate erklären zu können, gibt dem einzelnen eine erlöste Sachlichkeit. . . . Das völkerverbindende Zeichen für die neue, die technische Weltformel ist sicher der Formel-1–Rennwagen.[50]

A further influence cited by Jelinek is Handke's play *Über die Dörfer* (1980; *Across the Villages*), where Handke reflects on the transformation of Austria's rural regions by an aggressive building industry and the ensuing collapse of communal structures. Jelinek's play similarly acknowledges a transformation of this sort but locates its origins in a cultural and semiotic system whereby the myth of *Zugehörigkeit* is both desperately repeated and ruthlessly exploited.

Jelinek's perception of Austria's cultural impasse is acute, focusing on the total absence of any critical reflective dimension that would bring about a reversal of society and history. The illusion of collective identity, that figured so prominently in fascist ideology, as Jelinek's severe analysis shows, has not been critically and fundamentally questioned. It has merely been displaced onto the consumer who lays claim to a distorted sense of community by obsessively substituting leisure for reflection, spectacle for history and amnesia or melancholy for mourning. In this overly determined cultural climate marked by an inability to mourn, the victims, such as Hannah Arendt, are left not only with their lot of victimization but with the overburdening task of cultural reconstruction. As Jelinek remarks, Arendt did not have the luxury of pursuing pure thinking like Heidegger: "Sie hat — auch wenn es ihr möglich gewesen wäre — die Souveränität des reinen Ontologisierens nicht erreichen können."[51] Consequently, Arendt "[ist] negativ gesprochen, statt einer Philosophin nur eine sehr gute Essayistin im angewandten Denken geworden."[52]

Conversely, Austria and Western Europe's sanitized cultures appear less altruistic when meeting the demands of disinherited peoples and nations. Europe's fear of losing social and consumer comfort, however, as Jelinek attempts to show, is in reality unfounded: such comfort proves to be an illusion, demanding a grave human toll to keep pace with the social coercion of consumerism's self-perpetuating system and the illusions it promotes. Consumerism, in this sense, constitutes the imagined norm by which an entire culture measures and deludes itself. This illusion of consumerism is aggravated in its indebtedness to fascist ideology that reverberates persistently in the marketing of *Zugehörigkeit*, *Heimat*, *Gesundheit* and *Unversehrtheit*. Jelinek remains ultimately pessimistic about whether a reversal of cultural self-perception is possible in the presently over-coded consumer society of Austria.

## Jelinek's Early Work and Its Evolving Cultural Critique

In comparison to her earlier works, Jelinek's later writings have increasingly attempted to size up the complex phenomenon of cultural resentment. In *Die Liebhaberinnen* (1975; *The Lovers*), *Die Ausgesperrten* (1980; *Wonderful, Wonderful Times*) and *Die Klavierspielerin* (1983; *The Piano Player*), Jelinek mostly focuses on the self-destructive internalization of projected social norms and less on their general cultural import. By the time of *Oh Wildnis, oh Schutz vor ihr* (1985), *Lust* (1989) and, finally, *Wolken, Heim* (1990), Jelinek manages to project this self-inculcated cultural self-hatred aggressively back onto the entire cultural landscape, revealing its pornographic addiction and self-debasement in consumerism and nationalism. Her recent *Totenauberg* (1991) comes to terms with cultural self-hatred more directly by pointing more explicitly to its latent inscriptions of ethnic and national identity.

Elisabeth Spanlang's observation that "Die Beschäftigung mit der Problematik des Faschismus, bzw. seiner extremsten Ausformung, dem Nationalsozialismus, zieht sich wie ein roter Faden durch das gesamte Werk Elfriede Jelineks"[53] is essential in understanding Jelinek's acute critique of culture. However, Spanlang misses the point of Jelinek's cultural critique when she attacks her portrayal of fascists as strongly stereotyped. As Spanlang claims:

> Elfriede Jelineks idealtypischer Faschist, setzt sich aus den Versatzstücken verschiedener Faschismustheorien zusammen. Daraus resultiert nicht zuletzt die beklemmende Statik und die ärgerliche Eindimensionalität der Figuren.[54]

Jelinek's accomplices of fascism are indeed ready-mades in the manner of consumer products and merely mimic their mechanical reproducibility. This treatment makes the fascist a more threatening phenomenon of consumer society, a reified embodiment of the dehumanizing forces that permeate all of society and not merely an identifiable core of reactionaries.

In her attempt to expose fascism in the past, Jelinek has resorted to diverse strategies to unmask its deceptive rhetoric. Two early plays, *Was geschah nachdem Nora ihren Mann verlassen hatte* (1979) and *Clara S. Musikalische Tragödie* (1981), set in the 1920s, evoke a militant male chauvinist discourse that anticipates the discourse of the coming era of fascism. In *Die Ausgesperrten* (1980), Jelinek confronts us with a stereotypical pathological form of fascism in the sexual and sadistic perversion of the character Witkowski, a former SS officer and war criminal pathetically reduced to impotence and pornographic voyeurism in his now colorless life as a war invalid. The novel's outcome, the murder of the Witkowski family by their own son, reflects the new generation's inability to come to terms with its historical heritage. The immediate postwar generation of *Ausgesperrte* (excluded generation), as Jelinek demonstrates, has internalized the violence of the older generation and, in its self-hatred, brings about its own destruction.

This phenomenon of an unsuccessful mimetic struggle for identity has always played a central role in Jelinek's work. This struggle not only is shown to be the foundation of fascism but also of the self-hatred of minorities such as women or socially discriminated classes. Her early work *Die Liebhaberinnen* (1976) gives us an ironic reflection on the possibilities of social rise or descent through marriage. Reminiscent of Handke's *Publikumsbeschimpfung*, the language of this work is highly formulaic and predictable, mapping out in advance, and with little surprise, the twice-cursed fate that awaits women from economically disadvantaged classes. The women's only commodity in patriarchal society depicted by Jelinek is their sexual body that they must wisely invest and not expose foolishly to the hazards of romantic love, an empty illusion for the economically disadvantaged. In her enslavement to love and its concomitant fantasy of social rise, Paula ironically ends up as secret and occasional prostitute and is upon her discovery spurned by family and community. Unlike the more practical-minded Brigitte who understood the commodity value of her body and manages to secure financial success, Paula is forced to return to her old job in the sewing factory, acquiescing in exhaustion and self-oblivion.

Jelinek's early work shows a keen sensitivity for groups excluded from official discourse and their incomplete attempts at self-definition due to the lack of a legitimate language. Her understanding of linguistic deprivation and minority status resembles Handke's to some extent, although Jelinek grants this condition first to groups rather than individuals. This remaining trait of a collective ideology, however, eventually vanishes in her work, as Jelinek pays more attention to the social and cultural tensions that occur from within and between various discourses. Her work thus becomes post-ideological in that she begins to view the language of minority cultures as the internal and repressed reflection of the entire dominant discourse.

## Minority and Majority Language in *Die Klavierspielerin* and *Lust*

### A. *Die Klavierspielerin*

Jelinek's *Die Liebhaberinnen* is still rudimentary in its depiction of the struggle for social identity, focusing mostly on the discrepancy between social ambition and social reality. In *Die Klavierspielerin* (1983), the author eventually delves deeper into the social formation of identity by analyzing at length its complex dynamics of internalization and externalization. The novel can be described as a parody of the *Bildungsroman* (developmental novel) portraying the sadistic and masochistic socialization of Erika Kohut, an aspiring concert pianist and teacher at Vienna's Conservatory of Music. Jelinek makes the phenomenon of self-hatred on the part of women as a cultural minority explicit in the detached and farcical depiction of the pathological identity formation of Erika Kohut. This phenomenon is also revealed in the novel's reference to the over-coded dominant social and cultural discourse that restricts the articulation of any minority experience. In countering ideological and feminist idealizations in *Frauenliteratur* and its formulation of a gender-specific aesthetics, Jelinek depicts women more skeptically as helpless agents of patriarchal values that they promote as part of their internalized and displaced self-hatred.

Under the strict and tyrannic guidance of her mother, as the novel shows, Erika, the heroine, is forced early in her life into complete self-denial for the sake of her career as a classical concert pianist, a trademark of Austria's social and cultural elite. Erika's identity is one that is from its very inception forcefully designed and managed by her mother:

> Für Erika wählt die Mutter früh einen in irgendeiner Form künstlerischen Beruf, damit sich aus der mühevoll errungenen Feinheit Geld herauspressen läßt, während die Durchschnittsmenschen bewundernd um die Künstlerin herumstehen, applaudieren.[55]

Economic motives rather than genuine appreciation betray the mother's petit-bourgeois interest in the arts as a claim to social status. These motives are concealed from Erika, however, and adumbrated with rhetoric of cultural elitism that promises her a place above the *Durchschnittsmensch* (average person). The Kohuts, a family in which the mentally ill father no longer plays a decisive role, continue to repeat the patriarchal myths of cultural elitism and social status rather than breaking with their imposed identity. The tragicomic plot of the novel consists in Erika's failure to liberate herself from the bonds of her mother's tyrannical "fatherhood" that she had equally internalized.

The sacrifices demanded by an elite career in music are enforced not only by the mother, who tolerates no deviation from her goal of creating a profitable prodigy, but also by a society narcissistically entranced by the sublimity of its cultural canon. Erika's sacrifices are made to appear banal in the light of what is perceived as a tradition of art in which pain has been heroically suffered to a much greater extent. "Beethovens Schmerz, Mozarts Schmerz, Schumanns Schmerz, Bruckners Schmerz, Wagners Schmerz" (K 21), as one concert-goer savors the rhythm of this profound heritage of pain and sublimity. Moreover, this tradition of pain, asceticism and self-sacrifice represents the exclusionist and elitist value system of Erika's world of music, and it is ultimately said to elude anybody who is less than a genius:

> Eine Frau Doktor steht mit dem Schmerz schon lang auf du und du. Sie ergründet jetzt seit zehn Jahren das letzte Geheimnis von Mozarts Requiem. Bis jetzt ist sie noch keinen Schritt weitergekommen, weil dieses Werk unergründlich ist. (K 21)

Erika's attempts to comprehend the pain and self-denial that result from her ambitious artistic career are equally unsuccessful, yet they bear no mark of Mozart's elusive genius. Instead, Erika is reduced to acting out this pain physically rather than in a sublimated manner.

The novel leads us through a series of escalating self-degradations in which Erika increasingly transfers the severe and ascetic discipline of her musical training onto her body. Her female body becomes in consequence the transferred site of social contradictions surrounding high culture and its presumed purity. Erika's permanent exclusion from regular social life, due to her mother's anxiety over the contamination of her sensitive artistic nature, brings out in Erika a perverse pathological voyeurism through which she seeks to reconnect with the "base" world banished from her refined sphere of culture. On the sly, she visits peep shows in "infamous" Turkish districts and searches with her binoculars for lovemaking couples in the vicinity of Vienna's red light district of the Prater. Erika's visit to the Turkish district displays an additional facet of a self-hatred transferred onto other cultural minorities. The Turks, whom Erika fetishizes as the transgressive limit in her secret forays into degradation, must nevertheless keep their distance: "Sie verwest innerlich, doch die Türken weist sie mit Blicken zurück" (K 53). The obscene patriarchal gaze that dominates the perception of women is internalized and projected back onto one's own sex (nude models) and onto another cultural minority (Turks).[56]

The enforced postponement of sexual experience further triggers in Erika a perverse desire for a sexual conquest violently brought upon her. During her adolescence she performs a self-mutilating cutting routine — "Ihr Hobby ist das Schneiden am eigenen Körper" (K 88) — involving at one point her genitals as well. As a teacher, she later welcomes and tolerates, though not without some self-disgust, the aggressive sexual advances of her student Walter Klemmer. Her eventual relationship with Klemmer, which unfolds into a masochist scenario, reflects Erika's confused identity, which is torn between a desire for love and one for total subjugation and bondage.

Erika's deviations, however, must not be exclusively understood in their literal sense. They also point metonymically to a need for something deeper than mere sexual gratification. The cutting, the bleeding and the letter that she sends to Klemmer can be seen as a metonymic evocation of writing (knife=stylo, blood=ink) and as an attempt at an articulation of identity. Her letter describing her erotic fantasies, for example, proceeds endlessly and takes delight in the writing process rather than the acting out of her fantasies. It is this claim to language that also spoils the literal advances of Walter Klemmer who does not want to surrender his dominant male gaze, surprised "daß sie IHM Anweisungen erteilen möchte" (K 218). In the end, however, it is Erika's restricted language and her masochistic image of the female that brings upon herself physical abuse and rape by her student.[57]

Erika's identity is ultimately one that expresses itself only negatively through its total absence. Unlike Handke, who partially restores his mother's obscured identity in *Wunschloses Unglück*, Jelinek considers this entire restorative effort as premature in the current restricted cultural climate of Austria. As Ria Endres captures the ironic ending of the novel: "Ihr Körper schmerzt nicht. Auf Erika wartet nicht einmal ein tragisches Ende."[58] The banal story of Erika's unsuccessful emancipation unmasks farcically not only all social pretensions attached to art and high culture but also the bond presumed to exist among an oppressed minority. Instead, Jelinek's novel reveals the identity of women to be informed by a deep self-hatred that makes them perfect accomplices in the preservation of the patriarchal status quo, bringing about their own self-enslavement.

The experience of being a minority, lacking its own language of self-expression, perversely leads to a deeper sedimentation of reactionary consciousness and the repetition of the dominant discourse. It is this dominant discourse that Jelinek strives to undermine strategically in her novel. Like Kafka who saw merit in Karl Kraus' *mauscheln* or cultural double-talk and deployed its heteroglossic style in subverting the dominant officialese of the Habsburg Empire, Jelinek undertakes a similar subversion of Austria's rhetoric of high culture. Examples of linguistic contamination bring to the fore and mock implicit assumptions of cultural superiority. As Erika espies, for instance, the protruding genitals beneath her cousin's slim bathing suit, the high language of Goethe's Faust is invoked to commemorate this moment of proud male self-display: "Dieser Augenblick soll bitte verweilen, er ist so schön" (K 44). The music of Anton Bruckner is similarly ridiculed in its primitive phallocentric gestures described as "Elefantentrompeten" (K 71).

Jelinek here is indebted to Bernhard's irreverence that in *Holzfällen* spoke of the "fette, stinkende Bach" and parodied Beethoven's primitive martial rhythms. In Bernhard these parodies leave the aspiration towards an elite culture partially intact; in Jelinek, this critique becomes irreversible. Jelinek's consciously polluted discourse obliterates the artificial distinction between high and low cultural discourse. Polite Viennese is placed deliberately next to expressions of violence. "Er soll ihr seine Knie dabei in den Leib bohren, bitte sei so gut," (K 217) reads at one point Erika's masochistic fantasy of bondage.

In their study on *Kafka: Toward a Minor Literature* (1975), Deleuze and Guattari provide an exemplary analysis of how cultural and linguistic minorities find themselves without a proper discourse when it comes to defining their own identity. Instead, their language, as in the case of Kafka, already belongs to the dominant culture and provides only limited possibilities of self-articulation. What is required, therefore, is an entirely different approach to language. "In order to liberate a living and expressive material that speaks for itself," Kafka, as Deleuze and Guattari point out, created a "language torn from sense," one that resisted the territorial claims of the dominant culture.[59] The language of the minor writer, as Deleuze and Guattari suggest, can only come into its own if it first incorporates the discontinuities and ruptures of his or her cultural sense of homelessness. Coming home, for the minor writer, paradoxically lies in uprooting the hegemonically constructed institutions of the dominant culture along with their homogeneous discourse. Kafka does so through a metamorphic language that subverts the complacent humanism of Habsburg Austria and subjects it to the dehumanizing force of its bureaucratic master language, one re-assembled by Kafka into an intensified maze of contingencies.

Jelinek similarly takes delight in her subversion of what is commonly perceived as the dominant culture. In Kafka's work, the discourse of institutional authority still retains some positive identification, in spite of its demonstrated non-existence, as, for example, in the father, the law or the state. Jelinek's works offer no such positive identifications but only simulations. All the delusions of her characters are demonstratively announced in advance of their actions. Unlike Kafka's characters who are stuck in their search for a language or a plot, Jelinek's language scenarios do not wish to possess their characters. Each character in Jelinek is only the empty shell or *Schablone,* a mask that suggests his or her identity. Jelinek projects an even stronger sense of linguistic homelessness, one that cannot even begin to point to the roots of its absent home. This rootlessness also accounts for the voracious sense of pleasure (*Lust*) with which Jelinek's plots devour themselves and in which language becomes a site for an extreme heteroglossic tension that cuts through characters and identities.

If Jelinek's characters do not speak themselves, who ultimately does the speaking? As Jelinek has answered with regard to Heidegger or Arendt, her characters are mere *Sprachschablonen*, linguistic clichés dominating us everywhere but with no identifiable core or center. This sense of linguistic expropriation is typical of a minority. However, as Jelinek seems to imply, it is also typical of the majority. For instance, the apparent sense of freedom and mastery flaunted in popular leisure culture is shown to be entirely illusory:

> Sie können nicht umhin, solche Menschen als Abhängige zu bezeichnen, wenn sie sich auf die Berghänge begeben, wo sie abgleiten und sich auch noch wohl fühlen dabei. Doch abhängig wovon? Ja von ihren eigenen, nie genesenden Bildern, die ihnen, als wären sie nichts als Gehilfen der Wirklichkeit, jeden Tag aufs neue gezeigt werden, nur größer, schöner und schneller. So fallen sie von der Wasserscheide des Fernsehens gestoßen, auf die andere Seite hinunter, zu den Kleinen auf dem Idiotenhügel.[60]

Jelinek describes the gratification pursued in sports as a pathological dependence on a narcissistic image of oneself as a physically fit and self-determining agent. The origin of this image remains ultimately obscure since it is reinforced as much by the media as by our own desire to fashion the projected media world in our own image. The regressive image of the beginner's slopes (*Idiotenhügel*) where we join again the children (*den Kleinen*) suggests our inability to escape the infantile narcissism of our self-projections. Jelinek's extreme decontextualization of culture exposes its pathological thirst for identification through words and images, as parodied, for instance, in the obsessive circular language reminiscent of Heidegger in her *Wolken, Heim*: "Wir bezeugen uns: wir sind hier. Uns gehören wir."[61] It is from this perspective of excessive cultural self-definition, as our remaining analysis of *Lust* will show, that Jelinek imagines the comically forestalled homecoming of a culture as a potential cure to its obsessive desire to belong to itself.

### B. *Lust*

In opposition to her earlier *Die Klavierspielerin* where Jelinek demystified with a cold analytic eye any positive identification with women typical of *Frauenliteratur*, *Lust* proves more sympathetic to women as a socially disadvantaged group without a discourse of their own. In her caricature of the erotic commodification of women in Western society, Jelinek projects in this novel her boldest and most outspoken image of a pornographic society which has internalized the sexually fetishized and debased image of women as the general reference for any social exchange or interaction. The novel is as much a reflection of society's imprisonment in its own myths of power as it is a reflection on the oppression of women. As Jelinek explains the double bind of a dominant male culture: "Die Männer herrschen als Gefangene über die Frauen, die diesen Genuß kaum jemals haben."[62] Jelinek's violent amplification of male sexual discourse evokes the pathological image of a culture constructed around the myth of the male and his narcissistic delusion of agency. This fantasy of power enables the male, in spite of his own enslavement to the commodified and fetishized image of women, to possess at the expense of women a language and a discourse: "Der Mann. Er ist ein ganz großer Raum, in dem Sprechen noch möglich ist" (L 8).

It is by means of this deeply engrained grammar of sexual difference, as Jelinek suggests, that society construes all its other mirror images that subsequently make both man and nature readily available for instrumentalization and consumption. Her intent in *Lust* is to break this linguistic monopoly of male pornographic discourse and to separate the language of discourse from its meaning:

> die kommerzielle Pornographie . . . soll durch aesthetische Vermittlung sozusagen dem Leser ins Gesicht zurückschlagen . . . Das ist genau der Zweck, daß man sich darin nicht wälzen kann wie das Schwein in der Kuhle, sondern daß man blaß wird beim Lesen.[63]

Jelinek's strategy of writing is foremost one of subversion wherein the confidence of the dominant discourse is led to its own destruction by turning its underlying hatred of minorities into a critical form of self-hatred and self-disgust.

The epitome of the inflated male myth of agency in Jelinek's novel is the character of "Herr Direktor," the center of action towards which the entire village world depicted by Jelinek gravitates. The farcical plot of this mock-*Heimatroman* evokes a homecoming in which the Direktor is forced by the AIDS epidemic to abandon his sexual pursuits outside his marital confines and return to his original "Heimat nach seiner Heirat" where he can use "sein vertrautes Werkzeug. . . . wo noch kein anderer war" (L 129). Whatever excitement his previous sexual adventures may have afforded him, the Direktor is now ferociously demanding the same from his wife, gratifying himself at will in all of her available orifices. The omnipresent Direktor is also in charge of his son's violin training and cultural upbringing, the wily fate of employment at his paper factory, and the "Werkschor," which he commands to give beneficial concerts. He is the magical signifier that centers the community, the most advanced embodiment of man as the dominating and consuming animal.

The novel's comical subversion lies in the destruction of this magical signifier and its blend of unquestioned sexual, social and ontological self-legitimization, exploited to the fullest by the Direktor and poorly mimicked by his inferiors. The Direktor's perverse ontology of power meets its eventual challenge when his "Heimat" chooses "fremd zu gehen," when his wife betrays him with a young law student. The husband's worry, as Jelinek's pornographic-ontological language makes clear, lies deeper than with the mere infidelity at hand: "Es ist als könnte kein Schwanz mehr Ruhe finden, da vielleicht ein anderer in ihrer Fotze sich eingegraben hat und ihren Boden mit seinem Trumm Wurst verunreinigt hat" (L 139). It appears as if the entire grammar of sexual difference and its implied foundation originating in male superiority comes undone, thereby undermining the ground (*Boden*) of the Direktor's existence.

The latter part of the novel initially depicts the partial restitution of the Direktor's waning power and loss of control. Michael, the young lover, not only sexually humiliates the Direktor's wife in front of his skiing companions, thereby destroying any amorous illusions on her part, but, upon meeting with the original owner of Gerti, willingly cedes his claim. In a final grotesque culmination of the novel's building sexual violence, the Direktor forces his wife to perform sexual acts in front of Michael who, watching from his apartment window, is aroused by this obscene display of male dominance. The novel's compulsive repetition and intensification of sexual violence is reminiscent of de Sade and his evocation of a bizarre self-perpetuating institutional terror, or Nagisa Oshima's film *In the Realm of the Senses* with its incessant escalation of a couple's sexual acts leading to the male's eventual castration. Jelinek's *Lust* likewise ends with a necessary death, the murder of the Direktor's offspring by his wife Gerti, to break the spell of this otherwise unending cycle of violence.

*Lust's* excessive evocation of an overstimulated consumer society has brought Jelinek to the limits of her own writing. It is hardly possible, as she admits, to imagine a novel following further down the path of *Lust.* Jelinek has instead purged herself largely of the self-hatred that weighs on a minority discourse and soundly incorporated its destabilizing rhetoric into the discourse of the dominant culture. In doing so, as her recent works show, she has advanced to a much deeper cultural critique combining consumerism, ethnicity and nationhood. Unfortunately, the ethnic and national critique of Jelinek's work and its grounding in the Jewish tradition of critical *mauscheln* has so far received little attention from critics. As Jelinek explains: "Weil die jüdische Kultur vernichtet ist, . . . hat auch diese Form der Sprachkritik in der Sprache selbst keine Rezeption mehr."[64] It is this forgotten Jewish heritage of cultural critique, as I have tried to show here, that aligns itself with the other cultural discourses of gender and consumerism in Jelinek's work and accounts for a multi-layered and irreducible critique of culture beyond ideology. Like Handke's and Bernhard's, Jelinek's work is a critical attempt to forestall a homecoming to a cultural origin too quickly abused in the coercive administration of identity and sameness.

# Notes

[1] Yasmin Hoffmann, "'Hier lacht sich die Sprache selbst aus': Sprachsatire — Sprachspiele bei Elfriede Jelinek," *Elfriede Jelinek*, eds. Kurt Bartsch and Günther Höfler (Vienna: Droschl, 1991) 41.

[2] Kraus, quoted in Hoffmann, 41.

[3] Hoffmann, 43.

[4] Sigrid Berka, "Ein Gespräch mit Elfriede Jelinek," *Modern Austrian Literature* 26.2 (1993) 130.

[5] Such an interpretation of Jelinek as a proto-postmodernist is found, for instance, in Ingeborg Hoesterey's "Postmoderner Blick auf die österreichische Literatur," *Modern Austrian Literature* 23,3/4 (1990), and in John Pizer's "Modern vs. Postmodern Satire: Karl Kraus and Elfriede Jelinek," *Monatshefte* 86.4 (Winter 1994).

[6] Sigrid Berka, 137.

[7] Sander L. Gilman, "Jewish Writers in Contemporary Germany," *Anti-Semitism in Times of Crisis*, eds. Sander L. Gilman and Steven T. Katz (New York: New York UP, 1991) 313.

[8] Franz Kafka, *Briefe, 1902–1924*, ed. Max Brod (New York: Schocken, 1966) 335–38.

[9] Berka, 129.

[10] This observation by Henryk Broder in his essay "Die unheilbare Liebe deutscher Intellektueller zu toten und todkranken Juden" (originally published in *Semit* 3 (1989) 29) is further explored in Gilman's essay on "Jewish Writers in Contemporary Germany" from which I take this reference. In his inquiry into the expropriation of German Jews in present German cultural discourse, Gilman asks the provocative question "Who killed the remaining Jews in contemporary culture and why?" The terminology of liberalism, as Gilman points out, with its universal concerns has not allowed the particularism of an ethnic perspective to come to the fore other than in its typified representations of exemplary Jews of the past (339).

[11] Jean Baudrillard, *Simulations* (New York: Semiotext, 1983).

[12] Baudrillard, 11.

[13] Michael Fischer, *Trivialmythen in Elfriede Jelinek's Romanen* (St. Ingbert: Werner Röhrig Verlag, 1991).

[14] Fischer, 15.

[15] Quoted in Fischer, 15.

[16] Quoted in Fischer, 15.

[17] Quoted in Fischer, 15.

[18] Yasmin Hoffmann echoes here a common post-structuralist notion of the random play of signification entailing the destruction of the subject. Hoffmann refers specifically to Lacan's theory of language. See pages 51–53.

[19] Jean Baudrillard, *The Ecstasy of Communication* (New York: Semiotext, 1988) 22. With regard to Baudrillard there is no documented influence on Jelinek as given with Roland Barthes. Indeed, Jelinek's work parallels Baudrillard's as that of a contemporaneous and simultaneous discovery. Baudrillard's extended conception of pornography was developed in *The Ecstasy of Communication* and originally published as *L'Autre par lui-même* in 1987 (Éditions Galileé, Paris). It is preceded by *Jelinek's Die Klavierspielerin* which was published in 1983 and points already, although not as explicitly as the later *Lust* (1989), to a pervasive pornographic sense of reality.

[20] Luc Rosenzweig and Bernhard Cohen, *Waldheim*, trans. Josephine Bacon (New York: Adams Books, 1987) 177.

[21] Maxim Biller, "Sind Sie lesbisch, Frau Jelinek?" *Tempojahre* (Munich: dtv, 1991) 183.

[22] *Elfriede Jelinek*, eds. Kurt Bartsch and Günther Höfler, 13.

[23] *Elfriede Jelinek*, 18.

[24] Heidegger uses the term *zugehörig* in its double sense of reflective listening (*zuhören*) and belonging (*gehören*). Both of these notions are grounded in *Mitsein*, a collective "we" that through its disposition of listening to itself — "Das Aufeinanderhören indem sich das Mitsein ausbildet" — recovers itself: "Das Dasein ist in dieser Hörigkeit zugehörig" (*Sein und Zeit* (Tübingen: Max Niemeyer, 1986) 163). This circular structure, in which collective *Aufeinanderhören* apparently seamlessly grounds the *Zugehörigkeit* of a culture, identifies the hermeneutics of Heidegger as a fundamental one. Paul Ricoeur rightly points to the "question that remains unresolved in Heidegger's work": "How can a question of critique in general be accounted for within the framework of a fundamental hermeneutics?" (*Hermeneutics and the Human Sciences* (Cambridge: Cambridge UP, 1988) 59). In more explicitly political terms, Ricoeur's question could be rephrased as follows: Can one really argue that there is cultural authenticity in a culture that narcissistically succumbs to its self-identity in a collective *Mitsein*?

[25] Arendt sees the rootlessness and the vulnerability of European Jewish culture predominantly in its unsuccessful integration into the developing structures of the European nation-states, which never granted Jews full and equal membership, while relying heavily on their cosmopolitan and transnational resources. "Because of their close relationship to state sources of power," writes Arendt, "the Jews were invariably identified with power, and because of their aloofness from society and concentration upon the closed circle of the family, they were invariably suspected of working for the destruction of all social structures" (*The Origins of Totalitarianism* (New York: HBJ, 1968) 28).

[26] Sander L. Gilman, *Jewish Self-Hatred: Anti-Semitism and the Hidden Language of the Jews* (Baltimore: The Johns Hopkins UP, 1986) 3.

[27] *Jewish Self-Hatred*, 3.

[28] Elfriede Jelinek, *Totenauberg* (Hamburg: Rowohlt Verlag, 1991) 5. Hereafter quoted in text as T.

[29] Riki Winter, "Gespräch mit Elfriede Jelinek," *Elfriede Jelinek*, eds. Kurt Bartsch and Günther A. Höfler (Vienna: Literaturverlag Droschl, 1991) 13.

[30] Elfriede Jelinek, "Wir leben auf einem Berg von Leichen und Schmerz," interview in *Theater Heute* (September, 1992) 8. Jelinek's immediate family was spared persecution. Her father, a chemist, as Jelinek recounts, "hat als Jude überlebt, weil er als Fachmann für organische Chemie wichtig war für die Kriegsrüstung"(6). After the war, Jelinek's father developed a mental disease from which he eventually died. While it is difficult to speculate whether such a disease resulted from a traumatic experience of guilt and self-hatred, its potential origin is preserved in the writings of Jelinek which display strong masochistic and self-destructive tendencies, what Jelinek herself describes as a "wahnsinnigen Destruktionstrieb" that characterizes her work (6).

[31] Thomas Bernhard, *Alte Meister* (Frankfurt: Suhrkamp, 1985) 91.

[32] *Alte Meister*, 92.

[33] Martin Heidegger, "The Question Concerning Technology," *The Question Concerning Technology and Other Essays*, trans. William Lovitt (New York: Harper & Row, 1977) 19.

[34] Hannah Arendt, "For Martin Heidegger's Eightieth Birthday," *Martin Heidegger and National Socialism*, eds. Günther Neske and Emil Kettering (New York: Paragon, 1990) 209.

[35] *Heidegger and National Socialism*, xiv.

[36] *Theater Heute*, 8.

[37] *Theater Heute*, 2.

[38] *Austria: Facts and Figures* (Vienna: The Federal Press Service, 1993) 69; the service industry is here identified as the tertiary sector next to industry (39.4%) and agriculture and forestry (3%).

[39] *Austria: Facts and Figures*, 10.

[40] *Theater Heute*, 8.

[41] Theodor Adorno, "Culture Industry Reconsidered," *The Culture Industry: Selected Essays on Mass Culture*, ed. J.M. Bernstein (London: Routledge, 1991) 86.

[42] In *The Origins of Totaliarianism* (New York: Harcourt, Brace, Jovanovich, 1968), Arendt refers to the disintegration of Austria's Dual Monarchy after World War I. Its ensuing denationalization of ethnic minorities "became a powerful weapon in totalitarian politics" (Vol II, 149), leaving their identities both nationally and economically exposed and vulnerable. Having lost their

Habsburg protection, Jews were considered economically superfluous and portrayed in fascist propaganda as "unidentifiable beggars, without nationality, without money, and without passports [crossing the] frontiers" (from the *Schwarze Korps*, the official SS newspaper, quoted by Arendt in Vol II, 149). Likewise, Arendt points to economic discrimination among Jewish functionaries who collaborated with Eichmann on decisions concerning deportation. (Cf. *A Report on the Banality of Evil* (Harmondsworth: Penguin, 1963) 44–48).

[43] Jacques Derrida, *Of Spirit: Heidegger and the Question*, trans. Geoffrey Bennington and Rachel Bowlby (Chicago: U of Chicago P, 1989).

[44] Elfried Jelinek, *Ein Sportstück* (Hamburg: Rowohlt, 1998).

[45] See John M. Hoberman, *Sport and Political Ideology* (Austin: U of Texas P, 1984) 162–169. Hoberman offers an in-depth study of both Marxist and fascist ideologies of sport with a concentration on body, gender, ethnic and national exploitation of physical exercise. His study, however, does not discuss at length the cultic side of sport lending itself to spectacle and distraction.

[46] See Richard D. Mandell, *Sport: A Cultural History* (New York: Columbia UP, 1984)237–245. Mandell foregrounds the spectacle and aesthetic nature of the fascist appropriation of sports. Leni Riefensthal's six hour movie *Olympia* (1938) can be seen not only as an aesthetic accomplishment of visual documentation, as Mandell suggests, but more importantly as an implicit aesthetization of politics in the form of an iconic public spectacle. Hitler's decision to keep Theodor Lewald, of Jewish descent, on the Olympic Organization Committee and the half-Jewish Helene Mayer on the women's fencing team, indicates, as Mandell correctly points out, Germany's deceptive use of a public event to demonstrate to the whole world "that the new Germans were administratively capable, generous, respectable, and peace loving" (244).

[47] Sigmund Freud, "Mourning and Melancholia," *General Psychological Theory*, ed. Philip Rieff (New York: Collier Books, 1963) 164–179.

[48] Jelinek claims in her interview with Riki Winter that *Totenauberg* is "mein resignativster Text" (17) [my most resigned text].

[49] See, for instance, Arendt's essay "On Violence," where she attempts to guide the reaction through violence on the part of oppressed minorities towards the more constructive praxis of political action (*Crisis of the Republic* (New York: HBJ, 1972) 105–198). Also, Arendt's exemplary study of Eichmann's inability to communicate other than in the form of clichés points to the dangerous hollowing-out of a communicative competence dominated by administered standards.

[50] Peter Handke, "Das Öl des Weltmeisters," *Das Ende des Flanierens* (Frankfurt: Suhrkamp, 1980) 74–75. This essay explores Austria's fascination with its Formula 1 world champion race car driver Niki Lauda in connection with the jargon of technology.

[51] *Elfriede Jelinek*, 17.

[52] *Theater Heute*, 7.

[53] Elisabeth Spanlang, *Elfriede Jelinek: Studien zum Frühwerk* (Vienna: VWGÖ, 1992) 93.

[54] Spanlang, 101.

[55] Elfriede Jelinek, *Die Klavierspielerin* (Hamburg: Rowohlt, 1983) 25; hereafter quoted in text as K.

[56] For a more comprehensive analysis of the function of the gaze in the novel, turn to Sabine Wilke's "'Ich bin eine Frau mit einer männlichen Anmaßung' Eine Analyse des "bösen Blicks" in Elfriede Jelinek's *Die Klavierspielerin*," *Modern Austrian Literature* Vol. 26.1 (1993) 115–145. Wilke uses the concept of gaze as developed in film studies and its analysis of spectatorship. This analysis allows for pertinent insights into Jelinek's work, at the expense, however, of elucidating further Jelinek's double minority status as a Jewish female writer. By neglecting Jelinek's peculiar ethnic position within Austrian discourse, her project of writing is reduced to a feminist and ideological perspective alone. It is precisely the overlapping of a variety of discourses in Jelinek's work that makes her writing foremost post-ideological and irreducibly complex in its mode of cultural analysis.

[57] See Barbara Kosta, "Muttertrauma: Anerzogener Masochismus," *Mütter — Töchter — Frauen: Weiblichkeitsbilder in der Literatur*, eds. Helga Kraft and Ellen Liebs (Stuttgart: Metzler, 1993) 243–265. Kosta analyses in depth the masochistic identity formation in Jelinek's novel. Like Wilke, however, she ignores the overall context of Jelinek's writings and reduces it to a form of autobiographical *Frauenliteratur*. This analysis fits *Die Züchtigung* as discussed by Mitgutsch but not Jelinek's more culturally polyvalent novel.

[58] Ria Endres, "Ein musikalisches Opfer," *Elfriede Jelinek*, 207.

[59] Gilles Deleuze and Félix Guattari, *Kafka: Toward a Minor Literature*, trans. Dana Polan (Minneapolis: U of Minnesota P, 1986) 21.

[60] Elfriede Jelinek, *Lust* (Hamburg: Rowohlt, 1989) 62–63; hereafter quoted in text as L.

[61] Elfriede Jelinek, *Wolken, Heim* (Göttingen: Steidl, 1990) 12.

[62] Elfriede Jelinek, *Der Standard* (Vienna: 12/17/1988); quoted in Margarete Lamb-Faffelberger, *Valie Export und Elfriede Jelinek im Spiegel der Presse: Zur Rezeption der feministischen Avantgarde Österreichs* (New York: Peter Lang, 1992) 105.

[63] Elfriede Jelinek, *Stern* 37 (Hamburg, 1988); quoted in *Valie Export und Elfriede Jelinek im Spiegel der Presse*, 105.

[64] Berka, 130.

# *Closing Remarks: The Emergence of Recent Austrian Jewish Writing*

## Introduction

CHALLENGING ENTRENCHED cultural ideologies of national affiliation, political consensus, and social elitism, Bernhard, Handke and Jelinek have questioned through their strategic literary interventions Austria's complacent self-understanding. On the various levels of cultural self-representation (Bernhard), socialization and participation in social discourse (Handke), and minority experience and commodity discourses (Jelinek), they alert us to the imaginary construction of what is all too readily accepted as a self-evident national culture. In their dystopian and utopian vision, they push Austria towards a post-national era in which its cultural self-definition looses its traditional boundaries that are said to lie with a particular people, its occupied territory, its institutional powers, and its inherited history. These stable variants of cultural self-definition are subjected to a radical decontextualization in order to revive what is commonly felt to be a culture in its death-throes and reflected in symptomatic expressions of pervasive political apathy or right-wing extremism. Bernhard, Handke and Jelinek explode the traditional consensus that has guided Austria's postwar reconstruction, one that has imposed a radical harmonization of culture at the expense of the freedom of individuals and underrepresented collectives. More constructively, however, their literary visions have also facilitated an intellectual climate in which other, and heretofore neglected cultural voices can come to the fore. As an example of more recent modifications of the literary revolution set in motion by our three writers, I would like to discuss briefly two younger writers, Robert Schindel and Doron Rabinovici, and highlight aspects of their works that stress a continuity with the concerns of Bernhard, Handke and Jelinek.

## Postnationalism and the Revival of Ethnic Literature

In their introduction to an anthology of essays on the recent revival of Jewish culture in Germany, editors Sander L. Gilman and Karen Remmler speak of the "demand by many Jews that they be heard on their own terms" and the present "possibility of a vital Jewish culture in Germany."[1] While admitting that no consensus can be reached on the nature, course and success of this recent cultural development, Gilman and Remmler's anthology marks a major advance in German literary and cultural studies by placing "the reciprocal instability of Jewish and German identity" in the foreground.[2] Tireless self-analysis of German guilt by German authors has been refracted through and replaced by another unacknowledged Germany, asserting its distinct German-Jewish perspective concerning the interpretation of German history. Excessive focus on a vanished Jewish culture, as Jack Zipes correctly remarks, allowed Germans to install themselves as experts on Jewish culture: "It seemed that the deader the Jews, the more Germans could exhibit their interest in Jewish culture."[3] The recent emergence of a distinct Jewish discourse, it appears, paves the way for a corrective of this self-revolving national discourse in German culture. A monolithic aspect of Germany's postwar culture is finally more openly challenged and negated as a myth.

Gilman and Remmler show, however, that this act of Jewish self-inauguration is still marked by a problematic internalization of difference experienced from within German culture. It labors under the burden of having to negate and transform an ascribed or imagined difference (physical and cultural pathology, memorialization of Jews as dead and invisible) into a positive identity resisting reification. For example, Gilman's analysis of Jewish male discourse focuses on the construction and questioning of identity markers such as circumcision visibly inscribed onto the body. Remmler's analysis, conversely, focuses on the metaphorical transformation of the female Jewish body into a symbolic site of traumatic memory and mourning. Present Jewish literary discourse, Gilman and Remmler similarly conclude, is marked by a negative symbiosis that paradoxically achieves its desired recognition only by recourse to those cultural forces that negate its existence(stereotypes of race and gender, monolithic images of German culture). Seen critically, its discourse remains caught up in the struggle between national or official and ethnic or unofficial representations of German and German Jewish identity.

Focusing on the limited example of Austrian Jewish literature, I would like to explore other possibilities of recognition beyond those of positively or negatively asserted identities and beyond the polarity of national or ethnic contention. To be sure, I am not proposing Austrian Jewish literature as an alternative to its German counterpart. Nor do I wish to invalidate the importance of Gilman and Remmler's sobered understanding of identity claims and their inevitably ensuing cultural stereotypes. Instead, I am concerned with a complementary interpretive model that remains faithful to the immediate geographic and cultural topography of the writer which situates her or his body in the surrounding field of socialization (cultural heritage, discursive traditions, political and cultural public spheres, concrete social interactions).[4] By way of an analysis of the contemporary Jewish writers Robert Schindel and Doron Rabinovici, I wish to show how these writers are ill at ease with national or ethnic categorizations. Instead, they attempt to enlarge these definitions toward a metropolitan, transnational and transcultural identity as the result of their specific acculturation in the city of Vienna. With its unique urban culture, Vienna, much like New York, Paris or Berlin, has in many ways defied the national boundaries that are said to contain its identity. My argument here is that Schindel and Rabinovici reflect this cosmopolitan heritage in their writing and critically recover cultural positions prevalent in turn-of-the-century Vienna.

In this respect, Schindel and Rabinovici resemble other contemporary Austrian writers, such as Bernhard and Handke, who have little use for a national definition of their artistic endeavors. Handke, for instance, has produced a remarkable diasporic literature built on a self-chosen imaginative and, more recently, geographic exile from Austria. Bernhard, although he never left Austria for any length of time, strongly ridiculed Austria's so-called indigenous culture. The persona of the critical *Nestbeschmutzer*, the writer exposing the narrow provincial and nationalistic profile of his own country in the manner of Heinrich Heine or Karl Kraus, became Bernhard's lifelong vocation. Other writers like Peter Rosei or Christoph Ransmayr have settled their imaginations in abstract or concrete spaces beyond the Austrian territory such as the peripheral regions of the former Habsburg Empire (Turkey, Romania, Franz-Joseph-Land). Indeed, the uncertainty of national affiliation displayed in all these writers recalls the instability of cultural identity during Austria's imperial decline as reflected in Robert Musil, Joseph Roth and Hugo von Hofmannsthal. These writers, while flirting with an imperial Austrian identity, have ultimately shunned any sharp nationalistic contours and preferred instead to represent its inhabitants as men without qualities, exiles, or evasive eccentrics (*Schwierige*).

Here I will explore transcultural profiles of identity that resurface in Schindel and Rabinovici's examination of Jewish identity in present Austria. In my use of the term identity, I am referring to meaningful affirmations of social and cultural practices that are profoundly influenced by, though not exclusively limited to, affiliations of gender, race, and nationhood with their inevitable genetic and essentialist resonance. A transcultural identity would be characterized by the ability to function and interact in a variety of socio-cultural contexts, and particularly in those that are not immediate to one's background and experiences. This identity encompasses cross-cultural influence yet does not entirely eradicate difference. This transcultural identity is expressed through complex subject positions informed by multiple and overlapping discourses. And, unlike in the case of other contemporary Austrian writers adopting a similar perspective (Handke, Bernhard, Roth), I will stress that Schindel and Rabinovici also share a different legacy (Viennese Jewish culture, the Shoah) that makes an important difference in their negotiation of cultural boundaries. This difference, to be sure, is not merely part of an inherited tradition but grows out of active re-appropriation, interpretation and assertion.

This chapter will explore Jewish identity in present Austrian writing in two parts. First, in a brief review, I would like to point to the cultural instability of Jewish and Austrian identity as defined in various contexts of Austrian history (turn-of-the-century Vienna, inter-war and Nazi era, post-World War II and reconstruction era, Waldheim and present era). Such contexts will help us understand the complex patterns of recuperation that inform Jewish identity in Austria today. Second, an analysis of the three writers focusing on rhetorical and plot strategies will demonstrate both their confrontational and evasive staging of Jewish identity. These strategies allow them to demand recognition from within a disturbingly revisionist and "normalizing" cultural climate, on the one hand, while also stemming against equally dubious manifestations of ethnic fetishization and philo-Semitism on the other. The writers present an intriguing model of cultural diversity, aiming beyond any multiculturalism that does not take overlapping and shared zones of social definition into account.

## Jewish Identities in Austrian Culture

While the emphasis on a transnational tradition in Austrian literature would seem to account for Schindel and Rabinovici's cosmopolitan stance growing out of this tradition, this emphasis at the same time obscures the roots of this transnationalism, suggesting that it is essentially Austrian. The national labeling of a transnational identity conceals its cross- and multi-cultural origin. As Steven Beller has suggested, the origin of Austria's transnational culture must be located in the late Habsburg era. This historical period marks the encounter between indigenous Austrian traditions and a diasporic and cosmopolitan Jewish culture. "While there are other traditions and backgrounds which added to Vienna 1900," claims Beller, "it was the Jewish experience which was the most prevalent among its central figures and its audience, even when that experience is defined in social and not even ethnic terms."[5] Contrary to the myth of an exclusive Jewish assimilation to Austrian culture, Beller makes a compelling case for a similar reverse assimilation of Austrian culture to that of its Jewish residents. Within this multi-contextual space of cultural encounter and hybridity, nationalism did not have a chance to solidify in Vienna as it did in the various and more homogeneously structured territories of the empire.

Historians generally agree that the multinational and dynastic character of the Habsburg Empire did not allow for a strong, or at least clearly defined, sense of national identity as witnessed, for example, in late imperial Germany.[6] This uncertainty about the ultimate identity of Austria's supra-national monarchy also extended to its definition of Jewish ethnicity in a Vienna with its variety of Jewish communities ranging from ultra-orthodox to liberal, from Hungarian, Galician, Czech, Polish to Austro-German Jews. As Marsha L Rozenblit correctly points out, Jewish cultural assimilation in Vienna, unlike in Germany, did not imply the acculturation to a single national identity: "One could easily be an Austrian — an essentially supra-national identity not attached to a particular ethnic group — and also remain a Jew."[7] Ruth Beckermann notes a similar cultural diversity among Jews even in their traditional Viennese district and former ghetto, the Leopoldstadt, where a majority of Viennese Jews resided:

> Die Leopoldtstadt paßt in keine Schablonen. Ihre Bevölkerung läßt sich nicht soziologisch oder ethnisch in ein gemeinsames Korsett zwängen. In der Leopoldstadt war die Vielfalt Prinzip. Man konnte jüdischer Sozialist oder Kommunist sein, Chassid an einem der nach Wien emigrierten "Höfe," Mitglied der kleinen sephardischen Gemeinde oder Zionist. Man konnte auch Zionist und gleichzeitg in der Sozialdemokratie aktiv sein, man konnte sich als assimilierter Jude fühlen und von den Ostjuden distanzieren, man konnte sein Judentum ablegen, oder man wußte gar nicht mehr, daß man Jude war. Die Juden waren in den zwanziger Jahren bereits zu einer vielschichtigen Gemeinde gewachsen. Für manche war die Zugehörigkeit zu einer Klasse, einem Berufstand, einer politischen Gruppierung bereits verbindlicher als ihr Jude-Sein.[8]

Beller's, Rozenblit's and Beckermann's assessments of Viennese culture imply that while it was in many respects synonymous with Jewish culture, it was never reducible to a single definition of Jewish culture or tradition. For a brief period, the notion of a homogeneous national identity, already prevalent in other European countries (Germany, France, Italy, and England) and developing at the various peripheries of the empire (Hungary, Serbia, and Bohemia) was negated in Vienna with its multicultural diversity.

Nevertheless, Austria's post-imperial history produced its own peculiar pan-Germanic nationalism that made it an eventual ally of Germany's militant nationalism and led to the expatriation and extermination of the Jewish community that had helped to build and shape so decisively Austria's cultural heritage. Once faced with economic pressure, the multicultural experiment of Austria quickly came to a halt and gave way to ethnic polarization that had increasingly solidified in the shadow of Vienna's liberal bourgeois culture. In this climate of rising German nationalism, Jewish culture in Vienna was forcefully subjected to a conceptual collectivization that eventually allowed for its systematic extermination.[9] Along with it, the multicultural and cosmopolitan world of fin-de-siècle Vienna indebted to Jewish culture disappeared from the Austria's cultural landscape.

The reconstruction of a separate national identity in Austria's post-World War II society after this interlude of German nationalism appears at first as a contradictory enterprise. With regard to the supra-national heritage of the empire, one could only nostalgically recall a world in which a peaceful coexistence was possible among diverse cultures that were now, however, no longer represented to their former extent. With regard to Austria's post-imperial history, one had to confront both a problematic landscape of intense political polarization that led Austria into civil strife and the subsequent dictatorship of its corporate state. The attempt to revive Austria's national identity in the postwar era, one can thus safely say, was a revival *ex nihilo* based on no applicable prior model in Austrian history.

As critics have pointed out, the revival of a national identity was largely inspired by the pragmatic concern of emphasizing Austria's difference to and non-complicity with Nazi Germany. Austria could thereby regain its sovereignty as a state without having to account fully for its role in the Jewish genocide. Barbara Kaindl-Widhalm discerns in Austria's postwar history no endemic process of democratization but one that is merely administered from above: "Die außenpolitisch-militärische Niederlage bedingte die innenpolitischen Veränderungen."[10] Austria's national identity appeared to younger writers and intellectuals as an insidious ideological device covering up its problematic past rather than a positive set of national and constitutional tenets presumably shared by its citizens. The young Handke, for instance, already expressed his doubts and reservations at the very beginning of Austria's postwar republic:

> Davor war verkündet worden, daß wir durch einen Staatsvertrag mit den Besatzungsmächten endlich *frei* seien: Als sich aber bis jetzt nichts geändert hatte, außer daß ein Staatsfeiertag eingeführt worden war, man aber noch immer hörte, daß wir jetzt *frei* seien, hielt ich allmählich die Wörter 'frei' und 'unfrei' nur für Sprachspiele.[11]

Abstract expressions such as freedom, Handke claims in 1957, have contributed little to political change but have become arbitrary signifiers in a state machinery based on an equally arbitrary national identity.

During the Grand Party Coalition era of the 1960s and the subsequent Kreisky era of the 1970s, this atmosphere of pragmatic nationalism was perfected into what is known as Austria's consensus society with its efficient and smoothly coordinated economy and its extensive welfare apparatus guaranteeing social stability.[12] The model of consensus society in postwar Austria, while in many ways founded on a progressive attempt to avoid labor confrontation, still recalls a regressive side that harks back to the Nazi era and its engineered social consensus. In the context of furthering democratic practices from within such an instituted consensus society, the socialist chancellor Bruno Kreisky figured as a political innovator who left an indelible mark on Austria's history by inaugurating an unprecedented era of liberalism, social reform and cosmopolitan outlook. However, even the highly popular Kreisky ultimately did not touch upon the deeper problem of an unchallenged collective consensus upon which Austria's postwar society was built. The chancellor, who was also of Jewish descent, ultimately chose not to dwell on this heritage in an Austria that wished to forget its history. Instead, Kreisky promoted an international politics that, for instance, intervened in an unorthodox manner for the Palestinian right to self-determination. While avoiding the confrontation of his own ethnic heritage in Austria's public sphere, Kreisky, much to Israel's chagrin, responded sensitively to the plight of an ethnic minority on an international level. This critical and self-effacing stance towards his own Jewish heritage, as Robert S. Wistrich points out, was entirely coherent from within Kreisky's ideology:

> At most one could define the Jews as a Schicksalsgemeinschaft [a community of fate] . . . based on a common history of suffering. But they were emphatically not a world-wide people as many Zionists claim; . . . Indeed, the entire concept of Jewish peoplehood as it was interpreted by Zionism implied for Kreisky the inadmissible adoption of the Nazi fiction of a Jewish race.[13]

Kreisky's complex understanding of his Jewish heritage, clearly indebted to Vienna's turn-of-the-century cosmopolitanism, eluded Israel, however, that expected more solidarity for its newly founded and embattled nation. It also eluded the majority of Austrians who were content in not having to deal with the "problematic" background of their beloved chancellor. Indeed, Kreisky's liberal principles of socialism that looked beyond ethnicity facilitated a persistent mood of historical amnesia during this period of Austrian reconstruction and emerging affluence.

While writers like Ilse Aichinger, Paul Celan and Ingeborg Bachmann had early on confronted Austria with its problematic past, this examination never reached the wider political public sphere in a climate of instituted silence and amnesia until Waldheim became president in 1986.[14] With Waldheim, finally, Austria's silenced past became an open public theme and allowed writers to articulate their concerns with more national and international attention than ever before. Bernhard's drama *Heldenplatz* (1988), for example, triggered a national controversy over how Austria's heritage ought to be remembered. Since the main protagonists in Bernhard's play were Jewish, this controversy also had to acknowledge the continued presence of living witnesses to Austria's dubious history. Bernhard's play was only the beginning of an ethnic examination of Austria's identity that followed in the wake of Waldheim. This new attention to ethnicity was also as a result of the collapse of the Eastern Bloc and its repression of ethnic interests as well as Germany's reunification and its problematic stance on citizenship and asylum.[15] In the early 1990s, a more explicit preoccupation with Austria's Jewish history and its community of survivors and their descendants commanded the attention of media and public sphere.

And yet, while this ethnic focus has allowed one to transcend the monolithic myth of Austria's national identity, its collectivization of Jewish interests still remains problematic. Demographically, for example, Austria's present Jewish community "is largely made up of survivors of concentration camps, displaced persons or refugees who only arrived in Austria to begin a new life after 1945, 1956 [Hungary] or 1968 [Czechoslovakia]."[16] Austria's former Jewish community who went into exile has, for the most part, not returned to Austria. This rupture in the continuity of Austria's Jewish community, complicated by the varying subject positions of its present community with their diverse linguistic, cultural and political heritages, recapitulates the diversity of Vienna's Jewish community at the turn of the century. To speak of a contemporary Austrian Jewish literature appears almost impossible. As our brief historical review has shown, both Jewish ethnic and Austrian national identity never achieved stability in recent Austrian history and are subject to constant transformation.

## Jewish Identities in Present Austrian Writing

What unites contemporary Jewish communities beyond their apparent diversity is a common history marked particularly by traumatic persecution but also by practices of resistance and solidarity. Kreisky's notion of a community of fate (*Schicksalsgemeinschaft*) is indeed an example of this limited universal that cuts across cultural difference. In a concrete sense, Kreisky's loss of 21 family members, Jelinek's of 51 members, or Schindel's of his father and members of extended family unites their otherwise different biographies.[17] Peter Sichrovsky's work on the traumatic history shared by survivors and their descendants can be seen similarly as a unifying expression of otherwise diverse Jewish cultural identities.[18] This identity of a common fate of persecution also does more justice to assimilated Jewish populations and their secular and hybridized lifestyles as well as to those who were labeled and grouped as Jewish by the enforcement of racial laws. In addition, this shared traumatic history separates writers such as Jelinek, Schindel and Rabinovici from non-Jewish writers who are sympathetic to their position such as Handke, Bernhard, Reichart or Roth. While the latter may have suffered a cultural loss resulting from the persecution and marginalization of Jewish culture in Austria, they do not have the direct experience of ethnic victimization and persecution.

Jean Améry's critical remark on Hannah Arendt that Nazi violence can never be banal for those who have suffered it physically clarifies this difference also from within Jewish intellectual discourse that on occasion took on the detached position of sociological comment more commonly found among non-Jewish analyses of the Holocaust.[19] Améry's remark would further suggest a cross-cultural solidarity of Jewish suffering with other collectively victimized groups such as the Gypsies, Native American Indians or African Americans. It appears as if the definition of a Jewish community bound by fate would quickly dissolve due to its overly universal tendencies in which all victims become Jews.[20] What does it mean, then, when a person claims to be a Jew apart from traditional cultural and religious affiliations? How does a legacy of persecution (*Schicksalsgemeinschaft*) spell out an identity that is still different from other persecuted groups or individuals? "The social articulation of difference, from the minority experience," writes Homi Bhabha, "is a complex, on-going negotiation that seeks to authorize cultural hybridities that emerge in moments of historical transformation."[21] Bhabha, addressing minority identities in general, questions their demarcation through absolute boundaries of tradition or collectivization. Instead, a complex process of negotiation and recognition defines the tenuous boundaries of minority identities. In this context, being a Jew, as our examples will demonstrate, means to address a specific history and heritage that cannot be taken for granted as an already "authenticated cultural tradition"[22] but that defines itself in active communal negotiation and contention concerning its cultural and ethical significance. Jewish identity construed as such a cultural identity includes both its ongoing clarification and the resistance with which it is met by other competing social interests from within and without.

This emphasis on the notion that cultural negotiation is at the origin of any identity is displayed concretely through the use of multi-plot configurations (Schindel) and a conflicting semantics of identity (Rabinovici). Both writers, in fact, write against the grain, against the consensus that usually surrounds traditional identity politics with its already established semantic fields of inclusion and exclusion. Their performative language ruptures such a binary model that defines belonging and not belonging in a culture as well as minority and majority status. Cultural understanding, as their works suggest, is the direct outcome of interaction and negotiated boundaries. Demarcations of group identities are therefore strategic rather than final, dramatic rather than epistemic. Our examples will further point to this process of negotiation as part of a conflicting discourse landscape that we share as the negotiation of Jewish and non-Jewish encounters in everyday situations (Schindel), and as intra-Jewish differences on the significance of Jewish identity (Rabinovici).

Robert Schindel represents the first postwar generation of Jewish survivors in Austria. Born in 1944, Schindel escaped the Nazi genocide under an altered name that entitled him to state welfare. His parents, both communists, chose to return to Austria in order to join the resistance movement against Nazi rule. Schindel's father was murdered in Dachau in 1945, while his mother, though imprisoned, escaped extermination. This irregular and curious past is also reflected in Schindel's first novel *Gebürtig* (1992; *Born Where*), following to some extent the political commitment to Austria displayed by Schindel's father. Like his father, Schindel still sees hope for constructive intervention and resistance in a present climate of resurging nationalism and anti-ethnic sentiments. His novel, reflecting the author's own assimilated upbringing in Austria, proves sympathetic to the heirs of both victims and victimizers in their attempts of sorting out their complicated family histories.

*Gebürtig* takes a critical view of Austria's dubious normalization, belying a climate of enforced harmonized consensus: "Die Väter haben die Unsern in die Öfen geschoben, die Mütter haben den Rosenkranz gebetet, und die Söhne haben uns großzügig eingemeindet."[23] Nevertheless, Schindel still believes in the possibility of cultural rebirth to the extent that it involves a genuine engagement with history affecting the present and its sphere of intercultural encounter. Schindel's multi-plot novel shows most of his characters struggling for more viable forms of cultural identity in which difference and commonality can co-exist. The past is acknowledged but not necessarily the single determining avenue to Jewish identity: "Dürfen unsere Juden gelegentlich ein bißchen totsein oder müssen sie auch als Knochenmehl ständig gespitzt bleiben?"(G 16). Schindel's novel succeeds in presenting us with a credible intersubjective world interposing itself between the various negotiations of cultural identity ripe with contradictions and inconsistencies.

The appropriate vehicle for this tentative, diverse and flexible reconstruction of culture is the multi-plot narration with which Schindel highlights both progressive and regressive attempts in which public and private boundaries are negotiated between Jewish and non-Jewish characters. The centrality of social and cultural co-dependence is emphasized by the twin characters Sascha Graffito and Danny Demant who are symbiotically connected to one another as passive observer-narrator and acting character respectively, producing together a narrated life or story. This symbiotic model subsequently plays itself out in a series of other paired characters whose lives intersect with Danny's and Sascha's. At the outset, the novel depicts patterns of interaction typical of Austria's amnesiac society: "Er betonte seine jüdische Herkunft, sie sagte, damit könne sie nichts anfangen, sie interessiere sich nicht für Politik" (G 35). The work further highlights generation conflicts between survivors and their descendants such as Emmanuel Katz who becomes the indirect victim of his mother's traumatic memory or Susanne Ressel who questions her father's fond memories of communist activism and comradeship during the Spanish civil war.[24] Eventually, however, the novel presents more positive transformations such as the public outing of a repressed Jewish identity (Katz, Adel) or a hidden Nazi past (Konrad Sachs). The commitment to confront once again a traumatic past as a witness in a Nazi trial (Gebirtig) and the approximation of the Shoah experience, albeit highly ironized, as stand-ins in a Holocaust movie set, focuses the newly gained sense of ethnic identity and solidarity.

In Schindel's novel, the predominance of the characters' positive transformations along with the flippant, though ultimately benign, humor would appear to promote a false harmonization at the novel's end. Its intent to expose the historical amnesia of Austria's consensus society is undermined by what some critics may identify as sentimentality or ethnic kitsch. However, the novel's tone, admittedly not without its own problems, resists a sanctimonious quality that has become of late a cliché in the treatment of the Holocaust, turning critical reflection into iconic reverence for events claimed to be beyond human comprehension. Like his German colleague Maxim Biller, Schindel attempts to break this spell of unquestioning awe and reticence by means of irreverent satire so as to allow for a continued inquiry into Jewish history and identity. Compared to Jelinek's *Totenauberg*, Schindel's novel evokes a similar heteroglossia of commodified discourses surrounding cultural identities. Yet Schindel's more conciliatory work highlights the assimilative potential that Vienna harbored beneath its diasporic identity which allowed, apart from cultural tension, for hybridities and mutually enriched cultural contexts.

This transregional and cosmopolitan confidence is reflected in the novel's constant shifting of scenery between Vienna, Venice, Hamburg, Munich, Frankfurt and New York, all distinctive cities with distinctive traditions. Schindel's more easygoing cosmopolitan perspective, critically grounded in distinct regional settings, does not attempt to globalize or universalize its thematic of various cultural encounters between Jews and non-Jews. Indeed, each of the novel's encounters produces a unique negotiation of Jewish identity from within uniquely interpreted cultural settings. The novel's depiction of attempts at self-comprehension and identity is in this respect often linked to the reflective act of writing that creates a necessary distance to an immediate set of historical or personal circumstances. Emmanuel Katz, tyrannized by his mother's Auschwitz past, offers such an instance of an attempt to give birth to a new identity other than through the memory of victimization. After the death of his father and a series of forced attempts to assert his Jewish identity (growing a beard and accusing other Jews of denying their identity), Katz quits his banking profession and settles for writing a book on Holocaust survivors. The book explores their inability to escape their past, an insight that is tragically borne out by his mother who eventually dies of a "verspäteter Auschwitztod" (G 199). On the other hand, this attempt at emancipation is also more contingently linked to the matrix of desire that somehow subverts predictable boundaries of cultural identity and difference. Katz's emancipatory effort from an overwhelming heritage through the distance of writing is tainted by his private "Faible für schlanke Riesendamen . . . , je deutscher desto lieber" (G 27), revealing an ongoing tacit admiration for German culture.

In Schindel's *Gebürtig*, the apparent stability of cultural boundaries is shaken by various peripheral and centrifugal movements away from and towards Vienna, the novel's main locale, as well as by linguistic and regional differences. Schindel's novel presents a multi-contextual (rather than multicultural) negotiation of identity that occurs on many discourse levels and not merely on the level of bipolar oppositions between typified ethnic, national or regional identities. Renewing the significance of Jewish identity and its public visibility, Schindel ultimately manages to avoid a facile pluralism and a dogmatic politics of identity obliging every Jew to be Jewish in the same manner. Since Jewishness, as Schindel realizes, overlaps with other private and public identities, it recedes or moves into the foreground in accordance with changing subject positions influenced by age, gender, generation, community, region and language. Its visibility, while desirable in Austria's all too homogeneous cultural landscape, cannot be reduced to any single strategy or form of public disclosure.

Doron Rabinovici, born in 1961, represents a younger third generation of postwar Austrian Jewish culture. His stance, comparable to that of his German contemporary Maxim Biller, betrays less confidence in the reconstruction or normalization of Austro-Jewish relations. Rabinovici's collection *Papirnik: Stories* (1994) resists Schindel's sympathetic ironic treatment of the recently emerging politics of identity. Instead, from within an ambience of a seemingly secure banality, the author stages a return of violence, anxiety and repressed historical content. "Papirnik," for example, the framing story of the cycle, depicts a character made of books and scrolls and ends abruptly in the character's self-immolation and an evocation of Nazi book burning after his inner secret has been pried out of him by his companion Lola.

This haunting image of the total erasure of Jewish history and memory due to a lack of delicate treatment is taken up again in the book's epilogue as a traumatic scene of instruction from which the act of writing takes its ambivalent justification. Lola Varga, as a survivor and writer, views herself now implicated in Papirnik's death for having shamelessly devoured his textual body. The secret word, violently pried out of Parpirnik and which caused him to inflame himself, is now guarded by her more respectfully as a password for those who would wish to enter the forgotten history it represents. However, this desire to understand Jewish history on its own ground is not yet manifest in the largely indifferent public:

> Aussagen wird sie, wird es ausrufen, wird uns die Losung ausgeben, falls wir sie abverlangen. So schreibt sie ihre Bücher. So präsentiert sie ihre Arbeit. So sitzt sie in der Pressekonferenz. Aber niemand fragt Lola.[25]

Like Jelinek, Rabinovici expresses serious doubts about the visibility of a Jewish identity that is neither acknowledged nor sought after in a culture seemingly at home with itself.

Rabinovici stems against this invisibility by refusing likewise the legitimization of the dominant culture. Through his narrative style where the semantics of single words and names often receives heightened attention, the author subtly lays bare their implicit cultural and political connotations. In the story "Noémi," for example, the city of Vienna is mentioned only cryptically as "W" and thereby belittled in its significance and identity. A cafe location, so central in Schindel's work as a terrain of intersecting biographies, is in the same diminutive manner more critically defined by its proximity to the monument of Vienna's anti-semitic mayor (Lueger) that has without any challenge survived into the present. By means of these minimal rhetorical strategies, Vienna turns into a site of negativity and absence, reflecting a loss rather than a presence of culture.

In "Noémi," a story about two adolescents attempting to come to terms with their cultural and ethnic heritage, a single name similarly is at the center of its unfolding action. The story's vehicle, the name "Noémi" with its readily presumed Jewish origin, triggers a comedy of errors revolving around competing models of ethnic authenticity. As part of an intra-Jewish critique, Rabinovici critically explores in the story the phenomenon of an ethnic revival of identity and its own peculiar forms of betrayal. The separate and exiled identity of Jews in Austria is initially represented by the Zionist youth movement where its two protagonists Amos and Georg find a temporary yet ambivalent shelter: "Wie gespannter Stacheldraht schien die Geschichte zwischen ihnen und dem Rest der Stadt zu verlaufen" (P 36). This seemingly clearly demarcated exiled identity, however, is complicated by the Jewish community's own inner differences over what constitutes Jewish identity (historical heritage, geographical location, matrilineal bloodline). The protagonists' mimetic rivalry for the same girlfriend who, with her seemingly Jewish name "Noémi," embodies both the promise and the betrayal of their tenuous identity. Challenging Austria's nationalism with their transnational Zionist beliefs, Amos and Georg nevertheless succumb to an obsession with their own origin projected onto the presumably Jewish Noémi: "Er fragte . . . nach ihrem Namen. 'Noémi.' Daraufhin hatte er sie eingemeindet und alles darangesetzt, sie wieder zu treffen" (P 34). And as is recalled later in the story: "Georg sah, wie sein Freund ihr entgegenschaute, und ein noch namenloses Verlangen keimte zum ersten Mal in ihm auf" (P 50).

This erotic obsession with a legitimate origin, especially on the part of the half-Jewish Georg whose mother is not a Jew, ultimately undermines the construction of a common identity and solidarity. As in Schindel's work, a less stable matrix of desire subverts the seemingly more stable cultural identities. Both Amos's and Georg's initial Zionist aspirations are undone by a triangular desire in which Jewish identity is displaced onto a fetishized object and thus the focus of mimetic rivalry. The story's ending, in which the two adults now look back on this youthful episode, places the flirtation with Zionism into a similar adolescent and naive context. Both protagonists have in the meantime abandoned their desire to live in Israel and resigned themselves to a more settled secular identity.

However, apart from this sobering ending, the protagonists ultimately learn that identities cannot be innocently acquired nor revived. During their stay in Israel, they find out that they are after all Viennese Jews with a particular tradition that does not fully coincide with the tradition of Israel. Their urbane humor and sketch-like parody of anti-Semitism, for instance, is not appreciated during a community event in the kibbutz where the pressure of such an ideology is viewed differently. As both Amos and Georg come to realize: "Der Antisemitismus: Hier ließen sie ihn dumm sterben. Sie [Amos and Georg] wollten das Unreflektierte hohlspiegeln. Wollten es im Widerschein preisgeben. Jüdischer Selbsthaß wurde ihnen mit einem Mal vorgeworfen" (P 40–41). Internal dismantling of cultural stereotypes in the manner of a Karl Kraus, Amos and Georg must realize, is a restricted and not commonly shared Jewish practice. The acquisition of identity entails a necessary shattering of idols, reminding the protagonists of their specific geographic and cultural position in what appeared to be a seamless and unproblematic world of pan-Jewish solidarity.

While opening up Jewish cultural definition from within itself to a cosmopolitan perspective, Rabinovici, like Jelinek and Schindel, does not settle for a fashionable multicultural model that would be welcomed by more liberal elements in Austria. His major reservation is once again a semantic one, struggling with a tacit consensus underlying the notion of cultural pluralism. The desired harmonization of diverse cultural claims, as Rabinovici's stories demonstrate, does not necessarily guarantee recognition but demands assimilation to a norm, even if such a norm is now more heterogeneously articulated. Reflecting on the semantics of public debate, Rabinovici exposes this strategic elimination of difference and dissent in a story that highlights how the overruling force of consensus preserves difference only in the form of tokenism:

> Sie werden nur so lange verkraften, was ich zu sagen habe, bis sie mich in eine Ihrer konsensualen Lösungen eingebunden haben. Meine Position soll nicht an die Öffentlichkeit dringen, aber meine Teilnahme hier Ihrer Harmonie den passenden Kontrapunkt verleihen. (P 93–94).

Like Jelinek or Schindel, Rabinovici is acutely aware of the commodification of cultural identities which subjects them to commercial, national and ideological interests and rituals of democratic decision making. The assertion of Jewish identity in Austria is therefore further complicated by the horizon of cultural expectation that surrounds it. Is it always productive, for example, to represent a living Jewish community in a society that wants to forget its annihilationist politics of the past and now take pride in its present political freedom? Visibility of difference, as Rabinovici's stories indirectly suggest, can also be exploited for token democratic expressions of freedom and recognition. Rabinovici's analysis highlights the problematic semantic manipulation of cultural identities in which any positive assertion can possibly be turned into its opposite.

As this illustration of Schindel and Rabinovici has attempted to show, the politics of recognition in contemporary Austrian discourse does not rest entirely on an increased visibility in a culture or on any clearly marked ethnic collectivity, even if such a community is construed as a force of resistance. Instead, Schindel and Rabinovici attempt to foreground the complex work that underlies any negotiation of identity. To be Jewish, for these writers, means foremost to challenge one's own secure sense of identity defined by traditional affiliations and to enter the multi-contextual spheres of private and public cultures with their uneasy compromises and balances. They alert us to the increasingly post-ideological landscape of a new public sphere in which there is no longer any privileged perspective more innocent than others. At the same time, they remind us that any position is ideologically suspect unless it enters the challenge of cultural diversification and hybridization which makes cultural recognition, and therefore identity, possible.

The examples of Schindel and Rabinovici demonstrate that a redefinition of Jewish culture in Austria is only in its beginning stages and is marked by contradictory desires for dissent and harmonization. Along with their other fellow Austrian writers Gerhard Roth, Christoph Ransmayr and Maria Thérèse Kerschbaumer, Schindel and Rabinovici have just begun to show new facets in the ongoing challenge to Austria's consensus society. Modifications of its cultural identity can be said to follow along the path of the pioneers Bernhard, Handke and Jelinek who were the first to break openly with a climate of enforced public assent as part of Austria's cultural reconstruction.

The aim of this book has been to analyze this crucial cultural upheaval from within Austria. The cultural demolition of the myth of Austria undertaken by Bernhard, Handke and Jelinek has often been belittled as the expression of an overheated and subversive imagination. This demolition has, however, begun to leave its visible mark on Austria's political scene. As Werner A. Perger puts it: "Der Umbruch in Europa hat Österreich erfaßt. Das alte System bröckelt, ein neues ist nicht in Sicht."[26] Austria's once comfortable coalition arrangement between its major conservative and socialist parties is quickly nearing its end. The extreme right wing party of populist Jörg Haider has shown remarkable gains during recent elections. Bomb attacks against the mayor of Vienna and individuals of exposed ethnic background in 1995 have sharpened the political climate in a country once known for the absence of any crisis. In hindsight, it is ironic that all the signs of crisis were acutely identified during the 1970s and eighties by Bernhard, Handke and Jelinek, but ultimately not taken seriously by the public and its political representatives.

The crisis within Austria has been partially heightened as a result of the globalization made apparent since the fall of the East Bloc. The increased extraneous pressures on what was formerly known as an "island of the blessed" may be seen as the cause of defensive national attitudes. However, the consensus of what constitutes the essence of Austria's nation is quickly dwindling and complicated not only by the transnational imagination of writers. Multi-national conglomerates, a heavily Anglicized international media world and a pervasive consumer landscape make it difficult even on a simple level to identify what is unique to any region, community or national culture. In addition, Austria, like all of Europe, is haunted by its formerly inflated cultural significance that no longer can be taken for granted in the present diversified world market.

Bernhard, Handke and Jelinek, however, point in their works not only to a temporary political crisis that may well stabilize once Austria's economy has begun to settle down comfortably in the European community. As I have shown, these writers also question the very nature of our communal and political affiliations that tend to humanize some while dehumanizing others. Here, they alert us to a deep-seated communicative incompetence that cannot be mastered alone through instituted forms of democratic decision making. In their capacities as writers, they revolt against this specialization and instrumentalization of dialogue and public discourse. For unless one's entire culture is read and understood in the manner of a more complex narration, as they seem to suggest, little in it will be truly comprehended in its interdependence and therefore really matter to its citizens.

## Notes

[1] *Reemerging Jewish Culture in Germany: Life and Literature Since 1989*, eds. Sander L. Gilman and Karen Remmler (New York: NYU Press, 1994) 11.

[2] Gilman and Remmler, 2.

[3] Jack Zipes, "The Contemporary German Fascination for Things Jewish," *Reemerging Jewish Culture in Germany*, 18.

[4] Remmler, in her discussion, initially acknowledges "different geographical, political and cultural contexts" (186) as decisive factors in determining the author's specific Jewish identity. However, in her discussion, this consideration is overridden by a collective treatment of female Jewish identity, paralleling Gilman's discussion of male Jewish identity. Moreover, this identity is demarcated entirely collectively, ignoring the possibility of an individual's unique appropriation or revision of it. For example, Remmler claims: "For German Jewish women writing in German, the attachment, however ambiguous and painful, to German culture through memory, family, or language positions them in spaces not shared with non-German women of Turkish, African or Eastern European origin" (186). German Jewish women, in Remmler's view, have turned into a distinct sociological group, presumably preventing them in their absolute difference from sharing their own or assimilating experiences from any other minorities in Germany.

[5] Steven Beller, *Vienna and the Jews 1867–1938: A Cultural History* (Cambridge: Cambridge UP, 1990) 70.

[6] Benedict Anderson notes that "German's nineteenth century elevation by the Habsburg court, German as one might think it, had nothing whatever to do with German nationalism" (*Imagined Communities* (London: Verso, 1991) 78). William M. Johnston finds this absence of a strongly defined national identity once again in Austria's postwar republic that he terms a "nation without qualities." ("A Nation Without Qualities: Austria and Its Quest for a National Identity," *Concepts of National Identity: An Interdisciplinary Dialogue*, ed. Dieter Boerner (Baden-Baden: Nomos, 1986) 177).

[7] Marsha L. Rozenblit, "The Jews of Germany and Austria: A Comparative Perspective," *Austrians and Jews in the Twentieth Century*, ed. Robert S. Wistrich (New York: St. Martin's Press, 1992) 11. See also Dagmar Lorenz "The Legacy of Jewish Vienna." *Insiders and Outsiders. Jewish and Gentile*

*Culture in Germany and Austria*. Eds. Dagmar Lorenz and Gabriele Weinberger. Detroit: Wayne State UP, 1994: 293–300.

[8] Ruth Beckermann, *Die Mazzeinsel: Juden in der Wiener Leopoldstadt 1918–1938* (Vienna: Löcker Verlag, 1984) 13.

[9] See Gerhard Botz, "The Jews of Vienna from the *Anschluss* to the Holocaust," *Jews, Antisemitism, and Culture in Vienna*, eds. Gerhard Botz, Ivar Oxaal, and Michael Pollak (London: Routledge, 1987) 185–207.

[10] Barbara Kaindl-Widhalm, *Demokratie wider Willen: Autoritäre Tendenzen und Antisemitismus in der 2. Republik* (Vienna: Verlag für Gesellschaftskritik, 1990) 3.

[11] Peter Handke, "1957," *Ich bin ein Bewohner des Elfenbeinturms* (Frankfurt: Suhrkamp, 1972) 14.

[12] See, for example, Robert Menasse's study *Die sozialpartnerschaftliche Ästhetik* (Vienna: Sonderzahl, 1990) where the author extends the economic concept of cooperative consensus to the entire cultural landscape of Austria. The concept of social partnership, according to Menasse, lies at the root of Austria's political infrastructure. Its principle agency rests with an instituted parity commission which controls and settles wage and price negotiations in order to avoid open labor conflict. Social partnership, as Menasse concludes, aims for a total harmonization of social relations without, however, removing the original reasons for conflict (91). The social landscape, including Austria's democratic institutions, are thus said to be strongly marked by pre-arranged consensus, lack of critique and pseudo-democratic procedures. Incidentally, Menasse belongs to the same generation of Austrian Jewish writers that are discussed in this chapter.

[13] Robert S. Wistrich, "The Kreisky Phenomenon: A Reassessment," *Austrians and the Jews in the Twentieth Century*, 237.

[14] See, for example, Klaus Zeyringer's study *Innerlichkeit und Öffentlichkeit: Österreichische Literatur der achtziger Jahre* (Tübingen: A. Francke, 1992) which locates the turning point of Austria's consensus society at the end of the liberal Kreisky era (1985). Political corruption or *Verfilzung*, neoconservatism and the election of Waldheim, according to Zeyringer, contributed to a more outspoken engagement by writers and the redefinition of their task in terms of openly expressed cultural resistance.

[15] See Andreas Huyssen's "Nation, Race, and Immigration: German Identities after Unification," *Twilight Memories: Marking Time in a Culture of Amnesia* (London: Routledge, 1995) 67–84.

[16] *Jewish Life in Austria*, ed. Austrian Federal Press Service (Graz: Styria, 1992) 5.

[17] See Wistrich, "The Kreisky Phenomenon," 236; Elfriede Jelinek, "Wir leben auf einem Berg von Leichen und Schmerz," in *Theater Heute* (Sept., 1992) 8; and Schindel's autobiographical poem "Erinnerungen an Prometheus," *Im Herzen die Krätze: Gedichte* (Frankfurt: Suhrkamp, 1988): 11–16;

and the review "Die unterste Falte der Seele" (*Profil* 18 (28 April, 1992): 88–89) that provide biographical information on the author.

[18] See Peter Sichrovsky, *Wir wissen nicht was morgen wird, wir wissen wohl was gestern war: Junge Juden in Deutschland und Österreich* (Köln: Kiepenheuer & Witsch, 1985).

[19] Jean Améry, *At the Mind's Limit* (New York: Schocken Books, 1986) 25.

[20] Bernard Malamud, *The Assistant* (Harmondsworth: Penguin, 1959).

[21] Homi K. Bhabha, *The Location of Culture* (London: Routledge, 1994) 2.

[22] Bhabha, 3.

[23] Robert Schindel, *Gebürtig* (Frankfurt: Suhrkamp, 1994) 15; hereafter quoted in text as G.

[24] *Gebürtig*, 20, 92.

[25] Doron Rabinovici, *Papirnik* (Frankfurt: Suhrkamp, 1994) 134; hereafter quoted in text as P.

[26] Werner A. Perger, "Die Bomben, das Warten, die Angst," *Die Zeit* 12 (March 24, 1995) 3.

# *Works Cited*

Adorno, Theodor. *The Jargon of Authenticity.* Evanston: Northwestern UP, 1973.

———. *Aesthetic Theory.* Trans. C. Lehnhardt. London: Routledge, 1984.

———. "Culture Industry Reconsidered." *The Culture Industry: Selected Essays on Mass Culture.* Ed. J.M. Bernstein. London, Routledge, 1991.

Adorno, Theodor and Max Horkheimer. *Dialectic of Enlightenment.* New York: Continuum, 1972.

Améry, Jean. *At the Mind's Limit.* New York: Schocken Books, 1986.

Anderson, Benedict. *Imagined Communities.* London: Verso, 1991.

Arendt, Hannah. *Eichmann in Jerusalem: A Report on the Banality of Evil.* Harmondsworth: Penguin Books, 1963.

———. *The Origins of Totalitarianism.* New York: Harcourt Brace Jovanovich, 1968.

———. "On Violence." *Crisis of the Republic.* New York: Harcourt Brace Jovanovich, 1972.

———. "For Martin Heidegger's Eightieth Birthday." *Martin Heidegger and National Socialism.* Eds. Günther Neske and Emil Kettering. New York: Paragon, 1990.

*Austria: Fact and Figures.* Vienna: Federal Press Service, 1987.

———. Vienna: Federal Press Service, 1993.

Bartmann, Christoph. *Suche nach dem Zusammenhang: Handkes Werk als Prozess.* Vienna: Wilhelm Braumüller, 1984.

Barthes, Roland. *Mythologies.* New York: Granada, 1973.

Bhabha, Homi. *The Location of Culture.* London: Routledge, 1994.

Baudrillard, Jean. *Simulations.* New York: Semiotext, 1983.

———. *L'autre par lui-même.* Paris: Éditions Galileé, 1987.

———. *The Ecstasy of Communication.* New York: Semiotext, 1988.

Beckermann, Ruth. *Die Mazzeinsel: Juden in der Wiener Leopoldstadt 1918–1938.* Vienna: Löcker Verlag, 1984.

Beller, Steven. *Vienna and the Jews 1867–1938: A Cultural History.* Cambridge: Cambridge UP, 1990.

Beutin, Wolfgang et al. *Deutsche Literaturgeschichte. Von den Anfängen bis zur Gegenwart.* Stuttgart: J.B. Metzler, 1984.

Benjamin, Walter. "Über einige Motive bei Baudelaire." *Illuminationen. Ausgewählte Schriften I.* Frankfurt: Suhrkamp, 1977.

Berka, Sigrid. "Ein Gespräch mit Elfriede Jelinek." *Modern Austrian Literature* 26.2 (1993): 127–155.

Berman, Russell A. "The Vienna Fascination." *Modern Culture and Critical Theory*. Madison: U of Wisconsin P, 1991.

Bernhard, Thomas. "Der pensionierte Salonsozialist." *Profil* 4 (26 Jan., 1981): 52–53.

———. *Wittgensteins Neffe. Eine Freundschaft*. Frankfurt: Suhrkamp, 1982.

———. *Holzfällen. Eine Erregung*. Frankfurt: Suhrkamp, 1984.

———. *Alte Meister*. Frankfurt: Suhrkamp, 1986.

———. *Heldenplatz*. Frankfurt: Suhrkamp, 1988.

Biller, Maxim. "Sind Sie lesbisch, Frau Jelinek?" *Tempojahre*. Munich: dtv, 1991.

Blanchot, Maurice. *The Writing of Disaster*. Trans. Ann Smock. Lincoln: U of Nebraska P, 1986.

Böll, Heinrich. *Berichte zur Gesinnungslage der Nation*. Köln: Kiepenheuer & Witsch, 1975.

Bonn, Klaus. *Die Idee der Wiederholung in Peter Handkes Schriften*. Würzburg: Königshausen und Neumann, 1994.

Botz, Gerhard. "Die Ausgliederung der Juden aus der Gesellschaft." *Eine zerstörte Kultur*. Eds. Gerhard Botz, Ivar Oxaal and Michael Pollak. Buchloe: Verlag Obermayer, 1990.

———. "The Jews of Vienna from the *Anschluss* to the Holocaust." London: Routledge, 1987.

Broder, Henryk. "Die unheilbare Liebe deutscher Intellektueller zu toten und todkranken Juden." *Semit* 3 (1989): 29.

Camion, Arlette. *Image et écriture dans l'oeuvre de Peter Handke*. Berne: Peter Lang, 1992.

Cohen, Bernhard and Luc Rosenzweig. *Waldheim*. Trans. Josephine Bacon. New York: Adams Books, 1987.

Daviau, Donald. "Thomas Bernhard's Heldenplatz." *Monatshefte* 83.1 (1991): 29–44.

Deleuze, Gilles and Félix Guattari. *Kafka: Toward a Minor Literature*. Trans. Dana Polan. Minneapolis: U of Minnesota P, 1986.

Demetz, Peter. *Die süße Anarchie*. Berlin: Ullstein Verlag, 1970.

Derrida, Jacques. *Of Spirit: Heidegger and the Question*. Trans. Geoffrey Bennington and Rachel Bowlby. Chicago: U of Chicago P, 1989.

Dittmar, Jens. *Sehr gescherte Reaktion. Leserbrief-Schlachten um Thomas Bernhard*. Vienna: Edition S, 1993.

Durzak, Manfred. *Peter Handke und die deutsche Gegenwartsliteratur. Narziß auf Abwegen*. Berlin: Kohlhammer, 1982.

Fischer, Michael. *Trivialmythen in Elfriede Jelineks Romanen*. St. Ingbert: Werner Röhrig Verlag, 1991.

Endres, Ria. "Ein musikalisches Opfer." *Elfriede Jelinek.* Eds. Kurt Bartsch and Günther Höfler. Vienna: Droschl, 1991.

Foucault, Michel. "Preface." *Anti-Oedipus: Capitalism and Schizophrenia.* Minneapolis: U of Minnesota P, 1983.

Frank, Manfred. *What is Neostructuralism?* Minneapolis: U of Minnesota P, 1989.

Freud, Sigmund. "Mourning and Melancholia." *General Psychological Theory.* Ed. Philip Rieff. New York: Collier Books, 1963.

Gauss, Karl Markus. "Vorort-Vermessung und Reiseroman." *Profil* 46 (Nov. 14, 1994): 86–88.

Gilman, Sander L. *Jewish Self-Hatred: Anti-Semitism and the Hidden Language of the Jews.* Baltimore: The Johns Hopkins Press, 1986.

———. "Karl Kraus's Oscar Wilde: Race, Sex and Difference." *Vienna 1900: From Altenberg to Wittgenstein.* Eds. Edward Timms and Ritchie Robertson. Edinburgh: Edinburgh UP, 1990.

———. "Jewish Writers in Contemporary Germany." *Anti-Semitism in Times of Crisis.* Eds. Sander L. Gilman and Steven T. Katz. New York: New York UP, 1993.

Gilman, Sander L. and Karen Remmler. Eds. *Reemerging Jewish Culture in Germany: Life and Literature Since 1989.* New York: New York UP, 1994.

Greiner, Ulrich. *Der Tod des Nachsommers. Aufsätze, Porträts, Kritiken zur österreichischen Gegenwartsliteratur.* Munich: Hanser Verlag, 1979.

———. "Mangel an Feingefühl." *Die Zeit* (June 1, 1990): 13.

Habermas, Jürgen. *The Theory of Communicative Action.* Trans. Thomas McCarthy. Boston: Beacon Press, 1984.

———. *The Philosophical Discourse of Modernity.* Trans. Frederick G. Lawrence. Cambridge: The MIT Press, 1987.

———. *The Structural Transformation of the Public Sphere.* Cambridge: MIT Press, 1989.

———. "Further Reflections on the Public Sphere." *Habermas and the Public Sphere.* Ed. Craig Calhoun. Cambridge: MIT Press, 1992.

———. *The Past as Future.* Trans. Max Pensky. Lincoln: U of Nebraska P, 1994.

Handke, Peter. *Die Angst des Tormanns beim Elfmeter.* Frankfurt: Suhrkamp, 1970.

———. *Die Innenwelt der Aussenwelt der Innenwelt.* Frankfurt: Suhrkamp, 1971.

———. "Ein autobiographischer Essay." *Ich bin ein Bewohner des Elfenbeinturms.* Frankfurt: Suhrkamp, 1972.

———. "Die Literatur ist romantisch." *Ich bin ein Bewohner des Elfenbeinturms.*

———. "Zur Tagung der Gruppe 47." *Ich bin ein Bewohner des Elfenbeinturms.*

———. *Wunschloses Unglück.* Frankfurt: Suhrkamp, 1972.

———. *Langsame Heimkehr.* Frankfurt: Suhrkamp, 1979.

———. "Das Öl des Weltmeisters." *Das Ende des Flanierens.* Frankfurt: Suhrkamp, 1980.

———. *Versuch über die Müdigkeit.* Frankfurt: Suhrkamp, 1989.

———. *Versuch über die Jukebox.* Frankfurt: Suhrkamp, 1990.

———. *Versuch über den geglückten Tag.* Frankfurt: Suhrkamp, 1991.

———. "Gelassen wär ich gern." *Der Spiegel* 49 (Dec. 5, 1994): 170–176.

———. *Hier in der Niemandsbucht.* Frankfurt: Suhrkamp, 1994.

———. *Eine winterliche Reise zu den Flüssen Donau, Morawa und Drina oder Gerechtigkeit für Serbien.* Frankfurt: Suhrkamp, 1996.

———. *Sommerlicher Nachtrag zu einer winterlichen Reise.* Frankfurt: Suhrkamp, 1996.

———. *Die Fahrt im Einbaum oder das Stück zum Film vom Krieg.* Frankfurt: Suhrkamp, 1999.

Handke, Peter and Herbert Gamper. *Aber ich lebe nur von den Zwischenräumen.* Zürich: Ammann Verlag, 1987.

Handke, Peter and André Müller. *André Müller im Gespräch mit Peter Handke.* Weitra: Bibliothek der Provinz, 1993.

Hansen, Miriam. *Babel and Babylon: Spectatorship in Silent American Film.* Cambridge: Harvard UP, 1991.

Heidegger, Martin. "The Question Concerning Technology." *The Question Concerning Technology and Other Essays.* Trans. William Lovitt. New York: Harper & Row, 1977.

———. *Sein und Zeit.* Tübingen: Max Niemeyer, 1986.

Hoberman, John M. *Sport and Political Ideology.* Austin: U of Texas P, 1984.

Hoesterey, Ingeborg. "Postmoderner Blick auf die österreichische Literatur." *Modern Austrian Literature* 23.3/4 (1990): 65–76.

Hoffmann, Yasmin. "'Hier lacht sich die Sprache selbst aus': Sprachsatire bei Elfriede Jelinek." *Elfriede Jelinek.* Eds. Kurt Bartsch and Günther Höfler. Vienna: Droschl, 1991.

Hofmannsthal, Hugo von. "Die Briefe des Zurückgekehrten." *Gesammelte Werke, Prosa II.* Frankfurt: Fischer, 1951.

Hohendahl, Peter Uwe. "The Public Sphere: Models and Boundaries." *Habermas and the Public Sphere.* Ed. Craig Calhoun. Cambridge: MIT Press, 1992.

Honegger, Gitta. "This German Language . . . : An Interview with Elfriede Jelinek." *Theater* 25 (1994): 14–22.

Hüppauf, Bernd. "Peter Handkes Stellung im Kulturwandel der sechziger Jahre." *Handke: Ansätze, Analysen, Anmerkungen.* Ed. Manfred Jurgensen. Munich: Francke, 1979.

Huntemann, Willi. *Artistik und Rollenspiel.* Würzburg: Königshausen, 1990.

Huyssen, Andreas. "Nation, Race, and Immigration: German Identities after Unification." *Twilight Memories: Marking Time in a Culture of Amnesia.* London: Routledge, 1995.

International Commission of Historians. *The Waldheim Report.* Copenhagen: Museum Tusculanum Press, 1993.

Iser, Wolfgang. "Staging as an Anthropological Category." *New Literary History* 23 (1992): 877–888.

Janik, Allan. "Die Wiener Kultur und die jüdische Selbsthaß-Hypothese." *Eine zerstörte Kultur.* Eds. Gerhard Botz, Ivar Oxaal and Michael Pollak. Buchloe: Obermayer, 1990.

Janik, Allen and Stephen Toulmin. *Wittgenstein's Vienna.* New York: Touchstone, 1973.

Jelinek, Elfriede. *Die Liebhaberinnen.* Hamburg: Rowohlt, 1975.

———. *Die endlose Unschuldigkeit.* Munich: Schwiftinger Galerie-Verlag, 1980.

———. *Die Ausgesperrten.* Hamburg: Rowohlt, 1980

———. *Die Klavierspielerin.* Hamburg: Rowohlt, 1983.

———. *Burgtheater. Theaterstücke.* Köln: Prometh Verlag, 1984.

———. *Lust.* Hamburg: Rowohlt, 1989.

———. *Wolken. Heim.* Köln: Steidl Verlag, 1990.

———. *Totenauberg.* Hamburg: Rowohlt Verlag, 1991.

———. "Wir leben auf einem Berg von Leichen und Schmerz." *Theater Heute* 9 (Sept., 1992): 1–9.

———. "This German Language . . . : An Interview with Elfriede Jelinek." *Theater* 25 (1994): 14–22.

———. *Ein Sportstück.* Hamburg: Rowohlt, 1998.

*Jewish Life in Austria,* ed. Austrian Federal Press Service. Graz: Styria, 1992.

Johnston, William M. "A Nation without Qualities: Austria and Its Quest for a National Identity." *Concepts of National Identity. An Interdisciplinary Dialogue.* Ed. Dieter Boerner. Baden-Baden: Nomos, 1986.

Kafka, Franz. *Briefe*, 1902–1924. Ed. Max Brod. New York: Schocken, 1966.

Kaindl-Widhalm, Barbara. *Demokratie wider Willen: Autoritäre Tendenzen und Antisemitismus in der 2. Republik.* Vienna: Verlag für Gesellschaftskritik, 1990.

Klug, Christian. *Theaterstücke.* Stuttgart: Metzler, 1991.

Kolleritsch, Alfred. "Die Welt, die sich öffnet. Einige Bemerkungen zu Handke und Heidegger." *Peter Handke: Die Arbeit am Glück.* Eds. Gerhard Melzer and Jale Tükel. Königstein: Athenäum, 1985.

Kosta, Barbara. "Muttertrauma: Anerzogener Masochismus." *Mütter — Töchter — Frauen: Weiblichkeitsbilder in der Literatur.* Eds. Helga Kraft and Ellen Liebs. Stuttgart: Metzler, 1993.

Lämmle, Peter. "Gelassenheit zu den Dingen — Peter Handke auf den Spuren Martin Heideggers." *Merkur* 395 (April 1981): 426–428.

Lamb-Faffelberger, Margarete. *Valie Export und Elfriede Jelinek im Spiegel der Presse: Zur Rezeption der feministischen Avantgarde Österreichs.* New York: Peter Lang, 1992.

Löffler, Sigrid. "Öfter jemanden umbringen." *Profil* 36 (Sept. 3, 1984): 60–64.

———. "Farce. Tobsuchtsanfall. Weltblamage." *Profil* 42 (Oct. 17, 1988): 110–114.

———. "Das Werk hat ja auf wunderbare Weise triumphiert." *Der konservative Anarchist: Thomas Bernhard und das Staats-Theater.* Ed. Maria Fialik. Vienna: Löcker, 1991.

Lorenz, Dagmar. "The Legacy of Jewish Vienna." *Insiders and Outsiders. Jewish and Gentile Culture in Germany and Austria.* Ed. Dagmar Lorenz and Gabriele Weinberger. Detroit: Wayne State UP, 1994: 293–300.

Luhmann, Niklas. *Beobachtungen der Moderne.* Opladen: Westdeutscher Verlag, 1992.

Malamud, Bernhard. *The Assistant.* Harmondsworth: Penguin, 1959.

Mandel, Richard D. *Sport: A Cultural History.* New York: Columbia UP, 1984.

Mannheim, Karl. *Ideology and Utopia.* Trans. Louis Wirth and Edward Shils. New York: Harcourt Brace Jovanovich, 1985.

Menasse, Robert. *Die sozialpartnerschaftliche Ästhetik: Essays zum österreichischen Geist.* Vienna: Sonderzahl, 1990.

Menges, Karl. *Das Private und das Politische. Bemerkungen zur Studentenliteratur, zu Handke, Celan und Grass.* Stuttgart: Hans Dieter Heinz Akademischer Verlag, 1987.

Mitscherlich, Alexander and Margarete. *Die Unfähigkeit zu trauern.* Munich: Piper, 1968.

Mittermayer, Manfred. *Ich werden.* Stuttgart: Akademischer Verlag, 1988.

Moser, Samuel. "Das Glück des Erzählens ist das Erzählen des Glücks." *Peter Handke. Die Langsamkeit der Welt.* Eds. Gerhard Fuchs and Gerhard Melzer. Graz: Literaturverlag Droschl, 1993.

Musil, Robert. *Der Mann ohne Eigenschaften.* Hamburg: Rowohlt, 1988.

Nägele, Rainer and Renate Voris. *Peter Handke.* Munich: C.H. Beck, 1978.

Neske, Günther and Emil Kettering. *Martin Heidegger and National Socialism.* New York: Paragon, 1990.

Pail, Gerhard. "Perspektivität in Thomas Bernhards *Holzfällen.*" *Modern Austrian Literature* 21 (1988): 51–68.

Perger, Werner A. "Die Bomben, das Warten, die Angst." *Die Zeit* 12 (March 24, 1995): 3.

Pfaff, Peter and Gerhard vom Hofe. *Das Elend des Polyphem. Zum Thema Subjektivität bei Thomas Bernhard, Peter Handke, Wolfgang Koeppen und Botho Strauss.* Königstein: Athenäum, 1980.

Pizer, John. "Modern vs. Postmodern Satire: Karl Kraus and Elfriede Jelinek." *Monatshefte* 86.4 (Winter 1994): 500–513.

Rabinovici, Doron. *Papirnik. Stories.* Frankfurt: Suhrkamp, 1994.

Reich-Ranicki, Marcel. *Thomas Bernhard.* Zürich: Ammann Verlag, 1990.

Renner, Rolf Günter. *Peter Handke.* Stuttgart: Poeschel Verlag, 1985.

———. *Die postmoderne Konstellation. Theorie, Text und Kunst im Ausgang der Moderne.* Freiburg: Rombach Verlag, 1988.

Ricoeur, Paul. "Metaphor and the Central Problem of Hermeneutics." *Hermeneutics and the Human Sciences.* Trans. John B. Thompson. Cambridge: Cambridge UP, 1981.

———. *Lectures on Ideology and Utopia.* New York: Columbia UP, 1986.

———. "A Life: A Story in Search of its Narrator." *Paul Ricoeur: Reflection & Imagination.* Ed. Mario J. Valdes. Toronto: U of Toronto P, 1991.

Ringel, Erwin. *Österreichische Seele.* Vienna: Hermann Böhlaus, 1984

Rozenblit, Marsha. "The Jews of Germany and Austria: A Comparative Perspective." *Austrians and Jews in the Twentieth Century.* Ed. Robert S. Wistrich. New York: St. Martin's Press, 1992.

Rushdie, Salman. "De Pristina à Littleton." *Le Monde* (May 11, 1999) 17.

Sartre, Jean-Paul. *Baudelaire.* New York: New Directions, 1950.

———. *Mallarmé or the Poet of Nothingness.* Trans. Ernst Sturm. University Park: Pennsylvania State UP, 1988.

Schindel, Robert. *Gebürtig.* Frankfurt: Suhrkamp, 1994.

———. "Erinnerungen an Prometheus." *Im Herzen die Krätze: Gedichte.* Frankfurt: Suhrkamp, 1988.

———. "Die unterste Falte der Seele." *Profil* 18 (April 28, 1992): 88–89.

———. *Gott schütz uns vor den guten Menschen. Jüdisches Gedächtnis — Auskunftsbüro der Angst.* Frankfurt: Suhrkamp, 1995.

Schmid Bortenschlager, Sigrid. "Literatur(en) in Österreich und in der Schweiz." *Für und wider eine österreichische Literatur.* Ed. Gerhard Melzer. Königstein: Athenäum, 1982.

Schmidt-Dengler, Wendelin. *Der Übertreibungskünstler: Zu Thomas Bernhard.* Vienna: Sonderzahl, 1986.

Schmidt-Dengler, Wendelin and Martin Huber. *Statt Bernhard.* Vienna: Edition S, 1987.

Schorske, Carl E. *Fin-de-Siècle Vienna. Politics and Culture.* New York: Random House, 1981.

Sichrovsky, Peter. *Wir wissen nicht was morgen wird, wir wissen wohl was gestern war: Junge Juden in Deutschland und Österreich.* Köln: Kiepenheuer & Witsch, 1985.

Sorg, Bernhard. *Thomas Bernhard.* Munich: Beck, 1992.

Spanlang, Elisabeth. *Elfriede Jelinek: Studien zum Frühwerk.* Vienna: VWGÖ, 1992.

Taylor, Charles. "The Politics of Recognition." *Multiculturalism: Examining the Politics of Recognition.* Ed. Amy Gutman. Princeton: Princeton UP, 1994.

Timms, Edward. *Karl Kraus Apocalyptic Satirist: Culture and Catastrophe in Habsburg Vienna.* New Haven: Yale UP, 1986.

Weinzierl, Ulrich. "Bernhard als Erzieher: Thomas Bernhard's *Auslöschung.*" *German Quarterly* 63.3/4 (Summer Fall, 1990):455–461.

Wilke, Sabine. "'Ich bin eine Frau mit einer männlichen Anmaßung': Eine Analyse des "bösen Blicks" in Elfriede Jelineks *Die Klavierspielerin.*" *Modern Austrian Literature* 26.1 (1993): 115–145.

Winkelman, Christine. *Die Suche nach dem großen Gefühl.* Frankfurt: Peter Lang, 1990.

Winter, Riki. "Gespräch mit Elfriede Jelinek." *Elfriede Jelinek.* Eds. Kurt Bartsch and Günther Höfler. Vienna: Droschl, 1991.

Wistrich, Robert S. "The Kreisky Phenomenon: A Reassessment." *Austrians and the Jews in the Twentieth Century.* Ed. Robert S. Wistrich. New York: St. Martin's Press, 1992.

Zeyringer, Klaus. *Innerlichkeit und Öffentlichkeit: Österreichische Literatur der achtziger Jahre.* Tübingen: A. Francke, 1992.

Zürcher, Gustav. "Leben mit Poesie." *Text und Kritik* 24 (1976): 41–47.

Zweig, Stefan. *Die Welt von Gestern.* Hamburg: Fischer Verlag, 1970.

# Index